Second Edition

LIFE-SPAN DEVELOPMENT
Student Study Guide

Second Edition

LIFE-SPAN DEVELOPMENT

Student Study Guide

Prepared by
Michael G. Walraven

Jackson Community College

Wm. C. Brown Publishers
Dubuque, Iowa

Cover photo © Devon Jacklin/Folio

ISBN 0–697–00846–0

Printed in the United States of America

10 9 8 7 6 5 4 3

Contents

To the Student

By selecting this study guide, you have shown that you are serious about learning. Congratulations! This study guide is designed to help you learn the material in the textbook in the best possible way, and to remember it for later recall and application. In addition, this study guide is designed to help you improve and further develop your studying and learning skills, which will pay additional benefits for the rest of your life. As you have probably already discovered, learning is often the key to doing and enjoying.

Reading the text, listening to the instructor, and studying your notes are what many people think constitutes learning. Perhaps that is because they see students doing these things. Yet some students do these things for hours on end and do not learn, while other students do these things for a short period, and seem to learn very well. These differences often are not related to intellectual differences, but reflect differences in the strategy of studying. To help you improve your study strategy, this study guide contains a brief essay describing ways to be a better student.

To be effective, a study guide should be used properly. Often, very slight differences in how students use study guides (and other resources) can make the difference between success and failure. So, before you tear into this guide, please take a few minutes and read the section on using the study guide.

Many of us find the study of developmental psychology an exciting specialty. New discoveries are frequent, and we have the experience of being in the forefront of a very young science. I hope that you, too, will find this course of study an exciting one. Furthermore, I wish you hard work, consistent study, and resounding success. Most importantly, I wish you the satisfaction of learning.

How to Use this Study Guide

For each chapter in the textbook, you will find a corresponding chapter in this guide. Each chapter in the guide contains six major components; each with a specific goal and benefit for you.

The Preview

Each chapter begins with a preview. These few paragraphs capture the most important ideas and findings in the chapter. You should read the preview before you read the chapter in the text. Then, as you read the chapter in the text, your attention will be drawn to the most important elements. In addition, these important elements will seem familiar to you, since you will have read them before. Most important, the repetition of these key elements will give you a head start on your study of the chapter, and will serve as organizing pegs for the supporting material.

The preview is also a good way to review the chapter just before going to class for a discussion, or just before the test over that material.

Learning Objectives

The learning objectives provide you with a set of expectations about what you should be able to do after you have mastered the material in this chapter. Read them before reading the chapter itself, and you will find that as you read you will organize the information into strategic patterns which are based on the learning objectives. In other words, the learning objectives provide a format or strategy for learning.

The learning objectives are also the very best way to prepare for essay examinations, if your professor uses them. If you can actually provide written responses to the directives of these learning objectives, you will be very likely to do an excellent job on an essay exam.

Many students also find the learning objectives helpful in reviewing the material in the chapter. Accordingly, each learning objective is followed by a parenthetical number, which provides a reference to the text page on which the related information begins.

Key Terms

The next item you will find is a list of the key terms found in this chapter, with space to write in the definition of each. Simply thinking of the definition is a less successful way of using this section; the best way is to actually write in the definition. If you find a term you do not know, the numbers in parentheses will again refer you to the appropriate learning objective and text page on which you can find the term.

Guided Review

After you have read the preview, the learning objectives, and the key terms, read the chapter in the text itself. It is best to skim it first (the preview helps with this task); then read it in detail. Read all of it, including graphs, charts, and the captions under pictures.

After you have read the chapter, and allowed some time to pass for the material to incubate, it is time to tackle the guided review. This review is designed in a style called leaded. This means that when there is a shift of topic within the chapter, the first frame or two will provide the answer embedded in the statement. Then, after a few frames, there will be a review frame in which you will have to recall and organize answers from the preceding frames. Most students find this an excellent way to learn, but only if they do it correctly.

There is only one best way to use guided review frames. First, obtain a large index card or other piece of firm material, which is wide enough to cover the page of the study guide. Slide this card down the page, revealing only one frame at a time. Write the answers in the blanks. It is critical that you actually write in the answers. Simply saying the words out loud or to yourself will not produce the learning you want. If you actually write the answers in the blanks, you will find yourself remembering this material better than you could by any other method.

After you have written in the answers, slide the card down slightly to reveal the correct responses, and compare them with yours. If you had the correct answer, go on to the next frame. If you made an error, please go back a frame or two and follow the course of the material again, so that you see how the correct answer fits. Now, please write in the correct answer. This is important if you are going to learn it correctly.

Sometimes, the guided review will seem to go on forever. When you feel tired of it, be sure to take a break. Most students find that if they work consistently for more than twenty or thirty minutes without a break, their attention wanders and their time is wasted. Don't be afraid to take a short break, stretch, take a brief walk, or do something else just for a change of pace. When you come back to your work, you will find that it goes better.

If you find that some of the frames are unfamiliar, the numbers in parentheses at the end of each frame refer you to the appropriate learning objective and text page on which you can refresh your memory.

Self Test

After the guided review, you will find a self test. This is designed to help you prepare for a multiple-choice type test in class, and to give you some feedback about your knowledge of the material in this chapter. Each multiple-choice question has only one correct answer. (The answers to the multiple-choice self test are found at the end of each chapter in this study guide.) Each question is also referenced to the relevant learning objective and text page number, should you need to review.

Individual Learning Activity

Following the self test you will find an individual learning activity. If you choose to do this activity, you will find it helpful in learning the material in the chapter, usually in a way aimed at applications. These activities are also designed to stretch your mind a bit, and so to extend the material in the text. Most important to long-term memory is the way in which we learn the material, and the connections we make with other learned materials. These activities are designed to provide as many connections as possible, so you will be able to recall the materials more easily later on.

In summary then, the most efficient way to use this study guide is this. First read the preview and the learning objectives. Then read the chapter in the text. It is best to skim it first, then read it in detail. Next, write in the definitions of the key terms, checking your memory when necessary by referring back to the text. Next, complete the guided review, being careful to write in the answers in the appropriate blanks, to check your answers by sliding your cover sheet or card down slightly, and to correct any items you got wrong the first time. You may find it helpful to try the self test now, or you may wish to wait until you have reread the chapter in the text. Doing the individual learning activity will make the materials more meaningful, and help you to remember them better.

In preparing for essay examinations, use the learning objectives as sample essay items, and write out your responses to them. In preparing for multiple-choice tests, complete the self test in this study guide, and check your answers against those provided at the end of the chapter. Remember that each element of the study guide is referenced to learning objectives and pages in the textbook, to help you find material you want to review.

I hope that this study guide is helpful to you in this course. I wish you success in this course, and success in learning and in the enjoyable activities it makes possible.

How to Be a Better Student

Everyone who goes to college wants to be a good student. As you chose your college or university, and perhaps even an area of major interest or concentration, you had certain goals in mind. I would be willing to bet that three of them were to do well in school, earn good grades, and graduate.

Unfortunately, many students find that they do not do as well in college as they had hoped and expected. There are several reasons for this disappointment, and in examining them it is possible to see how to avoid them. It is possible, in other words, to know how to be a good student, and to guide our behavior so we improve the chances that we will achieve our goals.

The oldest known definition of *education* is: "how people learn stuff." For most of our history, educators have focused on the "stuff." Teachers were required to be masters of their respective academic fields. Even today, some states have requirements which speak only to the need to be qualified in the subject matter one teaches.

In the 1960s, we became more interested in the "people" part of the definition. This movement was made manifest by fads like open classrooms and free universities. The idea was that people just naturally learn, and need only the opportunity to do so. These experiments were dismal failures, but they taught us something.

The key to the definition of *education* is the word *how*. Today, thanks to a wealth of research on the principles which guide the phenomenon of learning, and on the nature of learning and memory, we know a considerable amount about how learning occurs and how we can make it better. It is by the application of these principles that we can become better students.

Formulating the Plan

Anything worth having is worth planning for. Whether you hope to learn to teach, to fly, to write for profit, or to change diapers correctly, you have a goal in mind.

Many students, from the earliest days in elementary school, are asked what they want to be when they grow up. This usually means what they want to do as work when they reach adulthood. Although I have been teaching at the college level for almost fifteen years, my father still asks me when I am going to get a steady job! The answer to these questions is one way of formulating a goal. Now that you are a college student, many people will expect that you know what you want to do for a profession or career. Yet, you may not have the foggiest notion, or you may have an idea which is still slightly foggy. That is OK. What is clear, however, is that you want to succeed in your college courses. This is a relatively long-range goal, and as such can serve a purpose in keeping you on track.

However, our day-to-day behavior is often hard to connect to our long-range goals. We need short-term goals to keep us organized, and to be sure that the flow of our activities is in the correct direction. I suggest that as students, you need three types of short-term (relatively speaking) goals. First, you need goals for the semester or term; second, goals for the week; and third, goals for the day. Let's look at each of these separately.

Goals for the Semester

At the beginning of each semester, we find ourselves immersed suddenly in many new courses. Often, we are confronted by several new professors with whom we have not worked before. It is difficult to sort out the expectations and demands of these several courses. However, organizing this information is critical to effectively completing all these requirements, and success.

If you can, obtain a large wall calendar, and mark on it all the dates of tests and exams, and term paper due dates. Be sure to write on the calendar for which course the date applies. Now, estimate how long it will take you to make final preparations for those exams, and mark those dates as warning or alert dates. Look over the dates on which papers are due, and see if they are bunched together. If your college is typical, they are. You can help yourself to avoid the last minute all-nighters, if you will simply determine a spread of due dates for yourself, and mark those on the calendar too. As you do this step, please be sure to avoid any days which have personal significance for you, such as birthdays, anniversaries, and the like. This calendar gives you an overview of major dates in your semester.

Goals for the Week

Students who are successful in college also schedule their time weekly. Sometime during the course of registration, you undoubtedly made up a schedule showing your classes arrayed over the week. If you also have a part-time or full-time job, you must allow time for that too. Also, everyone needs some time for relaxing, eating, and sleeping, not to mention life's essentials: ice cream and love. With all these things in mind, it is no wonder we find very little time to study.

But good students have all these things too, yet they study. Do they have more time? No, we all have the same amount of time; but successful students schedule their time carefully. So, make up a weekly schedule and block off time for all these necessary events: classes, work, relaxation, eating, sleeping, loving, ice cream, and studying. Is there any time left? If so, appoint a committee to decide what to do with it. If not, consider yourself a student.

As you make up your weekly schedule, you may find your study time in a large block. If this is true, please remember to take a short break every twenty to thirty minutes. This is called distributed practice, and is far more efficient than studying for hours on end. After the first twenty or thirty minutes, most of us become much less efficient anyway.

Goals for Today

It is also helpful to keep a daily checklist, as a reminder of what must be done that day. Check off the things as you accomplish them. A pocket calendar is most helpful for this task.

If you have followed this carefully, you now have a large semester calendar plastered on your wall, a weekly schedule of major life events, classes, and study times, taped over your desk, and a daily check list of must-do items in your pocket or purse. We have to hurry now; it's time to go to class!

Attending Classes

Many students believe that, since they are in college, they can decide whether to go to class at all. They are correct. Some students believe, furthermore, that attendance in class is not important to their grade. They are misled! Some instructors even announce that they do not adjust grades based on attendance. They do not have to! Students who do not attend class sessions almost always do poorly on the tests and exams. Perhaps they were absent when a crucial item was discussed, or when the instructor lectured about the material required for the examination. Moreover, if you are not there, the instructor cannot get to know you (sorry, instructors are not telepathic); and, therefore, cannot give you the benefit of the doubt on your answers.

In study after research study, the data clearly show that those students who attend class regularly, receive the highest grades, and actually learn more too! So, the first rule of effective studenthood is to attend classes. Besides, how else can you get your money's worth?

When you get to class, what do you do?

Benefiting from Lectures

Sometimes students attend lectures and just sit and pay attention. They reason that if they take notes they will miss much of what the instructor says. However, sitting and paying attention is difficult to do. For one thing, most people can think much faster than they can speak. While the instructor lectures at 80 words per minute, the student thinks at about 350 words per minute! If the student is using this extra "thinking capacity" to focus on what the instructor is saying, it is fine. This rarely lasts more than five minutes at a time, however. Most of the time, this extra "thinking capacity" is used in daydreaming! Daydreaming can be helpful in resolving our emotional problems, planning the course of our lives, and avoiding work. Most of the time it is motivated by the desire to avoid work. Whatever the motive, however, daydreaming is not compatible with attending a lecture. Human beings simply cannot attend to more than one stimulus at one time. Also, you have to admit, your daydreams can be ever so much more interesting than your professor's lectures.

Therefore, attending lectures is best done while taking notes. Use plenty of paper, and leave blank lines at regular intervals. You will use these lines later (they are not wasted!). If the instructor permits it, interrupt with questions if you do not understand what is being said. Lectures have a way of progressing. It is important to understand each point, or later points will be lost.

When you take notes, write out the major points, and try to just make simple notes on the supporting minor points. If you miss something, and you cannot ask a question about it, approach the instructor immediately afterward, when it is likely to still be fresh in both your minds.

Within one or two hours after the lecture, but for sure on the same day, go back over your notes, and do two things. First, fill in the rest of the minor points. This often amounts to completing the sentence or other element. Second, write brief summaries, and any questions that you now have, in the blank lines you left earlier (clever of you to leave those blank lines!). These few minutes spent reviewing and organizing your notes will pay off in greatly improved memory. You can ask the questions you have in class, or during the instructor's office hours, and reap two benefits. First, you will get the answers. Second, you will demonstrate that you are a serious student, and that will impress your instructor.

By the way, weren't we supposed to read something before the next class period? Oh yes, now where did I leave my text book? I sure hope I can get through all those pages before I fall asleep!

Reading for Learning

We all know how to read. You are proving it by reading these words. Hopefully, you are also realizing some ideas as a result of reading. If you are only reading words, please WAKE UP! STOP DAYDREAMING!

We can read a variety of things: newspapers, movie reviews, novels, sleazy paperbacks, and textbooks. Textbooks are unlike all the others, and must be read with a strategy all their own.

There are a multitude of reading and studying strategies, and all of them work to an extent. Perhaps you learned one or more in the course of going to high school. Perhaps you even took a how-to-study course as you entered college. If so, you probably learned one or two of these systems. If you have one you like, which works for you, keep it. If you are interested in learning a new one, read on.

The SQ3R Method

One of the most successful and most widely used methods of studying written material is the SQ3R method, first developed at Ohio State University. Researchers noted that students who were more successful were more active readers. This method teaches you the same skills which have made many thousands of students successful. If you use this method when you read and study, you will be more successful too. If not, there's always snake oil.

The S stands for SURVEY. After you have read the preview or chapter outline and the list of learning objectives, you should survey the chapter in the text. This is also called skimming. Look at the headings and subheadings, and get the gist of the major points in this chapter. If you have an outline of the chapter (some books provide them), check off each point as you pass it in the pages of the text.

The Q stands for QUESTION. Reading is greatly enhanced if you are searching for the answers to questions. For this text, the study guide provides learning objectives which can serve as questions. For other texts, make up questions for yourself, based on the chapter preview or on your own survey of the chapter. Be sure that you have at least one question for each major unit in the chapter, or you will find that you are less efficient in studying those units for which you do not have questions.

The first of the three Rs is for READ. As you read, look for the answers to the questions you posed, or to the study or learning objectives furnished for you. When you find material which answers these questions, put a mark (X) in the margin next to that material. This will help now, since you are actively involved, and later, when you review. It is a good idea to wait to underline or highlight lines of text until after you have read the entire chapter at least once, so you will know what is and what is not most important.

The second R is for RECITE. One of the oldest classroom techniques in the world (Aristotle used it) is recitation. In the classroom version, the teacher asks the questions and the students answer them. Unless you can get your teacher to study with you regularly, you'll have to play both roles. (Incidentally, if you do get your teacher to study with you regularly, please write and let me know how you accomplished it. Thanks.)

Stop periodically in your reading and say aloud (if possible) what the author is telling you. Try to put it in your own words, but be sure to use technical terms as you learn them. If you are not in a situation where you can recite out loud, do it in writing. Just thinking it is not enough. People who do not use recitation usually forget half of what they read in one hour, and another half of the half they remembered by the end of the day. People who use recitation often remember from 75% to 90% of what they studied. This technique pays off. By the way, if anyone questions why you are talking to yourself, tell them that a psychologist recommended it.

When should you pause to recite? A good rule of thumb is that each time you come to the end of a major subheading, you should recite. I like to encourage my students to recite at least one sentence at the end of each paragraph, and two or three or more sentences at the end of each subunit (when you come to a new heading). Who ever said that students should be seen and not heard?

The third R (in SQ3R, remember?) is for REVIEW. You should review a chapter soon after you have studied it (using the SQ and first two Rs). You should review it again the day or evening before a test. It is not usually helpful to cram the night before a test, and particularly not the day of the test! That type of study does not produce good memory, and is likely to make you more anxious during the test itself.

Taking Tests

One of the things students fear most is failure. Failure signifies that things are not going well, and alerts us to the possibility that we may not achieve our goals. Unfortunately, many students see tests and exams as opportunities to fail. They prepare by becoming anxious and fearful, and trying to cram in as much knowledge as possible as near as possible to the exam itself. These students rarely do well on the exam. They often fail, thus accomplishing just what they feared. Perhaps they should learn to fear success?

Taking tests requires some strategy and planning. First, it is helpful to know what type of tests you will have. Your instructor probably told you during the first class meeting, or perhaps is waiting for you to ask. If you do not know, ask and find out.

If you are going to be taking essay exams, the best way to prepare is by writing essays. Before you do this, it is a good idea to find out what types of questions the instructor asks, and what is expected in a response. Again, it is helpful to ask the instructor for this material. Perhaps you can even see some examples of essay questions from previous years. By finding out what is expected, you can formulate a model against which you can evaluate your answers.

Now, using the learning objectives, or some essay questions you wrote, actually sit down and write out the answers. HINT: If you usually feel more anxious during a test, it may help you to practice writing your essays in the room in which the test will be given. Simply find a time when the room is vacant, and make yourself at home.

If your instructor gives multiple-choice tests, then you should practice taking multiple-choice tests. For each chapter, either use questions provided in the student study guide, or make up your own. You may find it helpful to work out an arrangement to pool questions with other students, thereby reducing the amount of work you have to do, and developing a network of friends. Good for you!

Whichever way you do it, the important thing is to prepare for tests and exams. Preparation is about 95% of the secret to getting a good grade. (Yes, there is some actual luck or chance involved in test scores, as even your instructor will admit!) Preparation is not only a good study and review technique, but also helps to reduce anxiety.

Dealing with Test Anxiety

Some students find that the prospect of a test or an examination produces a set of responses which leave them feeling helpless, very anxious, and certain of failure. They find it hard to read the questions, often leave the examination incomplete, have stomach pains and other somatic problems, and contemplate drastic measures, such as dropping out.

Other students are less severely affected. For some, a little anxiety gives them the "edge" they need to do well. In fact, anxiety can be a helpful drive, when it occurs in low levels. In 1908, Yerkes and Dodson showed that the amount of anxiety which could benefit performance was a function of the difficulty and complexity of the task. As the difficulty of the task rose, anxiety became less helpful and more likely to interfere with performance.

If you have ever been so anxious in a test situation that you were unable to do well, even though you knew the information, you have test anxiety. If you get your exams back, and are surprised that you marked wrong answers when you knew the correct answers, or if you can only remember the correct answers after you leave the examination room, you too may have test anxiety. Short of dropping out of college, or seeing a professional counselor, what can you do? In fact, you can do three things.

Strategy Number One: Effective Study

Using study habits which promote learning, and make the best use of time, is a sure help. Such study strategies as we discussed above, including scheduling your time, and using the SQ3R system, reduce anxiety by increasing confidence. As you come to realize that you know the material, your confidence rises and anxiety retreats.

Strategy Number Two: Relaxation

Each of us develops a unique pattern of relaxation. Some people relax by going to a specific place, either in person or mentally. Others relax by playing music, or being with friends, or by using autogenic relaxation phrases, or by meditating. Whatever you do, be aware of it, and try to practice relaxation techniques. If you are good at relaxing, try thinking about those situations which make you anxious, and relax while you think of them. To do this, allow yourself to think only briefly (fifteen to thirty seconds at a time) of the situation which makes you anxious, and then relax again. After a number of such pairings, you will find that thinking about that situation no longer makes you anxious. At this point, you may be surprised to find that the situation itself also no longer produces anxiety. You may find that it is helpful to think about these anxiety-provoking situations in a sequence from those which produce very little anxiety to those which are more anxiety-evoking. Such a list, from low to high anxiety, might look something like this:

1. Your instructor announces that there will be a test in four weeks.
2. Your instructor reminds you of the test next week.
3. As you study, you see on the course outline the word *test,* and remember next week's test.
4. One of your friends asks you if you want to study together for the test which is the day after tomorrow.
5. You choose not to go out with your friends because of the test tomorrow.
6. As you get up in the morning, you remember that today is the day of the test.
7. You are walking down the hall toward the classroom, thinking about what questions might be on the test.
8. The instructor enters the classroom, carrying a sheaf of papers in hand.
9. The instructor distributes the papers, and you see the word *test* or *exam* at the top.
10. After reading the first five questions, you have not been able to think of the answer to any of them.

If you work at it gradually and consistently, pairing these types of thoughts (briefly) with relaxation, and remembering to let go and relax after each one, will dispel test anxiety and make test-taking a more productive and successful experience.

Strategy Number Three: Thinking Clearly

Most students who have test anxiety think in unclear and unproductive ways. They say to themselves things like: "I can't get these answers correct. . . . I don't know this stuff. . . . I don't know anything at all. . . . I'm going to fail this test. . . . I'm probably going to flunk out of school. . . . I'm just a dumb schmuck." These thoughts share two unfortunate characteristics: they are negative, and they are absolute. They should be replaced.

When we tell ourselves absolute and negative things, we find it impossible to focus on the test material. The result is that we miss questions even when we know the answers. Our thinking prevents us from doing well. A good strategy for replacing these negative and absolute thoughts is to practice thinking positive and honest thoughts, such as: "I may not know all the answers, but I know some of them. . . . I don't know the answer to that right now, so I will go on to the next one and come back to that. . . . I don't have to get them all right. . . . I studied hard and carefully, and I can get some of them correct. . . . I am a serious student, and have some abilities. . . . I am prepared for this test, and know many of the answers. . . . This test is important, but it is not going to determine the course of my entire life."

By thinking clearly, honestly, and positively, we quiet the flood of anxiety, and focus on the task at hand. Students who use this technique invariably do better on the tests. It takes practice to think clearly, but it is worth the effort. After a while, you will find that it becomes natural, and does not take any noticeable effort. As anxiety is reduced, more energy is available for studying and for doing well on examinations. The eventual outcome is more enjoyment in learning, better learning, more success in college, and the achievement of your goals.

1 Introduction, History, Issues, and the Life-Span Developmental Perspective

Preview

People study life-span development for many reasons: to prepare for a career, to gain insight into one's own development, or to satisfy curiosity. Life-span development encompasses many areas of contemporary concern: the well-being of children and adults, genetics, child abuse, divorce, and the aging population.

The concept of childhood as simply adulthood in miniature has persisted for many years. Our contemporary view of childhood has several sources. In Egypt, children were seen as helpless, and as having special needs. The Greeks viewed children as objects of affection, important family members, and symbols of the future. During the middle ages, in accord with the *original sin view,* the goal of child rearing became salvation, and the happiness of the child was not important. During the Renaissance, John Locke's view of the child as a *tabula rasa* became popular, as did Jean Jacques Rousseau's view of the *innate goodness* of the child. These three major viewpoints set the stage for the nature-nurture debate. We now conceive of childhood as a highly eventful and unique period, which forms the foundation for adulthood.

The scientific study of adolescence began early in the twentieth century. G. Stanley Hall referred to the period as one of *sturm und drang,* or storm and stress. More recently, researchers have shown that each person experiences adolescence in a highly individualized manner.

The life-span view of human development emphasizes changes that occur during adulthood. Philosophical interest in life-span development began in the late eighteenth century, and scientific studies have increased as the longevity of the typical person has. Actual studies of age-related changes in adulthood began in the 1940s.

It is now typical to divide the life span into several periods. The prenatal period extends from the moment of conception to birth, and is succeeded by infancy, which extends from birth to age eighteen or twenty-four months. Early childhood follows infancy, and ends at about age five or six years. Middle and late childhood extend from six to eleven years of age, and correspond to the elementary school years. Adolescence begins with puberty and ends at age eighteen to twenty-one years. Early adulthood follows adolescence, and lasts through the thirties, when middle adulthood begins. Late adulthood begins at age sixty or seventy, and extends until death.

The term *development* refers to a pattern of movement or change that begins at conception and extends throughout life. The pattern is complex, including both maturation, those changes dictated by the genetic blueprint, and experiences, which may arise from the biological or social environment. Without experiences, maturation would not occur. Both the amount of stimulation and its timing are important in determining development.

Development may also be thought of as consisting of several strands. Biological development emphasizes hereditary, neurological, and hormonal bases of behavior. Physical development refers to bodily changes, and cognitive development refers to changes in mental activity. Social, emotional, and personality development refer to overlapping spheres involving interaction with others, feelings, the development of the self, sex-typed behavior, and moral development.

Jean Piaget authored a major theory of cognitive development, focusing on qualitative changes in mental activity. His theory and other stage theories imply three elements: (1) that qualitative changes must occur in a certain sequence; (2) that there is some abruptness in transition from stage to stage; and (3) that there is concurrence in the appearance of patterns typical of a given stage.

Another important issue is whether development proceeds continuously or discontinuously. Stage theories imply discontinuity between stages; but to the extent that they assert that later development hinges on earlier development, stage theories also imply some continuity. Non-stage theories often argue that important characteristics are seen as important themes throughout development, unfolding in a continuous fashion. For many years, people believed that early experience dictated later development; we now believe that early experience, while important, does not have irreversible effects. Another aspect of the continuity-discontinuity issue involves whether human development is linked to that of other animals. Discontinuity can be generated by (1) social changes, (2) changes in life experience for the individual, (3) changes in life tasks at different ages, (4) biological changes, and (5) hierarchical development. On the other hand, continuity may result from (1) biological processes, (2) the continuing influence of early experiences, and (3) consistent experiences through childhood and adult life.

Although we look for consistent patterns of development, individual differences are not overlooked. Nonlinear patterns, with simultaneous declines in some functions and stability or improvements in others, apply both within and among individuals. In addition, some developmental changes can be modified or reversed.

Normative age-graded factors involve those elements of development which are linked to chronological age. Nonnormative life-event factors are those which affect only a few individuals, and may occur in the context of chance encounters. Normative history-graded factors are specific historical events, such as wars, and are important in comparing individuals of different ages. Life-span developmentalists are also interested in cohort effects; the term *cohort* refers to a group of people born at a particular time.

It should be clear that chronological age is not a good measure of development. Neugarten has proposed that we distinguish three perspectives of time: life time, social time, and historical time as measures of development during the life cycle. Life time is roughly approximated by age; social time refers to cultural expectations and demands at various ages, and historical time indexes major historical events in the life of individuals.

Learning Objectives

1. List three reasons for studying life-span human development. (p. 5)
2. Trace the history of the concept of childhood. (p. 6)
3. Describe the beginnings of scientific interest in life-span development. (p. 10)
4. Define the *prenatal period, infancy, early childhood, middle and late childhood, adolescence, early adulthood, middle adulthood,* and *late adulthood,* as those terms are used in the text. (p. 10)
5. Define *development,* and contrast maturation and experience. (p. 14)
6. Identify biological, physical, cognitive, and social and emotional strands of development, and appreciate their interaction. (p. 17)
7. Describe the issue of qualitative changes in development. (p. 20)
8. Specify the assumptions underlying a stage theory, and how they relate to the issue of continuity versus discontinuity in development. (p. 20)
9. List five factors which can contribute to discontinuous development. (p. 22)
10. List three factors which can contribute to continuity in development. (p. 22)
11. Describe the interest in individual differences and the malleability of developmental changes. (p. 23)
12. Give examples of normative age-graded, nonnormative life-event, and normative history-graded factors in development. (p. 24)
13. Recount what Neugarten means by life time, social time, and historical time. (p. 26)

Key Terms

For each key term, write the definition in the space provided.

original sin view (2, p. 7) _____

tabula rasa (2, p. 7) _____

innate goodness (2, p. 7) _____

prenatal period (4, p. 10) _____

infancy (4, p. 11) _____

early childhood (4, p. 11) _____

middle childhood (4, p. 12) _____

late childhood (4, p. 12) _____

adolescence (4, p. 12) _____

early adulthood (4, p. 12) _____

middle adulthood (4, p. 12) _____

late adulthood (4, p. 13) _____

development (5, p. 14) _____

maturation (5, p. 14) _____

experience (5, p. 14) _____

biological environment (5, p. 16) _____

social environment (5, p. 16) _____

biological development (6, p. 17) _____

physical development (6, p. 17) _____

cognitive development (6, p. 24) _____

social development (6, p. 17) _____

emotional development (6, p. 17) _____

personality development (6, p. 18) _____

qualitative change (7, p. 20) _____

stages of development (8, p. 20) _____

continuity versus discontinuity (8, p. 20) _____

individual differences (11, p. 23) _____

nonnormative life events (12, p. 24) _____

normative, age-graded factors (12, p. 24) _____

normative, history-graded factors (12, p. 24) _____

cohort (12, p. 24) _____

life time (13, p. 26) _____

social time (13, p. 26) _____

historical time (13, p. 26) _____

Guided Review

Before you begin this review, please be sure you have read, and understand, the instructions in the Introduction section of this study guide. Please remember that in order to get the maximum benefit from this section, you must write your responses in the blanks. Use a plain sheet of paper to conceal the answer and subsequent frames. Then, when you have written in your response to a frame, slide the cover sheet down to reveal the answer. If you responded correctly, go on to the next frame. If your response did not match the answer provided, write in the correct answer, then go on to the next frame.

1. We are beginning a course dealing with human development across the life span. We might ask, "How did the study of _____ development arise?" (1, p. 5)

   life-span

2. In looking at the history of developmental psychology, we find considerable interest in child development. In fact, there is a history of considerable research on the development of _____ . (2, p. 6)

   children (or the child)

3. Although the study of child development has a fairly long history, we have only recently begun to study human development across the _____ . (2, p. 6)

   life span

4. In early (prescientific) views of children, the uniqueness of childhood was not recognized. People thought of _____ simply as miniature adults. (2, p. 6)

children

5. In ancient times, children were often abused, abandoned, or even killed. We should remember, however, that in ancient times brutality was extended to adults as well as to _____ . (2, p. 7)

children

6. Not all societies treated children harshly. In Egypt, children were seen as helpless and having special needs. Also, children were viewed as objects of affection and symbols of the future by the _____ . (2, p. 7)

Greeks

7. Early scholars looked upon childhood from either a philosophical or theological perspective. They did not take a modern scientific approach to the study of the development of _____ . (2, p. 7)

children

8. One popular position held by early philosophers and theologians during the Middle Ages saw the goal of child rearing as salvation, and the child as afflicted by _____ _____ . (2, p. 7)

original sin

9. Another position held that the infant at birth is not sinful. John Locke claimed that the mind at birth is a tabula rasa, a blank slate. Thus, Locke denied that knowledge was _____ . (2, p. 7)

innate

10. Locke's argument for the acquisition of knowledge was embodied in his concept of tabula rasa, a Latin term which means _____ _____ . (2, p. 7)

blank slate

11. Others believed that children are inherently innocent and good, and that this good start must be supported and protected. According to Jean Jacques Rousseau, children will naturally grow up to be good persons if society will only support and _____ them from evil influences. (2, p. 7)

protect

12. These three viewpoints: the original sin view, the tabula rasa view, and the innate goodness view, set the stage for the nature-_____ debate. (2, p. 7)

nurture

13. Just as these debates gave way to an emphasis on scientific knowledge about children, the emphasis on child development also spawned an interest in adolescent and adult _____ . (3, p. 8)

development

4

14. Early in the twentieth century, the study of adolescence began. G. Stanley Hall saw the period of adolescence as one of *sturm und drang,* which means _____ and _____ . (3, p. 8)

storm, stress

15. By the 1940s, scientists were beginning to study age-related changes among _____ . (3, p. 10)

adults

16. As scientists studied development, they found it convenient to divide the life span into different phases. Your text also defines several _____ of the human _____ . (4, p. 10)

phases, life span

17. The first phase is the prenatal period. Extending from the instant of conception to birth, the _____ period is a time of tremendous growth. (4, p. 10)

prenatal

18. Most parents find themselves challenged by the demands of the period known as infancy. The period of extreme dependence, extending from birth to about eighteen or twenty-four months of age, is termed _____ . (4, p. 11)

infancy

19. The first few days after birth, the infant is called a neonate. Thus, a newborn baby may be called an _____ or a _____ . (4, p. 11)

infant, neonate

20. The two-year-old child, who walks well and speaks in short phrases, is ready to leave the phase we call _____ . (4, p. 11)

infancy

21. From about age two to age five or six, humans traverse the phase called early childhood. Another term for the preschool years is _____ _____ . (4, p. 11)

early childhood

22. Early childhood is considered over when the child, at age five or six, goes off to _____ . (4, p. 11)

school

23. Learning to care for oneself and developing school-readiness skills are important components of _____ _____ . (4, p. 11)

early childhood

24. Middle and late childhood corresponds roughly to the elementary school years. Thus, from age six through about age eleven, the child is in a phase called middle and late _____ . (4, p. 12)

childhood

25. Mastering reading, writing, and arithmatic skills are important components of _____ and _____ childhood. (4, p. 12)

middle, late

26. A period of major transition to adulthood is adolescence. Beginning with a period of rapid physical change, _____ leads to adulthood. (4, p. 12)

adolescence

27. Adolescence involves dramatic gains in weight and height, and the development of secondary sexual characteristics, which are examples of _____ changes. (4, p. 12)

physical

28. Adolescence also involves the development of abstract thought processes. Thus, both mind and body are readied for adulthood during _____ . (4, p. 12)

adolescence

29. Early adulthood begins in the late teens or early twenties, and lasts through the thirties. Personal and economic independence are important goals during _____ _____ . (4, p. 12)

early adulthood

30. Most Americans also select a mate, marry, and begin a family of their own during _____ adulthood. (4, p. 12)

early

31. Middle adulthood extends from about thirty-five or forty-five to fifty-five or sixty-five years of age. There is increased personal and social involvement during this phase, called _____ adulthood. (4, p. 12)

middle

32. Reaching and maintaining satisfaction in one's career also occurs during _____ _____ . (4, p. 12)

middle adulthood

33. The last phase of life is termed late adulthood. Adjusting to decreasing strength and reduced income are common developmental tasks of _____ adulthood. (4, p. 13)

late

34. Unlike earlier phases which have age-related terminals, late adulthood extends until death. Thus, preparing for one's own death may be an important consideration of a person during _____ _____ . (4, p. 13)

late adulthood

35. Psychologists use the term *development* to refer to a pattern of movement or change which occurs throughout the life span. Both growth and decay are involved in this pattern of movement or _____ we call development. (5, p. 14)

change

36. This pattern is the product of several processes, two of which are maturation and experience. Both maturation and experience contribute to the pattern we call _____ . (5, p. 14)

development

37. Maturation involves changes reflecting the genetic plan. The gradual specialization of the hemispheres of the cerebral cortex is an example of _____ . (5, p. 14)

maturation

38. Probably the broadest range of contributions to development comes from experiences. As the person interacts with the environment, these _____ produce developmental changes. (5, p. 16)

experiences

39. Maturation and experiences interact to produce a pattern of change called _____ . (5, p. 16)

development

40. As we look at development across the life span, we will follow various strands. Three different strands will be emphasized: biological and physical; cognitive; and social, emotional, and personality development. These areas are the three major _____ of _____ . (6, p. 17)

strands, development

41. Biological and physical development refers to simple changes in size and weight, and other anatomical changes. Changes in size of the brain would be a measure of _____ development. (6, p. 17)

physical

42. Cognitive development includes changes in mental activity. Changes in patterns of thought, or memory, or perception, or language, would be called measures of _____ development. (6, p. 17)

cognitive

43. Social development is involved in human relationships, in interactions between people. The development of close friendships would be an important aspect of _____ development. (6, p. 17)

social

44. Emotional development emphasizes a person's feelings or emotions. The increasing ability of the preschooler to identify and label personal feelings about events is an important feature of _____ development. (6, p. 17)

emotional

45. Personality development refers to many different aspects of individual development. In this text, the self and self-perception, sex-typed behavior and sex-role development, and moral development, will be emphasized as aspects of _____ development. (6, p. 18)

personality

46. These three aspects or strands of development interact to produce each unique person. As we look at various aspects of development, we must remember that these strands _____ to result in an integrated being. (6, p. 18)

interact

47. Early descriptions of child development were not scientific; they were philosophical. More recently, we have studied human development using _____ methods. (7, p. 20)

scientific

48. Recall that development is defined as a pattern of change. Piaget has proposed that cognitive development is characterized by _____ changes. (7, p. 20)

qualitative

49. Piaget also proposed that _____ development occurs in a fixed sequence of stages. (8, p. 20)

cognitive

50. We should expect to see a certain amount of abruptness as a person moves from one _____ to the next. (8, p. 20)

stage

51. We should also expect to see some concurrence in the appearance of behaviors that characterize a given _____ . (8, p. 20)

stage

52. Most people believe that _____ theories imply a certain element of discontinuity in development. (8, p. 20)

stage

53. In fact, the issue of continuity versus _____ is more complex than that. (8, p. 20)

discontinuity

54. To the extent that stage theories imply rather abrupt transitions between stages, they do support the notion that development is _____ . (8, p. 20)

discontinuous

55. But stage theories also imply that later development is dependent on earlier stages, and thus support the notion of a certain degree of _____ in development. (8, p. 21)

continuity

56. Non-stage theories assert that important characteristics are seen throughout development; thus, nonstage theories are typically perceived as supporting a view that development is _____ . (8, p. 21)

continuous

57. The third dimension of the continuity-discontinuity issue involves the extent to which human development is _____ with development in lower animals. (8, p. 21)

continuous

58. There are at least five factors which can generate discontinuity in development. Changes in society, such as the women's liberation movement, can result in _____ patterns of development. (9, p. 22)

discontinuous

59. An individual person can also have remarkable life experiences which cause that person's development to be _____ . (9, p. 22)

discontinuous

60. Our culture expects different things of us at different ages. These changes in demands produce _____ in our development. (9, p. 22)

discontinuity

61. Biological changes, such as the hormonal changes associated with puberty or menopause, can also produce _____ patterns of development. (9, p. 22)

discontinuous

62. On the other hand, at least three factors can generate continuity in development. Inherited characteristics or other innate features of the individual may account for some patterns of _____ development. (10, p. 22)

continuous

63. Early experiences may produce long-term effects, and, thus, may also have the effect of producing _____ patterns of development. (10, p. 23)

continuous

64. Also, if early experiences are followed by consistent experiences into adulthood, the effect will be seen in patterns of _____ . (10, p. 23)

continuity

65. The notion of patterns of development does not mean that we are all alike. The entire psychological testing movement is based on the premise that there are individual _____ between people. (11, p. 23)

differences

66. Nor should we assume that the effects of experience are permanent. There is good evidence that some aspects of development are _____ . (11, p. 23)

reversible

67. While we are only beginning to discover the extent to which developmental patterns can be changed or reversed, we are confronted by the ethical question of values and the need to make decisions regarding the desirability of _____ developmental patterns. (11, p. 24)

changing (or reversing, or modifying)

68. Life-span development involves the study of several types of factors. Traditionally, scientists have looked at normative, age-graded _____ . (12, p. 24)

factors

69. The types of events that are linked to a person's age and which are typical of most people, are called _____ age-graded factors. (12, p. 24)

normative

70. Those experiences which do *not* happen to most people are called _____ . (12, p. 24)

nonnormative

71. Experiences such as chance encounters, which happen to some people and not others, are referred to as nonnormative _____ _____ . (12, p. 24)

life events

72. Other normative events are linked to a specific time in history; these are called normative _____ factors. (12, p. 24)

history-graded

73. Normative history-graded factors will affect people differently depending on their age at the time. These different effects are often referred to as cohort differences, since a group of people born at a given time are referred to as a _____ . (12, p. 24)

cohort

74. The concept of chronological age as an index of development has fallen into disrepute. One way to deal with this complex issue is to refine our definition of time. Neugarten has proposed three types or measures of _____ . (13, p. 26)

time

75. According to Neugarten, the biological timetable for growth, of which age is a crude estimate, is termed _____ time. (13, p. 26)

life

76. That dimension of social demands and expectations which undergirds the age-grade system of a culture is called _____ time. (13, p. 26)

social

77. The timing of major historical events, such as wars and depressions, is reflected in the measure Neugarten calls _____ time. (13, p. 26)

historical

78. Thus, life time, social time, and historical time can provide a conceptual framework for moving beyond the reliance on _____ as an index of development. (13, p. 26)

age

Self Test

Instructions: Circle the number of the answer which best completes each item. When you have finished, check your answers against the key at the end of the chapter.

1. Early concepts of childhood were (2, p. 7)
   a. more complex than current concepts
   b. based entirely on Biblical teachings
   c. primarily philosophical and theological
   d. less well developed than concepts of adulthood

2. In ancient Egypt, children were viewed as (2, p. 7)
   a. helpless and deserving of affection
   b. miniature adults, to be punished frequently
   c. filled with original sin, requiring salvation
   d. blank slates, to be trained by their parents

3. Preparations for formal schooling occur during (4, p. 11)
   a. infancy
   b. early childhood
   c. middle childhood
   d. late childhood

4. Personal and economic independence are important life goals for people in the phase called (4, p. 12)
   a. late childhood
   b. adolescence
   c. early adulthood
   d. middle adulthood

5. Personal and social responsibilities become an important aspect of life for those in (4, p. 12)
   a. middle adulthood
   b. late adulthood
   c. early adulthood
   d. adolescence

6. The ultimate key to proper development is (5, p. 16)
   a. having the correct genetic information
   b. the maximum possible intensity and frequency of stimulation
   c. the timing of specific experiences
   d. avoiding unhappy adults

7. An emphasis on genetic elements, neurological patterns of development, and hormonal components of behaviors would be part of the strand of development called (6, p. 17)
   a. biological development
   b. cognitive development
   c. physical development
   d. emotional and personality development

8. The notion of stages of development implies all of the following EXCEPT (8, p. 20)
   a. the stages occur in a fixed sequence
   b. if a stage is missed, it can be made up later
   c. transitions between stages are abrupt
   d. patterns of behavior should appear in all people at about the same age or stage of development

9. An example of a nonnormative life event would be the situation in which a person (12, p. 24)
   a. retired at age sixty-five, and celebrated it with friends
   b. was attacked and beaten while walking home one night
   c. lived through a major depression as a young adult
   d. started school at age five

10. Neugarten's concept of historical time involves an assessment of (13, p. 24)
    a. normative life events
    b. normative age-graded factors
    c. nonnormative history-graded factors
    d. nonnormative life events

Individual Learning Activity

Having read about the history of human life-span development, most of us are at first confused about how we can ever be sure we know anything at all. So often we have been told things which scientific studies later disprove or reject. One way to approach the issue is to develop some questions which reflect our own interests, then try to design research to answer the questions. Unfortunately, this is not quite as easy as it sounds.

Asking the right type of question is a key to doing useful research. This chapter opened with some observations and some questions about the nature of human development. Perhaps you can improve on this list of questions, and at the same time, become more aware of your specific interests which may have brought you to this course. Most of us, when confronted with this type of request, initially formulate questions reflecting subject variables, particularly those of age and sex. For example, we might wonder at what age children begin to realize that they remember events? At what age do they begin to plan and hope for the future? In what ways are females superior to males in accomplishing developmental tasks? See how easy it is to generate questions about topics of interest? Now it is your turn. Please generate at least three questions.

_____

_____

_____

_____

_____

Having done that, let's try to generate some more complex questions. For example, does the ability to develop a particular fear, such as fear of snakes, change with age? Or, does having only one parent make you more vulnerable to emotional distress? At what point in life is stress most debilitating? What is the effect of divorce on physical health over the following decade? What factors in early childhood predict high academic success in adulthood? As you can see, these questions involve more than subject variables. They involve what we might think of as manipulable variables, factors which you as a developmental researcher could actually manipulate to test their effects. Now, give it a try yourself. Please generate at least three more questions you would like to know the answers to:

_____
_____
_____
_____

Now comes the most difficult (and most rewarding) part. If you were to design a research project to deal with any one of these questions, you would obviously want your research to be designed in such a way that the findings would be clear and unequivocal. So often we read conflicting findings in both popular and professional literature. How can two scientists discover findings that oppose one another? One way to approach this issue is to attempt to more carefully define what you mean by the terms you used in the questions you just wrote. For example, if you use terms like *punishment* or *aggression*, just what factors would you manipulate or measure in each of those. If you think about the task of instructing a research assistant to help you, you will at once see the difficulty involved. How do you teach someone to observe behavior and count instances of some specific category of event or behavior? You need to be certain that what is counted by one observer is the same thing that another observer would count while watching the same behavioral samples. In other words, the results of your observations must be reliable. Very often different researchers arrive at different conclusions because they used the same terms to mean different things.

Another problem researchers have is being clear about the assumptions underlying their questions or hypotheses. Look again at the questions you wrote above. What assumptions are you making in each of those questions about human development? Are you assuming that development occurs in stages? Do your questions imply continuity or discontinuity in development? What do your questions say about the relative importance of maturation and experience? You might also look for what you did *not* ask as clues to your assumptions. It is important to make explicit the assumptions we bring to research projects, but it is equally important to be alert for unstated assumptions and implications in the research of others. As you read this text, please be alert to these implications.

Answers to the Self Test

1. c	6. c
2. a	7. a
3. b	8. b
4. c	9. b
5. a	10. c

2 World Views, Theories, and Methods: The Science of Life-Span Development

Preview

The term *scientific* implies the use of theories and methods. Thus, the science of life-span development is characterized by a host of systematic theories and a variety of research methods. Like other sciences, its goals are to describe, predict, understand, and control or change aspects of development.

World views are highly abstract, grand models that transcend more precise and testable models. Life-span development is largely dominated by three major world views: mechanistic, organismic, and contextual. The mechanistic world view sees the individual as a passive responder to environmental events. The organismic world view sees the person as an active and mindful planner whose characteristics unfold according to a biological timetable. The contextual world view combines the other two, characterizing the person as both acting on and responding to the environment. This view is sometimes referred to as dialectical, indicating disequilibrium and change which are assumed to be normal.

Theories are less abstract than world views, and are sets of assumptions which can be tested and either rejected or supported on the basis of evidence.

The behavioral perspective emphasizes the influence of the environment. Behavior is assumed to be learned. Behaviorists apply rigorous methodology, behavior analysis, and view cognitive events as outside the realm of scientific study. Skinner's traditional behaviorism emphasizes that behavior is determined by its consequences, usually learned in the paradigm of operant conditioning. Bandura's cognitive social learning theory emphasizes both self-produced consequences of one's own actions and the consequences of the actions of others, as well as reciprocal determinism. He emphasizes imitation, also called modeling or vicarious learning.

The strengths of the behavioral perspective include the emphasis on specific behaviors and determinants, the observational method, the rigorous experimental approach, the information processing perspective, and the focus on the variability of the environment. Its weaknesses include the exclusion of cognition, the non-chronological perspective, the scant attention to biological foundations, its fine-grained reductionism, and its mechanistic views.

The cognitive approach stresses mental processes. Cognitive developmental theory focuses on rational thinking, and stresses the unfolding of development in a stage-like sequence. Piaget's views dominate cognitive developmental theory. According to Piaget, cognitive development proceeds through sensorimotor, preoperational, concrete operational, and formal operational stages. He believed that changes in thought processes were the result of adaptation, organization, and equilibration. According to Piaget, adaptation could be further divided into assimilation and accommodation.

The information processing approach is an outgrowth of the advances in computer science, and is concerned with how we attend to, store, retrieve, and reason about information. Piaget's views are the prototype of the organismic world view, while the information processing perspective of cognitive development involves the mechanistic world view. The strengths of cognitive theory include a new way of thinking about thinking, an emphasis on maturational changes in thought processes, a strong research orientation, and precision in concepts. The weaknesses of this viewpoint include some skepticism about the pureness of stages, loose definitions of concepts, the lack of an overall perspective on development, and a de-emphasis of environmental experiences.

Psychoanalytic theories emphasize biological and cognitive elements, primarily unconscious thoughts. Freud's classical psychoanalytic theory proposed that behavior is typically guided by instincts, particularly those related to sex and aggression. He saw people in constant conflict as they progressed through the oral, anal, phallic, latent, and genital stages. Neo-psychoanalytic theorists, such as Erikson, have de-emphasized the role of sexual and aggressive instincts, and included culture as an important determinant of development. Erikson's view encompasses the entire life cycle, emphasizing eight stages or psychosocial crises: trust vs. mistrust, autonomy vs. shame and doubt, initiative vs. guilt, industry vs. inferiority, identity vs. identity confusion, intimacy vs. isolation, generativity vs. stagnation, and ego integrity vs. despair. While Freud's views are particularly organismic, Erikson's are also contextual in nature. The strengths of psychoanalytic theories include emphases on the past, development, mental representation of the environment, the unconscious, and conflict. Psychoanalytic views have had significant impact on developmental psychology. The weaknesses of this perspective include the difficulty of testing its concepts experimentally, its lack of an empirical data base, overemphasis on the unconscious and sexuality, a negative and pessimistic view of human nature, and too much emphasis on very early experience.

Since no major theoretical perspective can account fully for human development, we must be eclectic, accepting the best of each viewpoint, testing these assumptions and predictions scientifically.

Much developmental research is conducted in the laboratory, though this presents a risk that people will behave artificially in response to the unnatural environment. Methods used include the interview, a set of questions asked of a person; and questionnaires which are similar to interviews, but the questions and answers are written. In both techniques, questions must be concrete, and answers must be assessed for veracity. Retrospective strategies are seriously affected by distortions in memory, and should be avoided. Standardized tests permit comparisons between individuals. Case studies involve an in-depth study of one individual, usually done by a clinical psychologist. The clinical method involves intense study of a small sample of people, using specialized interviewing procedures. Physiological research, and other research with animals, provides opportunities not available with humans, but risks not being generalizable. In testing terms, reliability refers to consistency, and validity refers to the ability of a test to measure what it claims to measure.

There are several research strategies. In an experiment, subjects are randomly assigned to one of two groups. The experimental group is subjected to the independent variable, the effect of which is measured in terms of the dependent variable. The control group provides a baseline for comparison because it is not exposed to the independent variable. The experiment allows us to make conclusions about causal relationships between variables. When the independent variable is not subject to experimental manipulation, but is a subject variable such as age, sex, or education, a quasi-experiment is conducted, with subjects matched on as many other relevant variables as possible. The quasi-experiment does not permit causal conclusions. The relationship of one variable to another is expressed in terms of the correlation coefficient.

Developmental research may involve any of a number of time spans. Cross-sectional studies involve testing subjects of varying ages in a brief time span and using age differences as indicators of developmental changes. This strategy cannot control for cohort effects, however. In a longitudinal study, members of a single cohort are tested repeatedly over a long time interval, but this strategy fails to control for the effects of repeated testing and time of measurement. Sequential designs combine the best of both cross-sectional and longitudinal designs, and are most efficient.

Learning Objectives

1. Define a world view, and describe mechanistic, organismic, and contextual world views. (p. 33)
2. Define a scientific theory, and describe behavioral, cognitive, and psychoanalytic theories. (p. 34)
3. List and describe strengths and weaknesses of behavioral, cognitive, and psychoanalytic perspectives. (p. 35)
4. List and summarize each of Piaget's stages of cognitive development. (p. 38)
5. Define what is meant by adaptation, assimilation, accommodation, organization, and equilibration. (p. 40)
6. Trace psychosexual development through the oral, anal, phallic, latency, and genital stages, explaining the major tasks of each stage. (p. 43)
7. List two ways in which Erikson's theory differs from Freud's. (p. 43)
8. Identify and describe each of Erikson's eight stages of human development, articulating the psychosocial crisis faced at each stage, and defining the conditions for positive resolution. (p. 44)
9. Describe the nature of scientific observation, and define interviews, questionnaire, standardized tests, case studies, and the clinical method. (p. 50)
10. Compare research designs, including the experiment, quasi-experiment, and correlational designs. (p. 56)
11. Create examples of cross-sectional, longitudinal, and sequential designs, showing the strengths and weaknesses of each. (p. 58)

Key Terms

For each key term, write the definition in the space provided.

science (1, p. 33) _____

world view (1, p. 33) _____

mechanistic world view (1, p. 33) _____

organismic world view (1, p. 33) _____

contextual world view (1, p. 34) _____

dialectical (1, p. 34) _____

theories (2, p. 34) _____

behavioral perspective (2, p. 35) _____

operant conditioning (2, p. 35) _____

instrumental conditioning (2, p. 35) _____

cognitive social learning theory (2, p. 36) _____

reciprocal determinism (2, p. 36) _____

imitation (2, p. 36) _____

sensorimotor stage (4, p. 38) _____

Guided Review

1. In this chapter we encounter a wide variety of world views. A highly abstract, grand model that transcends more precise models or theories, would be called a _____ _____ .
   (1, p. 33)

   world view

2. World views encompass more specific, testable models, often called _____ . (1, p. 34)

   theories

3. Three major world views currently are prominent in the study of life-span _____ .
   (1, p. 33)

   development

4. Mechanistic, organismic, and contextual are the names given these three grand models or _____
   _____ . (1, p. 33)

   world views

5. The notion that the individual is a passive machine, responding almost thoughtlessly to the environment, without planning, anticipating, or other complex internal activities is referred to as the _____
   world view. (1, p. 33)

   mechanistic

6. That world view which sees the individual as unfolding biological potential, and conceptualizes the person in active and mindful terms, is the _____ world view. (1, p. 33)

   organismic

7. The alternative world view that sees the individual as responding to and acting on the environment in which he or she lives, is the _____ world view. (1, p. 34)

   contextual

8. Another term for the contextual world view is _____ , which emphasizes that the individual is constantly changing, as are the contexts in which he finds himself. (1, p. 34)

   dialectical

9. Subsumed under world views are organized and logical sets of assumptions, laws, and axioms, called
   _____ . (2, p. 34)

   theories

10. The behavioral viewpoint is characterized by Skinner's traditional behaviorism and Bandura's cognitive social learning theory, both of which share the _____ world view. (2, p. 36)

    mechanistic

11. Behaviorists assert that the study of overt behavior is more important in understanding development than is the study of covert feelings and thoughts. "You are what you do" is a consistent maxim of _____ . (2, p. 35)

behaviorists

12. Human behavior is learned as a function of experience, according to _____ . (2, p. 35)

behaviorists

13. According to Skinner, stimuli and responses become linked in accord with laws and principles, particularly those of reinforcement and punishment. Operant conditioning accounts for the largest share of learned human response patterns, according to _____ . (2, p. 35)

Skinner

14. The key element of behaviorism, as expressed by B. F. Skinner, is that we are regulated by the consequences of our actions. The formal postulates of operant conditioning have been carefully researched and presented by _____ . (2, p. 35)

B. F. Skinner

15. According to the concept of reinforcement, behaviors which are followed by positive (desired) consequences are likely to recur. We can say that any behavior followed by a positive consequence is strengthened, or _____ . (2, p. 35)

reinforced

16. Cognitive social learning theory asserts that the social environment is very important. How our behavior is evaluated by others, and how we perceive those responses, are items of great interest to cognitive _____ _____ theorists. (2, p. 36)

social learning

17. Cognitive social learning theory also holds that self-reinforcement is just as important as reinforcement from others. Albert Bandura is a major proponent of _____ social learning theory. (2, p. 36)

cognitive

18. Bandura proposes the concept of reciprocal determinism. He says that the person's psychological development is best understood by analyzing the continuous interaction between behavior and its controlling conditions. This interaction affects both the behavior and the environment, so Bandura calls it _____ determinism. (2, p. 36)

reciprocal

19. Bandura also believes that people learn by imitating models. When a child sees an act of violence on TV, and then acts violently to another, we call this learning _____ . (2, p. 36)

imitation

20. Psychology is currently in the midst of a cognitive revolution. Behavioral perspectives are having to share the center stage with a renewed interest in _____ psychology. (2, p. 37)

cognitive

21. A focus on mental processes as key ingredients of development is the hallmark of _____ developmental theory. (2, p. 37)

cognitive

22. The major architect of cognitive developmental theory was Jean Piaget. A major theory of intelligence and its development has been the primary focus of the work of _____ . (2, p. 37)

Piaget

23. Piaget was concerned with the development of intelligence, not its measurement. He was concerned with how children think, rather than their ability to do well on an intelligence _____ . (2, p. 37)

test

24. Piaget was also interested in the general nature of thought at a given stage, rather than how children at each stage differed. The basic processes in the development of intelligence were the focus of the work of _____ . (2, p. 38)

Piaget

25. Piaget proposed several stages in the development of _____ . (4, p. 38)

intelligence

26. The first stage is called sensorimotor, lasting for about the first two years of life. Infants develop the ability to associate and coordinate sensations and motor responses during the _____ stage. (4, p. 38)

sensorimotor

27. From age two to seven years, the preoperational stage ensues. The child begins to symbolize events during the _____ stage. (4, p. 38)

preoperational

28. Children display egocentrism in their thinking during the preoperational stage. When the child cannot imagine how a scene would look to a person with a different vantage point, he is exhibiting _____ . (4, p. 38)

egocentrism

29. During the concrete operations stage, egocentrism is replaced by relativism. When the child can visualize another person's perspective, or can think about more than one aspect of a problem at once, the child is demonstrating _____ . (4, p. 39)

relativism

30. With adolescence comes the stage called formal operations. Thinking logically, manipulating abstract propositions, and generating and testing hypotheses, are all manifestations of the stage of _____ _____ . (4, p. 39)

formal operations

31. According to Piaget, three major processes transcend the stages of intellectual development. Adaptation refers to effective interaction with the environment. Assimilation and accommodation are the two components of _____ . (5, p. 40)

adaptation

32. Assimilation refers to the strategy of fitting new experiences into existing categories. When a child calls a butterfly a "birdie" because it can fly, the child is using _____ . (5, p. 40)

assimilation

33. When assimilation fails, accommodation works. Creating new categories, and redefining the parameters of existing categories, is called _____ . (5, p. 40)

accommodation

34. Organization is another major process, which occurs in each stage and across stages. In order to make use of knowledge, and to strategically solve problems, the child must have a way to _____ what is known. (5, p. 40)

organize

35. Equilibration helps explain the progression to a more advanced stage. When the person is aware that current abilities and strategies do not resolve all problems, and when the person is thus motivated to resolve the conflict to reach a balance of thought, _____ has occurred. (5, p. 40)

equilibration

36. The information processing approach is concerned with how we process what we know about the world. Research into how we attend to, store, retrieve, or reason about information is subsumed under the _____ _____ approach. (5, p. 40)

information processing

37. The first major modern theory of human development was proposed by Sigmund Freud. This theory is called psychoanalytic theory, or _____ theory, after its author. (6, p. 41)

Freudian

38. Freud proposed that our behavior is motivated by instincts. Freud called the strong biological forces which initiate and guide our behavior _____ . (6, p. 42)

instincts

39. Freud saw human development as the result of changes in the way the energy from _____ is channeled. (6, p. 42)

instincts

40. Freud detailed five stages of what he called psychosexual development. During each of the first three of these stages, pleasure arises from a different body region, called an erogenous zone. Psychosexual development can be thought of as a progression through different _____ zones. (6, p. 43)

erogenous

41. The first year of life is termed the oral stage. A small baby receives pleasure from lip stimulation, sucking, and biting during the _____ stage. (6, p. 43)

oral

42. The second and third years of life are called the anal stage. Pleasure with elimination, or voluntary retention, of waste matter is a feature of the _____ stage. (6, p. 43)

anal

43. Toilet training is a potential conflict during the _____ stage, just as weaning is during the _____ stage. (6, p. 43)

anal, oral (in that order)

44. During the third or phallic stage, pleasure is obtained from manipulation of the genitals. Conflicts about self-stimulation and about sex roles are common during the _____ stage. (6, p. 43)

phallic

45. During the phallic stage, boys experience the Oedipus complex, and girls experience the Electra complex. These complexes refer to vacillating feelings of affection and hatred for the parent of the same sex that occur during the _____ stage. (6, p. 43)

phallic

46. Freud believed that young children secretly want to eliminate and replace the parent of the same sex during the _____ stage. (6, p. 43)

phallic

47. These desires produce internal conflict and fear that the parent of the same sex will retaliate and punish the child. This fear is repressed or pushed out of consciousness. The child is able to identify with the parent of the same sex only after the fear is _____ . (6, p. 43)

repressed

48. This repression, Freud said, marks the onset of the latency stage, which lasts from age six through about age twelve. Freud believed that there was little sexual interest during the _____ stage. (6, p. 43)

latency

49. With puberty and adolescence, we enter the genital stage. Freud proposed that the last major stage of development begins at puberty and lasts throughout adult life, a stage he called _____ . (6, p. 43)

genital

50. Freud observed the sharp increase in interest in sexual matters which forces the individual to formulate a personal and sexual identity, and which characterizes the _____ stage. (6, p. 43)

genital

51. Freud said that some love of self, which characterizes earlier stages, is transformed into real love for another, during the _____ stage. (6, p. 43)

genital

52. Recall that Freud proposed that all behavior is motivated by unconscious drives and instinctual needs, and we can rarely be aware of why we actually do things. Many psychologists disagree with this strong emphasis on _____ motivation. (6, p. 43)

unconscious (or instinctual)

53. One person who disagreed with Freud's emphasis on unconscious influences was Erik Erikson, who has proposed major revisions to psychoanalytic theory. Erikson puts more emphasis on culture and society, and less on _____ aspects. (7, p. 44)

unconscious

54. Erikson's theory also differs from Freud's in its life-span perspective. Whereas Freud emphasized development in infancy and childhood, Erikson discusses development across the entire _____ . (7, p. 44)

life span

55. Erikson postulates eight stages of development. At each stage the individual faces a psychosocial conflict. Thus, at each major stage of development, we face one issue which overshadows all others, an issue which Erikson calls a _____ _____ . (8, p. 44)

psychosocial conflict

56. Erikson's first stage involves the development of trust or mistrust. If the infant's needs are met regularly and consistently, the infant will develop a sense of _____ in the world. (8, p. 44)

trust

57. If the infant's needs are ignored or not met consistently, the infant will learn to _____ . (8, p. 44)

mistrust

58. This first stage, trust vs. mistrust, occupies the first year of life, and corresponds to Freud's _____ stage. (8, p. 44)

oral

59. Corresponding to Freud's anal stage is Erikson's stage of autonomy vs. shame and doubt. A child who is given small doses of freedom and encouraged to make appropriate decisions will develop a sense of _____ . (8, p. 45)

autonomy

60. The child who is always told that he is not capable of much, or who is measured against impossible expectations, learns to feel _____ or to doubt that he is capable of independent action. (8, p. 45)

shame

61. The third stage of Erikson's theory is focused on the conflict of initiative vs. guilt. Here the child tries new activities and learns to feel capable of taking the _____ , particularly in solving problems. (8, p. 45)

initiative

62. The child who is not successful at solving problems, or who does not have the encouragement and support to try out ideas, learns to feel _____ as a result of these inabilities. (8, p. 45)

guilt

63. During middle childhood, the conflict of focus is industry vs. inferiority. If the child has the opportunity to apply newly learned facts and skills, and to evaluate these applications positively, then a sense of _____ will develop. (8, p. 46)

industry

64. If on the other hand the child does not have the opportunities to learn and apply new information, or if these applications are evaluated negatively by parents, peers, or self, then a sense of personal _____ will emerge, and may distort the child's sense of self for years to come. (8, p. 46)

inferiority

65. The confidence and assurance needed to meet new situations and challenges in a positive way, results from the development of a sense of _____ in late childhood, according to _____ . (8, p. 46)

industry, Erikson

66. During early adolescence, each of us struggled with the question of who we are. Erikson calls this the conflict of identity vs. identity confusion. In order to plan our futures, each of us had to establish a personal _____ . (8, p. 46)

identity

67. Failure to discover or define or decide who we are, results in a state Erikson calls _____
_____ . (8, p. 46)

identity confusion

68. Following the establishment of personal identity, the individual is ready, in early adulthood, to confront the issue of intimacy vs. isolation. Both a number of friendships, and a significant, intimate relationship with another person are crucial to the development of _____ . (8, p. 47)

intimacy

69. Failure to establish a sense of intimacy can result in _____ . (8, p. 47)

isolation

70. During middle adulthood, the focus is often on child rearing. Erikson reflects this focus by emphasizing the struggle between generativity and stagnation. The person who is productive and who has influence on the development of children is likely to develop a sense of _____ . (8, p. 47)

generativity

71. The adult who does not have the sense of influence on the next generation may develop a feeling of being a person of no lasting consequence, which Erikson refers to as a sense of _____ . (8, p. 47)

stagnation

72. In old age, the person reviews his or her life history, and develops a sense of either ego integrity or despair. If in retrospect life has been basically successful, and has made sense to the individual, then _____
_____ is the result. (8, p. 47)

ego integrity

73. Unfortunately, some people look back over their lives with bitterness and resentment, focusing on what might have been or what they wish they had done. These individuals risk ending life on a note of _____ .
(8, p. 47)

despair

74. Some students also despair when they confront the wide variety of theoretical perspective we have just reviewed. It is clear that no single _____ can account for all the evidence of life-span developmental research. (2, p. 50)

theory

75. But the variety of theories does help in the generation of ideas, postulates, and hypotheses (testable ideas) for research. In fact, a major use of theories is to obtain hypotheses to test with _____ . (2, p. 50)

research

76. The earliest scientific method is observation. When we systematically observe some aspect of behavior in a real-life setting, we are using scientific _____ . (9, p. 50)

observation

77. For observation to qualify as scientific inquiry, it must meet several requirements. First, the observer must be trained to look for certain behaviors. When we define for an observer exactly what we mean by aggression, and instruct that person to record only aggressive behaviors meeting our definition, our observations become more s _____ . (9, p. 50)

(s)cientific

78. Focusing on observable behaviors is one way to increase reliability. When two or more observers agree on their observations, we say the observations are _____ . (9, p. 50)

reliable

79. Much of the research in life-span development is conducted in the laboratory, where much greater control is possible than is the case with simple _____ . (9, p. 50)

observation

80. There are some costs involved in such research, however. There is quite a bit of difference between the real world and the setting of the _____ . (9, p. 50)

laboratory

81. Thus, in such an "unnatural" environment, the behavior of people might also be _____ . (9, p. 50)

unnatural

82. In addition to observation, there are several other techniques for collecting information. When we ask someone a set of questions and record the person's responses, we are using the _____ technique. (9, p. 51)

interview

83. If we write the questions down, and the person responds by marking answers on a sheet of paper, the procedure is termed a _____ . (9, p. 51)

questionnaire

84. Questions must be very specific, and there should be some assessment of the veracity of the replies, when one conducts large scale surveys with _____ . (9, p. 51)

questionnaires

85. When we want to compare one person with others, we can use a standardized _____ . (9, p. 52)

test

86. By allowing comparisons of one person with large numbers of other people, standardized tests provide information about individual _____ . (9, p. 52)

differences

87. Sometimes it is helpful to take an in-depth look at one particular person. This procedure, used mainly by clinical psychologists, is called the _____ _____ . (9, p. 52)

case study

88. Clinical psychologists also use another method, which involves reports summarizing a small number of similar cases. This procedure, involving specialized observing and interviewing skills, is called the _____ method. (9, p. 52)

clinical

89. Some psychologists conduct physiological research and other types of research with animals. Assessing the behavioral impact of a new drug is an example of _____ research. (9, p. 52)

physiological

90. In many other cases, too, we cannot ethically subject humans to some procedures, such as selective breeding of genetic defects; so the research is conducted on _____ . (9, p. 52)

animals

91. There are a number of strategies of research design currently used in life-span development. The nature of our inquiry and what we want to learn help us to choose the most appropriate research _____ . (10, p. 56)

design

92. Observation cannot tell us what aspects of the environment cause which behaviors to occur. Only the experimental design can give us information about _____ and effects. (10, p. 56)

causes

93. If we want to know what causes what, we must conduct an _____ . (10, p. 56)

experiment

94. In an experiment, the scientist specifies or manipulates one variable, the independent variable. The experiment is designed to discover the effect of such manipulation of the _____ variable. (10, p. 56)

independent

95. The experimenter measures the effect of the independent variable on the behavior of interest, called the dependent variable. The measure of behavior that changes as a result of the manipulation of the independent variable is called the _____ variable. (10, p. 56)

dependent

96. If an experimenter varied the level of difficulty of test items and measured the effect on the students' feelings of confidence after the test, the difficulty of the items would be the _____ variable. (10, p. 56)

independent

97. In the example of test item difficulty and students' feelings of confidence, the feelings of confidence would be the _____ variable. (10, p. 56)

dependent

98. In an experiment, all other variables other than the independent variable are held constant, or controlled. We also need to control for differences between research participants. The easiest way to do this is to assign participants (subjects) to experimental conditions by _____ selection. (10, p. 56)

random

99. In an experiment, we are basically comparing two groups on the dependent variable. One group receives the independent variable, and is called the experimental group. The other group does not experience the independent variable, and is called the _____ group. (10, p. 56)

control

100. If the independent variable has an effect, there will be a difference between the experimental group and the control group on the _____ variable. (10, p. 56)

dependent

101. Sometimes we cannot randomly assign subjects to conditions or groups. If the independent variable is one such as age or sex or marital status, we cannot assign subjects to various conditions of these variables by a _____ system of assignment. (10, p. 56)

random

102. In this type of situation, the procedure is called a quasi-experiment, because we cannot _____ assign subjects to conditions. (10, p. 56)

randomly

103. In a quasi-experiment, variables other than the independent variable may be influencing the dependent variable, so we cannot draw conclusions about cause and effect from a _____ . (10, p. 56)

quasi-experiment

104. Sometimes it is not feasible to conduct an experiment or quasi-experiment, but we want to know whether two variables are related. A correlation coefficient can tell us the nature and strength of the _____ between two variables. (10, p. 57)

relationship

105. The nature and degree of relationship are reflected in the algebraic sign and numerical value of the _____ coefficient. (10, p. 57)

correlation

106. In many cases, the relationship is direct. If one variable increases as the other increases, the correlation is positive, and the relationship is said to be _____ . (10, p. 57)

direct

107. Sometimes, however, the relationship is inverse, and the correlation has a _____ sign, showing that one variable increases as the other decreases. (10, p. 57)

negative

108. The correlation coefficient ranges from +1.0 to -1.0. The stronger the relationship between the two variables, the closer the correlation coefficient is to _____ . (10, p. 57)

1.0

109. Correlations cannot reveal cause-and-effect relationships. Causality can only be determined by conducting an _____ . (10, p. 57)

experiment

110. All these procedures are useful for different purposes and to discover different types of information. All can be used in designs involving different time spans. Based on the time span of the inquiry, we may select one of three major strategies of _____ . (11, p. 58)

research

111. The most simple and quick design is cross-sectional. When we compare people of different ages, testing them all within a short time period, we are using the _____ design. (11, p. 58)

cross-sectional

112. The cross-sectional design has limits, however. How do we know whether differences between age groups are the result of development or are due to differences in experiences due to the time of birth? These questions cannot be answered by the _____ design. (11, p. 58)

cross-sectional

113. An obvious way to approach the problem of focusing directly on developmental changes is with a longitudinal design. If we follow a group of people over several years, periodically measuring some aspect of their behavior to determine developmental changes, we are using a _____ design. (11, p. 59)

longitudinal

114. However, longitudinal designs cannot control for cohort effects. The specific differences between people due to time of birth or generation, but not to age, are called _____ effects. (11, p. 59)

cohort

115. It is possible to combine the best features of cross-sectional and longitudinal designs in using sequential designs. We can control for both repeated testing and cohort effects using a _____ design. (11, p. 59)

sequential

116. Schaie promotes the use of what he calls the most efficient design, which is the most elaborate of the _____ designs. (11, p. 60)

sequential

Speaking of sequences, this review has been a long one. Take a break, then be sure to review the learning objectives before doing your best on the self test.

Self Test

1. The mechanistic world view (1, p. 53)
   a. is best represented by Piaget's theory
   b. perceives the individual as master of the environment
   c. encompasses traditional behaviorism and cognitive social learning theory
   d. is closely allied with psychoanalytic theory

2. According to Freud, the central feature of human motivation is (2, p. 42)
   a. instinctual
   b. rational thinking
   c. intellectual development in stages
   d. reasoned reaction to the violence of others

3. Erikson's theory differs from Freud's in that Erikson (7, p. 44)
   a. emphasized sexual and aggressive motives
   b. does not accept the notion of the unconscious
   c. disregarded the role of culture
   d. emphasized development throughout the life span

4. According to Erikson, adolescence is a time for developing (8, p. 46)
   a. a sense of trust in the world
   b. a sense of our own identity
   c. intimate relationships
   d. career goals and opportunities

5. In middle adulthood, according to Erikson, emphasis is on (8, p. 47)
   a. ego integrity
   b. success at work
   c. child rearing
   d. dealing with the death of parents

6. Piaget's theory originated from his (4, p. 37)
   a. desire to measure individual differences in children's academic potential
   b. concern about how children think at different stages
   c. interest in the unconscious elements in children's dreams
   d. work assignment of correctly placing children in school levels

7. The shift from egocentrism to relativism occurs during which stage? (4, p. 39)
   a. sensorimotor
   b. preoperational
   c. concrete operations
   d. formal operations

8. A behaviorist would say (2, p. 35)
   a. we must develop insight into our unconscious impulses
   b. to self actualize we must escape routine contingencies of life
   c. our behavior is governed by the nature of its consequences
   d. most of our behavior is shaped by evolutionary forces of which we can be only partially aware

9. When we repeatedly measure some aspect of behavior of a particular group of subjects over several years, we are using a (11, p. 58)
   a. cross-sectional design
   b. longitudinal design
   c. sequential design
   d. cohort effects model

10. In an experiment, the researcher manipulates and tests the effects of the (10, p. 56)
    a. subject variables
    b. independent variable
    c. dependent variable
    d. correlation coefficient

Individual Learning Activity

Each of the theories we have studied differs from the other theories in several ways: comprehensiveness, clarity, researchability, and others. One key difference has to do with the underlying assumptions. For example, Freud's theory assumes we are in a constant struggle between instinctual drives and social constraints, that there is an unconscious, and so forth. To discover which theory can account for most anecdotal (rather than scientific) evidence, it is useful to find out which assumptions are widely held by nonscientists.

One way to do this is to ask at least ten people of varying ages what they consider to be the basic characteristics of human nature. There are many ways to ask this same question: What is the basic quality which makes us human? What accounts for the reality of our lives? What makes people tick? Why do people develop the way they do?

Your task is to interview at least ten people, and list their assumptions about human nature. How do these assumptions align with the major theories we have studied in this chapter? Which theories would most appeal to the people you questioned?

You could also write a brief list of assumptions, or test, based on the assumptions you have discovered, or on those implicit in the theories you have studied, and ask people to what extent they agree or disagree with each statement. This gives you an easier-to-handle set of data. The key here is to be clear about the differences in assumptions between the major theories.

Answers to the Self Test

1. c	6. b
2. a	7. c
3. d	8. c
4. b	9. b
5. c	10. b

3 Biological Foundations of Development

Preview

In evolutionary terms, human history is very brief, yet humans have established themselves quickly as a very successful and dominant species. Looking backward at evolution, Haeckel proposed that ontogeny, the development of an individual organism, recapitulates phylogeny, the development of the group of organisms or species. This belief, as well as that of terminal addition, are no longer viable. According to Darwin's observations, evolution is the result of natural selection of adaptive characteristics from the range of genetic diversity. Evolution is the key to ethology. The concept of critical periods originated in the study of embryology; and it is used less rigorously in terms of human development, where we find optimal periods for the development of attachment, language, and vision. Ethologists have also articulated the phenomena of imprinting and the triggering of fixed action patterns by sign stimuli.

Newborns have a number of behavioral capabilities that are preadapted. Many characteristic abilities appear before they are needed; thus, maturation is said to occur with a forward reference. As development unfolds, behavior becomes more differentiated, and at least neurologically, more hierarchically organized.

Our inherited genetic code is carried by biochemical agents called chromosomes and genes. Each human cell contains twenty-three pairs of chromosomes, each consisting of thousands of genes. The genes are constructed of DNA, and are transmitted from parents to offspring in gametes or sex cells; each of which, as a result of meiosis, contains half the genetic material of its parent cell. Reproduction occurs when sperm and ovum meet and merge to form a zygote.

The complement of inherited genes constitutes the genotype, while those ultimately expressed as measurable characteristics comprise the phenotype. Some genes are dominant over other, recessive, genes; some genes are sex-linked, carried on the twenty-third pair of chromosomes. Most characteristics are influenced by more than one gene, a phenomenon called polygenic inheritance.

Human characteristics are the result of an interaction of hereditary and environmental influences. The genetic material generates a reaction range within which environmental forces determine the final expression of the characteristic or trait. The concept of reaction range is most evident in the development of intelligence, and in the modification of the effects of genetic diseases such as phenylketonuria (PKU). Some human characteristics are canalized, and are not sensitive to environmental forces.

Behavior genetics is that discipline concerned with the degree and extent of the hereditary determination of behavior. Behavior geneticists use several techniques, including selective breeding, which is the mating of organisms of similar characteristics, and inbreeding, which involves the mating of siblings. Of course, these two techniques can be used only with nonhuman animals. With humans, behavior geneticists use twin studies, comparing monozygotic and dizygotic twins, family of twins designs, involving all nuclear family relationships, and kinship studies, which involve family members of even distant relationship. Adoption studies permit a direct comparison of the relative influences of hereditary and environmental variables. The goal of all this research is the determination of heritability, a mathematical estimate of the degree to which any characteristic is genetically determined or influenced. In humans, intelligence, schizophrenia, vocational interests, and personality have significant, known heritability factors.

It is crucial to remember that development depends on the interaction of genetic and environmental variables, both of which are necessary for development to proceed. We do not yet have genetic or evolutionary models of development across the life span.

Sociobiology is the controversial view that all social behavior is genetically influenced, and is motivated by the opportunity to insure the future survival of the individual's genes.

Learning Objectives

1. Describe the course of evolution, and comment on the viability of statements linking phylogeny and ontogeny. (p. 70)
2. Define and give an example of natural selection, showing its relationship to evolution. (p. 71)
3. Describe ethology, and define critical periods, fixed-action pattern, and sign stimulus, showing how each relates to human development. (p. 72)
4. Explain preadaptation and the development of hierarchical organization. (p. 75)
5. Define *chromosome, gene, dominant, recessive, genotype, phenotype,* and *gene pool.* (p. 76)
6. List and describe the sequence of events by which sperm and ovum combine to form a new life. (p. 76)
7. Explain that some inherited characteristics are sex-linked, resulting in disproportionate incidences among males or females. (p. 79)
8. Give an example of polygenic inheritance and explain the concepts of reaction range and canalization. (p. 79)
9. Describe and differentiate selective breeding and inbreeding designs used in genetic research with animals. (p. 81)
10. Identify two strategies of genetic research used with human subjects. (p. 82)
11. Define *heritability* and provide some examples of ranges of heritability coefficients for intelligence, schizophrenia, vocational interests, and personality. (p. 83)
12. Describe sociobiology and its major tenets, and compare it to the traditional nature/nurture debate. (p. 87)

Key Terms

For each key term, write the definition in the space provided.

ontogeny recapitulates phylogeny (1, p. 70) _____

ontogeny (1, p. 70) _____

phylogeny (1, p. 70) _____

terminal addition (1, p. 70) _____

natural selection (2, p. 71) _____

ethology (3, p. 72) _____

critical periods (3, p. 72) _____

fixed-action pattern (3, p. 74) _____

sign stimulus (3, p. 74) _____

preadapted (4, p. 75) _____

forward reference (4, p. 75) _____

differentiation (4, p. 75) _____

hierarchical organization (4, p. 75) _____

chromosomes (5, p. 76) _____

genes (5, p. 76) _____

gametes (6, p. 76) _____

meiosis (6, p. 76) _____

reproduction (6, p. 76) _____

genotype (5, p. 78) _____

phenotype (5, p. 78) _____

dominant-recessive (5, p. 78) _____

sex-linked genes (7, p. 79) _____

polygenic inheritance (8, p. 79) _____

reaction range (8, p. 80) _____

phenylketonuria (8, p. 80) _____

canalization (8, p. 80) _____

behavior genetics (9, p. 81) _____

selective breeding (9, p. 81) _____

inbreeding (9, p. 82) _____

monozygotic (10, p. 82) _____

dyzygotic (10, p. 82) _____

twin studies (10, p. 82) _____

family-of-twins design (10, p. 82) _____

kinship studies (10, p. 82) _____

adoption studies (10, p. 83) _____

heritability (11, p. 83) _____

neuroticism (11, p. 85) _____

extraversion (11, p. 85) _____

sociobiology (12, p. 87) _____

Guided Review

1. Against the backdrop of the evolution of many other species, humans have arrived only lately. We are not very far advanced in our own _____ . (1, p. 70)

   evolution

2. People have tried many ways to conceptualize human evolution. Haeckel's suggestion that ontogeny recapitulates phylogeny is one attempt to clarify the course of human _____ . (1, p. 70)

   evolution

3. Ontogeny refers to the development of any specific organism. Since each of us has a unique course of development, we could refer to our individual _____ . (1, p. 70)

   ontogeny

4. By contrast, the evolutionary history of a group of organisms, perhaps a species, is called its _____ . (1, p. 70)

   phylogeny

5. Haeckel's view was based on mistaken observation of the embryonic form, in which folds of tissue were interpreted to be gill slits, like those on fish. Today, we do not believe that ontogeny recapitulates _____ . (1, p. 70)

   phylogeny

6. Evolution can be explained in terms of natural selection. The process by which some characteristics survived over many generations and others were lost is referred to as _____ _____ . (2, p. 71)

   natural selection

7. Those characteristics which were adaptive permitted those organisms having them to survive and reproduce to a greater extent than those organisms lacking the adaptive _____ . (2, p. 71)

characteristics

8. Thus, nature selected some to survive and reproduce, hence the term _____ selection. (2, p. 71)

natural

9. Evolution is the key to ethology. According to ethologists, many forms of behavior are transmitted and sustained by the processes of _____ . (3, p. 72)

evolution

10. One of the most important concepts of ethology is that of critical period. A time during development when specific forms of stimulation are needed for normal development is called a _____ _____ . (3, p. 72)

critical period

11. In humans, the concept of critical period is not used as rigorously as in embryology, but language development in early childhood is an example of a _____ _____ . (3, p. 72)

critical period

12. Another ethological concept is that of the fixed-action pattern. Unlearned behavior that is universal in a species is called a _____ _____ . (3, p. 74)

fixed-action pattern

13. A fixed-action pattern is triggered by a sign stimulus. According to ethologists, behavior such as sex recognition is triggered by _____ _____ such as body contour or breast size. (3, p. 74)

sign stimuli

14. Newborns come into the world preadapted in many respects. When behavior is preparatory or anticipatory, we say that the organism is _____ . (4, p. 75)

preadapted

15. Indeed, sucking reflexes are well developed during the prenatal period. This forward reference of neurological maturation is a good example of the organism being _____ for life. (4, p. 75)

preadapted

16. As development unfolds, it becomes differentiated. The language of the ten-year-old permits more precise descriptions of events than that of the five-year-old, thanks to the _____ of language. (4, p. 75)

differentiation

17. Also, development involves hierarchical organization. We know from studies of memory as well as of motor behaviors, that most behavior patterns are organized in _____ . (4, p. 75)

hierarchies

18. Each of us carries the genetic code we inherited from our parents. Many of our characteristics and traits, as well as some specific behavior patterns, may be directly linked to our _____ code. (5, p. 76)

genetic

19. Hereditary codes are activated for a specific person at the time of conception. The joining of a sperm and ovum constitutes the event we call _____ . (6, p. 76)

conception

20. Sperm cells and ova (the plural of ovum) are gametes. Unlike other body cells, _____ have only 23 chromosomes in each nucleus. (6, p. 76)

gametes (or sperm, ova)

21. Other body cells contain 46 chromosomes, or 23 pairs. All of the cells of the body, except gametes, contain 23 pairs of or 46 _____ . (5, p. 76)

chromosomes

22. Chromosomes are structures composed of smaller molecules, called genes. Each chromosome contains thousands of _____ . (5, p. 76)

genes

23. A gene is also a complex structure. The basis for the genetic information which directs the development of each person is carried in these _____ . (5, p. 76)

genes

24. Each of us inherits a unique combination of genetic instructions called a genotype. We could say that our _____ is like a blueprint for our development. (5, p. 78)

genotype

25. However, not all genetic instructions are carried out. Some are recessive and are superceded by dominant instructions. Those which are realized and are observable constitute the phenotype. The phenotype is a subset or component cluster of the _____ . (5, p. 78)

genotype

26. Of the genetic instructions contained in the genotype, those which are realized in physical or psychological characteristics of the individual constitute the _____ . (5, p. 78)

phenotype

27. Each parent contributes exactly half of the hereditary material. Recall that sperm cell and ovum each contain 23 _____ . (6, p. 76)

chromosomes

28. All of the other body cells contain _____ _____ . (6, p. 76)

46 chromosomes (or 23 pairs)

29. When sperm and ovum unite to form a zygote, this new structure also has _____ chromosomes. (6, p. 76)

46

30. Just as different voices carry for different distances, so are some genetic instructions stronger than others. Those which are expressed in the _____ are called dominant, while those which are found only in the _____ are called recessive. (5, p. 78)

phenotype, genotype (in that order)

31. Some genetic instructions are linked to the chromosomes which determine the sex of the individual, so they are called sex-linked. Color blindness is a _____ characteristic. (7, p. 79)

sex-linked

32. The chromosomes responsible for sex determination are usually referred to as the 23rd pair. In females these are both shaped like an X, so a female would have two X chromosomes in the _____ pair. (7, p. 79)

23rd

33. Males have one X chromosome and one Y chromosome. Many sex-linked characteristics are tied to the X chromosome. Since _____ have only one X chromosome, they are more likely to manifest a sex-linked characteristic. (7, p. 79)

males

34. Not all characteristics are determined by one pair of genes; some characteristics are polygenically determined. When a characteristic is controlled by several genes, we say it is _____ determined. (8, p. 79)

polygenically

35. With many genes interacting to determine a single characteristic, dominance and recessiveness become relative, not absolute. Therefore, dominance and recessiveness are relative in _____ determined characteristics. (8, p. 79)

polygenically

36. Genetic influences also interact with environmental variables. Most psychological characteristics are the result of this type of genetic-environmental _____ . (8, p. 80)

interaction

37. Just as some genes are dominant and some recessive, so is the genetic blueprint for some characteristics more emphatic than it is for other _____ . (8, p. 80)

characteristics

38. In the interaction, then, the environment may play a major role, or have relatively little influence in the course of development of a characteristic primarily determined by _____ . (8, p. 79)

heredity

39. For each characteristic, it is wise to think in terms of a reaction range determined genetically. Environmental influences can only affect development for that characteristic within its genetically determined _____ _____ . (8, p. 80)

reaction range

40. In many cases the reaction range is quite broad, so the impact of the _____ is significant. (8, p. 80)

environment

41. In other cases, the effect of the environment is minimal, and we say that the characteristic is canalized. Hair and eye color are two obvious characteristics which are dominated by genetic influence to the extent that they are _____ . (8, p. 80)

canalized

42. Behavior genetics is that specialty interested in determining the heritability of various characteristics, which is to say the extent to which they are determined by _____ influence. (9, p. 81)

genetic

43. There are several research strategies used by specialists in _____ _____ . (9, p. 81)

behavior genetics

44. Some of these strategies are for use only with animals. In genetic research with _____ , two types of experimental research designs are used. (9, p. 81)

animals

45. In selective breeding experiments, animals are mated on the basis of their similarity in a given characteristic. After several generations, a strain of animals emerges in which all members of the strain are similar in this characteristic. This demonstrates that we can restrict variability by _____ _____ . (9, p. 81)

selective breeding

46. A second design is inbreeding. Here parents and offspring, or siblings, are mated. After a number of generations, a genetically pure (identical) strain can be produced by _____ . (9, p. 82)

inbreeding

47. Animal experiments demonstrate the extent to which a given characteristic is inherited. We can also determine heritability from research with humans. The extent to which a given characteristic is genetically determined is computed as the coefficient of _____ . (10, p. 83)

heritability

48. In trying to determine the amount of importance heredity plays, four research strategies are used with human subjects. One strategy, the twin study, involves comparing identical and fraternal twins. Since identical twins are produced from the same fertilized ovum, they are genetically _____ . (10, p. 82)

identical

49. Fraternal (nonidentical) twins are produced from separate ova fertilized by separate sperm, so they are not genetically _____ . (10, p. 82)

identical

50. On any characteristic we choose to study, if heredity is relatively important, we would expect more similarity among the _____ twins than among the _____ twins. (10, p. 82)

identical, fraternal

51. The second research strategy is called a family-of-twins design. The first strategy, studying twins, is expanded in the _____ design. (10, p. 82)

family-of-twins

52. In a family-of-twins study, twins, siblings, half-siblings, and children and their parents are compared. The closer the blood relationship, the more similar the genetic makeup and the more _____ the hereditary characteristics will be. (10, p. 82)

similar

53. Kinship studies extend the relationship variable to include more than one generation. If you were involved in a study and were paired with your grandfather, you would know that you were a subject in a _____ study. (10, p. 82)

kinship

54. Adoption studies permit careful comparisons between biological parent-child pairs and adoptive parent-child pairs who are not related. We can identify characteristics sensitive to either genetics or environment using an _____ study. (10, p. 83)

adoption

55. The goal of all such designs is to discover and compute the heritability coefficient. This mathematical derivative which reflects the relative importance of genetic influence on a given characteristic is the coefficient of _____ . (11, p. 83)

heritability

56. While there is some dispute and confusion regarding the computation of the heritability coefficient, there are some areas of general agreement. For example, the family-of-twins design has provided a good measure of the _____ of intelligence. (11, p. 83)

heritability

57. It is now generally accepted that intelligence has a _____ factor of about .50, ranging from .30 to .60. (11, p. 83)

heritability

58. The incidence of schizophrenia follows the genetic model closely; the more closely related to someone with the disorder you are, the more likely you are to get _____ . (11, p. 84)

schizophrenia

59. We have also explored the heritability of vocational interests, finding in an adoption study that young people's interests are most like those of their _____ parents. (11, p. 84)

biological

60. In the personality area, measures of neuroticism and extraversion show substantial coefficients of _____ . (11, p. 85)

heritability

61. It is very important to remember that heredity and environmental influences do not compete in any simple fashion. Rather they interact in a complex fashion. In order to develop, any organism needs both a genetic blueprint and an _____ in which it can be expressed and fostered. (11, p. 86)

environment

62. We are just beginning to see the importance of an evolutionary and genetic perspective on the life span, which will lead us to a better understanding of life-span _____ in years to come. (11, p. 85)

development

63. Sociobiology is the view that all social behavior is genetically influenced. Charles Wilson generated a considerable controversy with his publications regarding _____ . (12, p. 86)

sociobiology

64. The basic motivation of organisms is to attempt to promote the survival of their genes into the next generation, according to _____ . (12, p. 87)

sociobiology

65. Many people see the sociobiology debate as another form of the nature/nurture debate which has a long history in the field of _____ . (12, p. 87)

psychology

Self Test

1. The statement: "ontogeny recapitulates phylogeny" (1, p. 70)
   a. has been proven by genetic researchers
   b. was proposed by Darwin as an explanation for evolution
   c. has generally been rejected as incorrect
   d. is exactly reversed; phylogeny recapitulates ontogeny

2. In the process of natural selection, (2, p. 71)
   a. subjects are mated on the basis of matched characteristics, which is natural
   b. adaptive characteristics are more likely to survive
   c. genetic diversity is a disadvantage and is reduced
   d. sociobiologists attempt to reproduce using only natural techniques

3. If you stick your tongue out at a three-week-old infant, he or she will probably mimic you. This may well be an example of a fixed-action pattern (3, p. 74)
   a. and your behavior would be the sign stimulus
   b. which can be learned very early in life
   c. and as such reflects preadaptation
   d. but only occurs when the infant has gas

4. The nucleus of a sperm cell or ovum contains _____ chromosomes. (5, p. 76)
   a. 23
   b. 46
   c. 2
   d. X and Y

5. The total constellation of chromosomes and genes and their unique configuration in an individual is called the person's (5, p. 78)
   a. conceptus
   b. phenotype
   c. genotype
   d. gene pool

6. Polygenic determination means that (8, p. 79)
   a. only one or two genes are involved
   b. more than two genes are involved
   c. only the genes from large, colored birds are involved
   d. scientists have not yet determined whether the characteristic is inherited

7. If a characteristic is sex-linked, it means that it (7, p. 79)
   a. affects members of one sex more than the other
   b. is transmitted by sexual contact, and does not harm virgins
   c. is carried on the twenty-second chromosomal pair
   d. is transmitted by genes which are not attached to chromosomes

8. If a characteristic is not very sensitive to the effects of different environments, we are likely to say that it (8, p. 80)
   a. has a very large reaction range
   b. is not subject to genetic research
   c. only appears in studies of twins, primarily monozygotic
   d. is canalized

9. In a kinship study, as opposed to other behavior genetic research designs, (10, p. 82)
   a. identical twins reared together are compared with identical twins reared apart
   b. identical twins are compared with fraternal (nonidentical) twins
   c. related pairs of individuals are compared with each other and with unrelated pairs
   d. inbred rats are compared with selectively bred rats

10. The major tenet of sociobiology is that the major motive for most behavior, particularly social behavior, is (12, p. 87)
    a. the survival of the individual
    b. the opportunity to mate randomly
    c. the survival of the individual's genes
    d. altruistic expressions of feelings among family members

Individual Learning Activity

Many people respond rather strongly and negatively to the concept of heritability and the tenets of sociobiology. One reason why they may respond this way may be their sense that acceptance of such ideas reduces apparent personal freedom. Indeed, this is much the same reaction B. F. Skinner experienced upon publication of *Beyond Freedom and Dignity,* in which he discussed his scientific observations regarding the control of behavior by its consequences. It would appear that humans do not readily accept ideas which explain some behavior by concepts other than personal choice. This is, at least, a testable hypothesis. A curious person may well ask what assumptions a typical individual makes about the heritability of behavior patterns or the possibility that social interactions are primarily motivated by the underlying concern for the perpetuation of one's own genetic material. We should be able to find out rather easily.

The simplest way to do this is to prepare a series of statements (some would call them reflected attitudes or belief statements) with which people are asked to indicate the degree to which they agree or disagree. Typically, a five or six point scale is used, so for each person's responses, some numerical score can be ascertained. For example, such an instrument might look something like this:

	Strongly Agree					Strongly Disagree
Intelligence is primarily inherited	1	2	3	4	5	6
Most behavior is influenced by genetic factors	1	2	3	4	5	6
Inherited factors are not important in most behaviors	1	2	3	4	5	6
Personality is entirely learned	1	2	3	4	5	6

As you can see, it is conventional to word some statements to which agreement indicates one perspective, and some to indicate another. This helps to make sure that the subject is really responding to the statements, and not just following a pattern of marking one side of the page. The direction of the statements should not simply be alternated, but randomly positioned. Now it is your turn; please write at least ten such statements related to sociobiology and heritability, focusing on whatever classes of behaviors you choose.

Now you are almost ready to collect some data. Before you do, however, you might think about some of your assumptions about these types of beliefs. Will there be sex or age differences in what people believe and how they respond to your items? What other types of variables might index or predict differences in how people respond? If you have any hunches, you might plan to include some space on your questionnaire to collect information about these variables. Later, you might compare responses from people on the basis of these variables.

The actual collection of data requires some care, too. First, you need to recruit some subjects. It is only polite to ask people to participate in your project. It is important, however, to give them some idea of the design of your efforts. You might say that you are gathering the responses of several people (or several dozen if you are highly motivated) to some simple statements, and you would appreciate it if they would take a minute or two to respond. You should assure them that their responses will be held in confidence, and will be pooled with other responses to provide a pattern or group response. It is crucial to use the same explanation and instructions with all subjects, since altering them would introduce another uncontrolled variable which could account for differences in response patterns.

It is customary not to discuss the items or to help the person interpret them. If asked what an item means, or how the reader should "take" it, the best response would be that the person should respond however they understand the item. While this doesn't help to clarify vague items, it does help to avoid the introduction of variability in the task itself. Remember, we are looking for patterns of responses, so we have to keep the stimulus constant.

After you have collected some responses, examine them for patterns. Are there sex or age differences? Often these two variables interact to produce some very interesting effects. What other patterns can you discern from your data?

The most challenging part of any research is the interpretation of the findings. What do your data tell you? How can you make sense of these findings? What implications do your findings have for various theories? If you were going to pursue this line of research, what would you look at next? If you were going to do this project again, what would you do differently?

If you have had the courage and interest to proceed this far, good for you! You have learned some important aspects of research, and are gaining an appreciation for the role of the research scientist.

Answers to the Self Test

1. c	6. b
2. b	7. a
3. a	8. d
4. a	9. c
5. c	10. c

4 Physical Development

Preview

Life processes begin with the merging of a sperm from the father and an ovum from the mother. This act of fertilization, also called conception, occurs in the Fallopian tube, usually at the midpoint between menstrual periods, and heralds the onset of the germinal period, which proceeds for two weeks. The embryonic period follows, during which a primitive human form emerges and the placenta is formed. The fetal period lasts from about the eighth week of prenatal life until birth.

Although well protected in the uterus, the fetus is sensitive to some aspects of the outer environment, such as maternal nutrition and emotional status. The time of year of conception is also an important predictor of birth weight and rate of malformations. Teratogens include maternal diseases and disorders, diet, irradiation, drugs, and temperature and oxygen levels.

The term *premature birth* has been discarded as imprecise. Babies born after less than normal gestational period are called short-gestation babies, while those who weigh less than five and one-half pounds (2500 grams) are called low-birth-weight or high-risk infants. All newborn infants are assessed with the Apgar scale, which gives further indications of immediate risk.

In contrast to past views of the newborn as helpless and confused, the neonate is now seen as an active explorer of the environment. During the first year, growth proceeds in fits and starts following the cephalo-caudal (top to bottom) and proximodistal (midline to extremities) patterns. During the second year of life, the rate of growth decelerates, but gross and fine motor performance continues to improve.

Sensation is the detection of information by sensory receptors, and perception is the interpretation of sensory information. Infants have visual preferences, and soon develop perception of higher-order information. Newborns have visual acuity of about 20/600, but this improves to about 20/100 by age six months. Visual accommodation is not a significant problem, due to the small pupil size which provides great depth of field. Recent research shows infants able to detect color, but in the fashion of tritanopes, i.e. unable to detect blue, until about age three months. By age four months, infants can apparently detect all colors and can also view partly occluded objects as whole units.

Fantz has shown that newborns prefer to look at faces rather than other images, and by age two months they prefer normal faces to rearranged facial features. By age three months, object perception is present; and by five and one-half months, infants prefer a novel face to an habituated face. Depth perception is present by the age of crawling, although it may well be present earlier. In a creative series of experiments, Bower has shown that very young infants have size constancy.

While adults use both egocentric and objective frames of reference, Piaget speculated that infants in the first year of life are limited to an egocentric view. Acredolo and her associates have shown that six- and eleven-month-old infants use egocentric frames of reference, while sixteen-month-old infants consistently used objective frames of reference. She also showed that objective frames of reference were used more often when infants were tested in their own homes.

Newborns can hear, but only loud sounds. By age twenty-four months, the range of hearing approaches that of an adult. Infants can discriminate between voiced and unvoiced sounds, and quickly demonstrate recognition of the mother's voice, an ability which may begin to develop prenatally. By age four months, infants can perceive auditory and visual events in an integrated manner.

Taste sensitivity may be present before birth, and newborns are very sensitive to sweetness. Newborns also make reflexive movements in response to touch.

Learning Objectives

1. Describe conception and list the critical features of each stage of prenatal development: conception, germinal period, embryonic period, and fetal period. (p. 94)
2. Explain two different ways a mother's experiences could influence the development of her fetus. (p. 98)
3. Define *teratogen* and give two examples. (p. 99)
4. Trace the process of labor and describe the typical newborn. (p. 100)
5. Describe differences between full term, short-gestation, and low-birth-weight or high-risk infants. (p. 101)
6. Trace infant physical development through the first two years of life. (p. 107)
7. Define and differentiate the cephalo-caudal pattern and the proximodistal pattern of development. (p. 107)
8. Trace the course of gross and fine motor development in the second year of an infant's life. (p. 108)
9. Distinguish between *sensation* and *perception* as psychologists use those terms. (p. 110)
10. Describe the visual preferences, acuity, and accommodation of an infant during the first year of life. (p. 111)
11. Explain the experimental use of habituation and dishabituation to learn about color vision in infants. (p. 112)
12. Describe infant perception of objects, including size constancy and spatial relations. (p. 112)
13. Trace the development of sensory abilities for hearing, smell, taste, and touch. (p. 116)

Key Terms

For each key term, write the definition in the space provided.

in vitro fertilization (1, p. 92) _____

conception (1, p. 94) _____

germinal period (1, p. 95) _____

embryonic period (1, p. 95) _____

fetal period (1, p. 96) _____

teratogen (3, p. 99) _____

teratology (3, p. 99) _____

premature birth (5, p. 101) _____

short-gestation babies (5, p. 101) _____

gestation (5, p. 101) _____

low-birth-weight infants (5, p. 102) _____

high-risk infants (5, p. 102) _____

cephalo-caudal pattern (7, p. 107) _____

proximodistal pattern (7, p. 108) _____

sensation (9, p. 110) _____

perception (9, p. 110) _____

acuity (10, p. 111) _____

accommodation (10, p. 111) _____

habituation (11, p. 112) _____

dishabituation (11, p. 112) _____

size constancy (12, p. 114) _____

spectogram (13, p. 117) _____

bimodal perception (13, p. 118) _____

Guided Review

1. Let's follow the course of life from conception onward. When the sperm and ovum unite, usually in the Fallopian tube of the woman, _____ has occurred. (1, p. 94)

   conception

2. The two weeks following conception are called the germinal period. The fertilized ovum begins cell division, continues its journey down the Fallopian tube, and eventually imbeds in the wall of the uterus, bringing the _____ period to an end. (1, p. 95)

   germinal

3. At the time the fertilized ovum imbeds in the uterine wall, it is a small sphere about the size of the point of a pin. The outer part of this spherical mass of cells becomes the medium of exchange between the mother and embryo, while the inner mass becomes the _____ itself. (1, p. 95)

   embryo

4. The embryonic period lasts from the point of implantation (about 2 weeks after conception) until about 8 weeks after conception. The outer layer of cells in the spherical mass now forms the placenta. All exchanges of nutrients and waste products between mother and embryo take place across the semipermeable membranes of the _____ . (1, p. 95)

   placenta

5. There is no direct intermingling of blood between the mother and the _____ . (1, p. 96)

   embryo

6. By the end of the eighth week, all the body parts are present, and the first bone cells begin to replace the soft cartilage in the skeleton of the _____ . (1, p. 95)

embryo

7. This completion of form marks the end of the _____ period. (1, p. 95)

embryonic

8. The fetal period extends from the end of the eighth week until birth at about the end of the ninth month (40 weeks). The longest of the prenatal stages is the _____ period. (1, p. 96)

fetal

9. By the end of the fourth month, a number of reflexes can be felt by the mother. At this time, the _____ is only about six inches long and weighs about four ounces. (1, p. 96)

fetus

10. At the end of the fifth month, the skin structures have formed. At the ends of the fingers and toes are found _____ . (1, p. 97)

nails

11. Also by this time the fetus has selected its favorite position, called the *lie*. The mother can usually detect when the fetus is in its _____ because it quiets and is relatively still. (1, p. 97)

lie

12. By the end of the sixth month, the fetus is about fourteen inches long and weighs about two pounds. Growth is most rapid at the beginning of the _____ period and slows down over time. (1, p. 97)

fetal

13. The end of the seventh month is called the age of viability. The fetus, about 16 inches long and weighing about three pounds, could probably survive now, thus the term: _____ _____ _____ . (1, p. 97)

age of viability

14. At birth, the average fetus is about 20 inches long and weighs about 7 pounds. At birth, the average fetus has spent about _____ weeks in the uterus. (1, p. 98)

40

15. During pregnancy, many women wonder what effect their experiences might have on the development of the fetus. They want to produce a healthy _____ . (2, p. 98)

fetus (or baby)

16. A pregnant woman should be careful about her diet. If she does not eat sufficient nutrients, a woman is more likely to deliver a premature infant, an infant with low birth weight, or to have her pregnancy complicated by anemia or toxemia. Thus, she must consume sufficient _____ . (2, p. 98)

   nutrients

17. Mothers-to-be must also be careful about their emotional health, since severe upsets and distress can influence the development of the _____ . (2, p. 98)

   fetus (or baby)

18. The time of year of conception is also important. The heaviest children at birth are those conceived in the _____ . (2, p. 99)

   summer

19. The rate of fetal malformations is also least among those infants conceived during the _____ months. (2, p. 99)

   summer

20. Mothers and scientists wonder about the extent to which a mother's emotional state can affect the fetus. There is clear evidence that the fetus can be influenced by the _____ state of the mother. (2, p. 98)

   emotional

21. Emotional arousal in the mother triggers the secretions of hormones. The mother's blood carries these _____ to the placenta. (2, p. 99)

   hormones

22. Even though the blood cells cannot cross the placenta, the _____ can, and are picked up by the blood cells of the fetus. (2, p. 99)

   hormones

23. These hormones then produce the same physiological effect in the _____ as they did in the mother. (2, p. 99)

   fetus

24. Babies born to highly anxious mothers cry more and are more active than are babies born to less _____ mothers. (2, p. 99)

   anxious

25. Many authorities now recommend that pregnant women try to avoid circumstances in which they will be chronically _____ . (2, p. 99)

   anxious

26. A teratogen is any agent which produces birth defects. Certain drugs, including alcohol, can act as
_____ . (3, p. 99)

teratogens

27. Thalidomide, a mild tranquilizer thought to be safe, was discovered to be a serious _____
when used during pregnancy. (3, p. 99)

teratogen

28. The culmination of pregnancy is birth. During birth, strong contractions of the muscles of the uterus push the
_____ down through the cervix, and out through the vagina (birth canal). (4, p. 100)

fetus (or baby)

29. The newborn emerges, typically, into a bright, noisy delivery room, and is immediately handled, weighed,
and evaluated. The Apgar scale is one technique used to evaluate the human _____ .
(4, p. 102)

newborn

30. Some infants are born before term, or having very light birth weights. We used to call any infant born before the
normal expected due date _____ . (5, p. 101)

premature

31. In recent years, this term has fallen into disuse, and we now refer to infants born early as short-gestation
_____ . (5, p. 101)

infants

32. The time between conception and birth is referred to as the time of _____ . (5, p. 101)

gestation

33. By contrast, infants who at birth weigh less than five and one-half pounds (2500 grams) are called low-birth-
weight _____ . (5, p. 102)

infants

34. The term *high-risk* is also applied to _____ infants. (5, p. 102)

low-birth-weight

35. Contrary to popular belief, a short _____ period does not necessarily harm the infant.
(5, p. 102)

gestation

36. Indeed, neurological development of the _____ infant continues after birth at the same
rate as if the infant were still in the womb. (5, p. 102)

short-gestation

37. Very few (less than 10%) infants have any abnormality, and most _____ disappear during later development. (5, p. 102)

abnormalities

38. Newborns used to be thought of as passive creatures who were confused by the stimuli in their environment. Now we view the newborn as an _____ seeker and processor of information. (5, p. 103)

active

39. In addition to birth weight, newborns are evaluated using the Apgar scale. Five signs: heart rate, respiratory effort, reflex irritability, muscle tone, and body color make up the _____ scale. (5, p. 102)

Apgar

40. Apgar ratings at one and five minutes after birth are important predictors of health and development. This development follows predictable patterns. One of these is the cephalo-caudal _____ . (7, p. 107)

pattern

41. The process of development from the head downward is referred to as the _____
_____ . (7, p. 107)

cephalo-caudal pattern

42. Another pattern is the proximodistal pattern. The fact that development, particularly in fine motor control, proceeds from the midline of the body outward to the extremities, is called the _____
_____ . (7, p. 108)

proximodistal pattern

43. A prone infant can lift its head before it can lift its chest and abdomen, this is a reflection of the _____ pattern. (7, p. 107)

cephalo-caudal

44. Infants can swing their arms at objects long before they can reach and carefully grasp an object, this is a reflection of the _____ pattern. (7, p. 108)

proximodistal

45. During the first year of life, the infant gains control of the head, trunk, arms, legs, and develops some fine motor skills. Infants can usually crawl, pull themselves up, and walk with assistance by the end of the _____ year of life. (6, p. 107)

first

46. Growth decelerates during the second year. Walking skills mature, so that most toddlers can run and climb by the end of the _____ year. (6, p. 108)

second

47. In order to understand the development of infants, we must understand what the infant senses and perceives. Most people are surprised to learn of the sensory and perceptual abilities of _____ . (9, p. 110)

infants

48. Sensation refers to the acquisition of information by the senses. The functions of eyes, ears, nose, tongue, and skin can be summarized as _____ . (9, p. 110)

sensation

49. Perception is the interpretation of what is sensed. While sensation occurs at the level of the receptors, the cortex and other brain areas are responsible for _____ . (7, p. 110)

perception

50. The most frequently explored sense is vision. Newborns have poor visual acuity. In fact, their visual _____ is in the area of 20/600. (10, p. 111)

acuity

51. During the first three or four months, visual _____ improves dramatically. (10, p. 111)

acuity

52. One important aspect of visual acuity is the distance from the eyes to the target. In newborns, visual _____ does not apparently vary as a function of viewing distance. (10, p. 112)

acuity

53. The depth of focus of the newborn's eyes may be good due to the small diameter of the opening of the eye, the _____ . (10, p. 112)

pupil

54. Researchers have wondered whether infants can see in color. A normal person, who can detect all the primary _____ , is termed a trichromat. (10, p. 112)

colors (or hues)

55. Many adults are partially color blind. Dichromats can detect only two _____ . (10, p. 112)

colors

56. Those who cannot see red are called protanopes, while deuteranopes cannot see green, and tritanopes cannot see _____ . (10, p. 112)

blue

57. The investigation of the infant's ability to see _____ has used a phenomenon known as habituation. (11, p. 112)

color

58. The waning of a response after repeated presentation of a stimulus is called _____ .
(11, p. 112)

habituation

59. Thus, an infant who looks repeatedly at the same stimulus, and then stops looking at it when it is presented, is said to have demonstrated _____ . (11, p. 112)

habituation

60. If we take away the habituated stimulus for a while then reintroduce it, the infant may again look at it. This is called _____ . (11, p. 112)

dishabituation

61. Bornstein's research with three-month-old infants suggests that they can see all the colors, and are thus _____ . (11, p. 112)

trichromats

62. However, Pulos and his associates have shown that two-month-olds cannot see blue, and are thus _____ . (11, p. 113)

dichromats

63. When we see only part of an occluded object, we recognize it as a whole. This may be because we have had experience with that _____ . (12, p. 113)

object

64. Kellman and Spelke have shown that by four months of age, human infants can also perceive partly _____ objects as units. (12, p. 113)

occluded

65. Thus, we believe that _____ perception is present by three months of age. (12, p. 113)

object

66. Fantz has shown that newborns prefer to look at a normal human _____ rather than a novel rearrangement of features. (12, p. 113)

face

67. One technique for investigating the infant's sense of vision is the visual cliff. The apparatus uses a solid sheet of strong glass, under which are presented patterns of fabrics indicating a deep side and a shallow side, giving the _____ impression of a _____ . (12, p. 114)

visual, cliff

68. Infants as young as two months demonstrate by heart rate changes that they can see the _____ _____ . (12, p. 114)

visual cliff

69. A related area of perceptual study is the issue of size constancy. When we see the same person or object at different distances, we compensate for the different retinal image sizes and perceive the person or object as the same size under all conditions, a phenomenon called _____ _____ . (12, p. 114)

size constancy

70. In a very creative set of experiments, T.G.R. Bower demonstrated by having six- to eight-week-old infants respond to cubes of various sizes and distances, that the infants did have _____ _____ . (12, p. 115)

size constancy

71. However, attempts to replicate _____ research have not been successful, so the issue of size constancy is still open. (12, p. 115)

Bower's

72. We perceive relations between objects in space. But do infants perceive these spatial _____ ? (12, p. 115)

relations

73. When we locate objects with reference to our own bodies, we are using an _____ frame of reference. (12, p. 115)

egocentric

74. Using some external object as a locator for another object constitutes the use of an objective frame of _____ . (12, p. 115)

reference

75. Depending on the situation, an adult may use either the _____ or objective frame of reference. (12, p. 115)

egocentric

76. Jean Piaget, who theorized about intellectual development, suggested that in the first year of life infants can use only the _____ frame of reference. (12, p. 115)

egocentric

77. Research by Acredolo has supported the hypothesis first put forth by _____ . (12, p. 116)

Piaget

78. Acredolo also found that the use of an _____ frame of reference is enhanced when the infant is in familiar surroundings. (12, p. 116)

objective

79. Infants can hear immediately after _____ , although their sensory thresholds are higher than those of adults. (13, p. 116)

birth

80. By age one day, infants can hear high frequency sounds as well as _____ can. (13, p. 117)

adults

81. A spectrogram is useful in discerning the types of sounds that infants can _____ and distinguish. (13, p. 117)

hear

82. Both time and frequency of the sound wave are reflected in the sound's _____ . (13, p. 117)

spectrogram

83. Infants can distinguish the mother's voice. Moreover, infants as young as three days of age actually _____ the mother's voice. (13, p. 118)

prefer

84. Spelke has shown that infants as young as four months may demonstrate bimodal perception, in which auditory and _____ events are perceived in an integrated fashion. (13, p. 118)

visual

85. Newborns are also sensitive to strong odors. They turn away from onion and ammonia, demonstrating that they can _____ these stimuli. (13, p. 118)

smell (or sense)

86. A baby also quickly learns to discriminate the odor of the mother's breasts, demonstrating a practical application of the ability to _____ . (13, p. 118)

smell

87. Newborns can also taste, although their taste buds are more widely distributed on the tongue than those of older children or adults. The ability to distinguish sugar, lemon, salt, and quinine demonstrate that newborns can _____ at least strong flavors. (13, p. 118)

taste

88. Newborns are sensitive to touch. Although there is some disagreement, there is evidence to suggest that females may be more _____ to touch than _____ . (13, p. 118)

sensitive, males

89. Many people are curious to know whether newborns experience pain. The crying and fussing which accompanies typical circumcisions indicates that newborns are at least somewhat capable of experiencing _____ . (13, p. 118)

pain

Speaking of pain and other sensations, we have come to the end of this guided (and I hope painless) review. Please take a few moments to look over the learning objectives, then do your best on the self test.

Self Test

1. The fusion of a sperm cell and an ovum usually occurs in the (1, p. 94)
   a. womb
   b. Fallopian tube
   c. embryonic chamber
   d. ovary

2. The fertilized ovum becomes firmly imbedded in the wall of the uterus during (1, p. 94)
   a. conception
   b. the germinal period
   c. the embryonic period
   d. the Fallopian period

3. The age of viability is considered to be the end of the _____ month of pregnancy. (1, p. 94)
   a. third
   b. fifth
   c. seventh
   d. eighth

4. Women who smoke during pregnancy have infants who (3, p. 99)
   a. weigh less for a few months
   b. have much slower heart rates
   c. have trouble orienting to sounds and sights
   d. weigh more than the average infant

5. That an infant can slap at an object before he can grasp it between thumb and forefinger is referred to as the (7, p. 107)
   a. physiogenetic pattern
   b. developmental law
   c. proximodistal pattern
   d. cephalo-caudal pattern

6. Psychologists define sensation as the (9, p. 110)
   a. pickup of information by sensory receptors
   b. interpretation of sensory information
   c. startling headlines in the newspaper
   d. production of sensory impulses by the brain

7. At birth, infants can see clearly an object held at almost any distance, because of (10, p. 111)
   a. size constancy
   b. their very low thresholds for distances
   c. the innate preference for complexity
   d. the small pupil diameter

8. As infants get older, they have more experience with objects and may stop responding to some of them demonstrating (11, p. 112)
   a. size constancy
   b. depth perception
   c. habituation
   d. higher-order perceptions

9. The typical three-month-old infant, according to several habituation studies, is probably described best as (11, p. 112)
   a. a deuteranope
   b. a tritanope
   c. a trichromat
   d. color-blind

10. Piaget proposed, based only on his observations, that during the first year of life the infant was bound to (12, p. 112)
    a. an egocentric frame of reference
    b. the absence of size constancy
    c. crawling without depth perception
    d. dishabituating frequently due to limited memory

Individual Learning Activity

The early development of infants is fascinating to observe, yet few of us have a ready supply of human infants available for observation. Fortunately, infants can be found almost everywhere, particularly in late morning and late afternoon. Shopping malls, grocery stores, and medical office buildings are great places to see infants.

While it would be best to observe the same infants over some time (a longitudinal approach), this is also not very feasible for most college students, unless you have a private source (of infants). In order to make cross-sectional observations meaningful, you will have to take careful notes and remember a few things.

First, there are clear-cut sex differences. One of these is that boys are slower to mature than girls. These differences are most noticeable at times of fastest growth, for example in the first year or two of life and again in early adolescence. Second, as age increases, human variability increases. Two-week-olds are much more alike than are two-year-olds, who in turn are much more alike than twenty-year-olds.

With these two caveats in mind, then, let's observe some infants. It is a good idea to record each observation as quickly afterward as you can, while memory is still fresh. Let us suppose that we go to a grocery store. If you want to be truly surreptitious, you can put a few items in a cart and pretend to shop. Follow that mother with the young infant up and down a few aisles. Notice what the infant does, and how the mother and infant interact. Make a few notes. If you choose not to be surreptitious, you might even approach a few mothers and introduce yourself. Children in the second year of life are likely to be less apprehensive of strangers than children late in the first year. You may even be able to get some parental reports (bragging?) about the child's prowess. Can these be trusted? How could you verify them? (Hint: Are there photographs?)

After you have made at least ten observations, take some time to compare your notes. Did you observe sex differences? Did you find similarities between children of approximately the same age? Did you see evidence of cephalo-caudal and proximodistal patterns? What did you see that most surprised you? Were the infants able to communicate with their mothers even before language? Were you ever surprised at the age of the child, after observing the behavior?

These questions, and their answers, will lead you to both a deeper appreciation of the nature of the first two years of life, and to a curiosity about child development which will encourage further study. Thanks for your effort.

---

5 Cognitive Foundations and Language Development

Preview

Learning can be defined as a relatively permanent change in behavior that occurs through experience and cannot be accounted for in terms of reflexes, instincts, and maturation or the effects of fatigue, injury, disease, or drugs. Classical conditioning is a process of association between the unconditioned and conditioned stimuli, and results in the conditioned stimulus being capable of eliciting the conditioned response. Repeated presentation of the conditioned stimulus without the unconditioned stimulus leads to extinction of the conditioned response. Following this extinction procedure, an interval of rest may be followed by spontaneous recovery of the conditioned response. Classical conditioning has a great deal of survival value, but may also be responsible for the development of phobias.

Operant conditioning involves the organism operating on the environment, and differs from classical conditioning in at least two ways. First, while classical conditioning deals with reflexive types of responses, operant conditioning is involved with voluntary responses. Second, in operant conditioning the reinforcement depends on the response; while in classical conditioning, the reinforcing effects of the unconditioned stimulus depend on the design of the experience, or on the conditioned stimulus.

Operant conditioning is a powerful procedure to change almost any behavior, and its effectiveness can be demonstrated by collecting evidence of baseline levels of a response, then providing a series of conditioning trials during which the response results in reinforcement. In operant conditioning, extinction occurs when the reinforcement is no longer contingent on the response.

Bandura has demonstrated that imitation is also an important mode of learning, requiring the coordination of motor activity with a mental picture of what is being imitated. Very young children do not imitate others. Piaget has theorized that infants cannot imagine objects until about nine months of age. Collectively, classical and operant conditioning and imitation account for many types of learning. Other approaches to the study of learning emphasize cognitive processes to a much greater extent than these do.

Piaget believed that the child passes through a series of stages of cognitive development, motivated by biological pressure to adapt to the environment and to organize structures of thinking. The first of these stages, the sensorimotor stage, corresponds to the period of infancy, extending from birth to about two years of age. The sensorimotor stage is itself divided into six substages, each of which exhibits some change in the organization of basic schemes, or basic patterns of sensorimotor functioning.

During the first substage, the infant exercises basic reflexes and develops an ability to produce behavior that mimics reflexes in the absence of eliciting stimuli. In the second substage, the infant learns to coordinate sensation and types of schemes. Now habits emerge as basic schemes that are completely separate from the original stimuli. Primary circular reactions, schemes based on an infant's attempt to reproduce a chance but interesting event, also emerge. These habits and circular reactions are stereotyped.

In the third substage, that of secondary circular reactions, the infant becomes more object oriented, but the schemes still lack an intentional, goal-directed quality. Substage four deals with the coordination of secondary reactions, and the emergence of clear intentionality. The fifth substage involves tertiary circular reactions, schemes in which the infant purposefully explores new possibilities with objects. Piaget saw this substage as the onset of curiosity. It is clear that the tertiary reaction is the basis for trial-and-error learning. In the sixth and final substage, the infant develops the ability to use symbols, which Piaget defines as an internalized sensory image or word representing an event.

One of the most important accomplishments of infancy is the development of the object concept, often called object permanence, the ability to understand that objects continue to exist even when not physically present or in direct contact with the infant. Object permanence is usually studied by observing the infant's response when an interesting object is removed or hidden.

Two important cognitive processes used by infants are attention and memory. Attention is focused perception to produced increased awareness of a stimulus, and is manifested in part by the orienting reflex and saccadic movements. Memory is a central feature of cognitive development, and is assessed in newborns using the conjugate reinforcement technique. Memory in the strict sense, or conscious memory, does not appear to emerge until one and one-half to two years of age, earlier than Piaget had predicted. Adult memories of childhood events rarely include events prior to age three. Cognitive development in infancy may be assessed with developmental scales such as the Bayley Mental and Motor Scales.

Language is a complex set of rules used in speaking, listening, and writing characterized by infinite generativity and displacement. Rules cover the use of basic sounds or phonemes and units of meaning or morphemes. Rules of syntax involve how words are combined, and refer to both deep and surface structures. Pragmatics govern how language is used socially.

Three major theories have addressed language development by children. The behaviorist perspective assigns language to the category of learned behavior, citing shaping and reinforcement, as well as imitation, as major processes in language learning. Nativist theory asserts that humans are prepared genetically to develop language, based on four assumptions: language universals, lateralization of language in the brain, critical periods in language development, and the limited communication abilities of nonhuman species. Cognitive theory argues that in evolutionary terms language is too recent to provide support for specific structures, and instead is a manifestation of more general cognitive abilities. Each of these theories undoubtedly carries some truth; none of them is adequate by itself.

Language development includes several milestones. Babbling is biologically controlled, and begins at three to six months of age. An infant's first words at about ten to thirteen months provide the basis for holophrastic communication. During this time, concept learning may outstrip language ability, and children may overextend or underextend the meanings of words. By eighteen to twenty-four months of age, two-word telegraphic speech begins, setting the stage for the appreciation of syntax.

Learning Objectives

1. Define and give examples of classical conditioning, operant conditioning, and imitation as three major forms of learning, and show how each explains human infant development. (p. 130)
2. Review each of the six substages of Piaget's sensorimotor stage of cognitive development, citing the essential feature which distinguishes each substage. (p. 134)
3. Describe the use of the orienting reflex and saccadic movements to assess attention in infants. (p. 140)
4. Show how the conjugate reinforcement technique can be used to assess memory in a newborn, and contrast memory in the wide sense with memory in the strict sense. (p. 141)
5. List at least five measures on the Bayley Mental and Motor Scales, and indicate the aspect of development each is designed to assess. (p. 142)
6. Define *language* and its essential features and components: phonemes, morphemes, syntax, grammar, deep structure, surface structure, semantics, and pragmatics. (p. 145)
7. Briefly summarize the behavioristic view of language development, showing how shaping, reinforcement, and imitation account for some aspects of language. (p. 147)
8. List and characterize four arguments supportive of the nativist position on language development. (p. 148)
9. Describe the position of the cognitive theory of language development, citing at least two supporting arguments. (p. 152)
10. Trace the course of language development in infancy, listing at least three milestones and describing the growing contributions to communication ability. (p. 155)

Key Terms

For each key term, write the definition in the space provided.

learning (1, p. 128) _____

classical conditioning (1, p. 130) _____

unconditioned stimulus (UCS) (1, p. 130) _____

conditioned stimulus (CS) (1, p. 130) _____

unconditioned response (UCR) (1, p. 130) _____

conditioned response (CR) (1, p. 130) _____

extinction (1, p. 130) _____

spontaneous recovery (1, p. 130) _____

phobias (1, p. 131) _____

baseline (1, p. 132) _____

conditioning trials (1, p. 132) _____

extinction (1, p. 132) _____

imitation (1, p. 132, 148) _____

modeling (1, p. 132) _____

observational learning (1, p. 132) _____

scheme (schema) (2, p. 134) _____

primary circular reaction (2, p. 135) _____

secondary circular reactions (2, p. 135) _____

coordination of secondary reactions (2, p. 135) _____

intentionality (2, p. 136) _____

tertiary circular reactions (2, p. 136) _____

symbol (2, p. 137) _____

object permanence (2, p. 137) _____

attention (3, p. 140) _____

orienting reflex (OR) (3, p. 140) _____

saccadic movements (3, p. 140) _____

externality effect (3, p. 140) _____

memory (4, p. 141) _____

conjugate reinforcement technique (4, p. 141) _____

infantile amnesia (4, p. 143) _____

developmental scales (5, p. 142) _____

language (6, p. 145) _____

infinite generativity (6, p. 145, 148) _____

displacement (6, p. 145) _____

phonemes (6, p. 146) _____

phonology (6, p. 146) _____

morpheme (6, p. 146) _____

morphology (6, p. 146) _____

grammar (6, p. 146) _____

surface structure (6, p. 146) _____

deep structure (6, p. 146) _____

semantics (6, p. 146) _____

pragmatics (6, p. 147) _____

Guided Review

1. Learning may be defined as a change in behavior as a function of experience. Although the behavior change should be relatively permanent, that is not required for a behavior to be called _____ . (1, p. 128)

   learning (or learned)

2. Some behaviors are not learned. One class of unlearned behaviors is reflexes. Behaviors which are wired into a person's nervous system, and are elicited (evoked) by specific stimuli, are called _____ . (1, p. 128)

   reflexes

3. Other behaviors are maturational. Behaviors such as walking, which emerge eventually independent of practice, and seem based on the readiness of the infant, are called _____ behaviors. (1, p. 128)

   maturational

4. There are at least three basic mechanisms of learning. Classical conditioning, operant conditioning, and imitation are _____ _____ of learning. (1, p. 128)

   basic mechanisms

5. Classical conditioning is a way of modifying reflexive behavior. We can train a reflexive response to a neutral stimulus using _____ _____ . (1, p. 130)

   classical conditioning

6. In a reflex, an unconditioned stimulus (UCS) elicits an unconditioned response (UCR). When a puff of air against your cornea elicits an eye-blink, we have witnessed a _____ . (1, p. 130)

   reflex

7. Now if we pair a neutral stimulus, such as a bell, with the puff of air, the neutral stimulus will become a conditioned stimulus (CS). Eventually the bell will be able to elicit the _____ , which will now be called a conditioned response (CR). (1, p. 130)

   eye-blink

8. If we present only the CS, extinction will occur. Without the reinforcing action of the UCS, repeated presentations of the CS will result in weakening of the CR, and finally _____ will occur. (1, p. 130)

extinction

9. After the CR has been extinguished, we can look forward to spontaneous recovery. When the CR returns after a period of rest following extinction, we call the phenomenon _____ _____ . (1, p. 130)

spontaneous recovery

10. This process of association of stimuli, by which reflexes are modified, is called _____ _____ . (1, p. 130)

classical conditioning

11. Many phobias and other affective responses in children and in adults are the result of the form of learning, called _____ _____ . (1, p. 131)

classical conditioning

12. Another form of learning is operant conditioning. While reflexes are used as the basis for classical conditioning, freely occurring responses are the basis for _____ _____ . (1, p. 132)

operant conditioning

13. In operant conditioning, the probability or intensity of a response is influenced by its consequences. Reinforcers and punishers are the two major types of _____ . (1, p. 132)

consequences

14. A reinforcer is any event which follows a response and increases the likelihood that the response will occur again. An event which follows a response and decreases the likelihood that the response will be repeated is called a _____ . (1, p. 132)

punisher

15. These definitions are functional. Any definition which hinges on the effect of some event, rather than on its apparent value or desirability, is called a _____ definition. (1, p. 132)

functional

16. Reinforcement is more effective than punishment for changing behavior. Because punishment may involve undesired arousal, aggression, fear, anxiety, and eventually avoidance behavior, _____ is preferred. (1, p. 132)

reinforcement

17. There are two types of reinforcement. When an increase in or presentation of some stimulus (cookie, money, hug) follows a response and increases its rate of occurrence, the effect is called positive _____ . (1, p. 132)

reinforcement

18. But when a decrease or removal of a stimulus (pain, tedious work) follows a response and increases the rate of occurrence of the response, the effect is called _____ reinforcement. (1, p. 132)

negative

19. Thus, the terms *positive* and *negative* reflect whether the consequence involved an increase or decrease in the value of the stimulus event, while the effect on the behavior is called _____ or _____ . (1, p. 132)

reinforcement, punishment (either order)

20. Learning experiments often have several phases. Baseline, conditioning, and extinction are typical names of these _____ . (1, p. 132)

phases

21. In the baseline phase, the behavior of interest is simply observed and recorded. No intervention occurs in the _____ phase. (1, p. 132)

baseline

22. In the conditioning phase, intervention takes place. Consistent and contingent punishment or reinforcement is applied to the target behavior during the _____ phase. (1, p. 132)

conditioning

23. Extinction is like baseline, which means that no intervention, either reinforcement or punishment, occurs during the _____ phase. (1, p. 132)

extinction

24. The third major format of learning is called imitation. Bandura (recall that name?) is a strong advocate of learning by _____ . (1, p. 132)

imitation

25. In order to learn by imitation of a model, the person must first pay attention to the model. Warm, powerful, atypical individuals command more _____ . (1, p. 132)

attention

26. In addition to attention, retention is required. The coding and storing of information in memory defines _____ . (1, p. 132)

retention

27. Motoric reproduction is also required. Particularly in infancy, maturational readiness may limit the ability to do what the model does. In other words, young infants may be unable to accomplish _____ . (1, p. 132)

motoric reproduction

28. Another way of studying infancy is that proposed by Piaget. In fact, the entire field of cognitive development owes its existence to the theory first proposed by _____ (2, p. 133)

Piaget

29. Piaget's theory emphasizes qualitative changes in cognitive functioning. Rather than focusing on measurements or quantitative changes, Piaget focuses on _____ changes. (2, p. 133)

qualitative

30. Piaget posits a series of stages of cognitive development. Biological pressures to adapt to the environment and to organize structures of thought impel the individual through these _____ . (2, p. 133)

stages

31. Piaget's first stage of cognitive development is the sensorimotor stage. According to Piaget, during the first two years of life the infant is in the _____ stage. (2, p. 133)

sensorimotor

32. Six substages comprise the _____ stage. (2, p. 133)

sensorimotor

33. Substage 1 involves simple reflexes. The infant practices basic reflexes, and develops a penchant for voluntary behaviors which look like the reflexive behaviors, during substage _____ . (2, p. 134)

1

34. From age one to four months, the infant is in substage 2. The infant develops habits during substage _____ . (2, p. 135)

2

35. A scheme based on simple reflexes, which has become independent from any eliciting stimulus, is Piaget's definition of a _____ . (2, p. 135)

habit

36. A primary circular reaction is a scheme based upon the infant's attempt to reproduce an interesting or pleasurable event which had occurred by chance. Substage 2 involves both habits and _____ circular reactions. (2, p. 135)

primary

37. Substage 3 involves secondary circular reactions. Unlike earlier substages, objects in the world are involved in substage _____ . (2, p. 135)

3

38. Thus, a fascination with a rattle or overhead mobile may form the basis of a _____ circular reaction. (2, p. 135)

secondary

39. Substage 4 involves the coordination of secondary reactions. Previously learned schemes are now combined in a _____ way. (2, p. 135)

coordinated

40. Intentionality is also seen for the first time in substage _____ . (2, p. 136)

4

41. Substage 5 involves tertiary circular reactions. Schemes which involve purposeful exploration of new possibilities are called _____ circular reactions. (2, p. 136)

tertiary

42. Piaget claims that human curiosity and interest in novelty have their beginnings in the _____ _____ _____ of substage 5. (2, p. 136)

tertiary circular reactions

43. Substage 6 involves the internalization of schemes. The advent of language and other symbol systems permits the child to _____ schemes. (2, p. 137)

internalize

44. Throughout the sensorimotor period, one of the most important accomplishments is object permanence. The understanding that objects and events continue to exist even when not in the immediate presence of the infant defines _____ _____ . (2, p. 137)

object permanence

45. Psychologists often hide a toy in the presence of the infant, to test for the development of _____ _____ . (2, p. 137)

object permanence

46. In contemporary research on cognitive development, both attention and memory are important constructs. The focusing of perception to produce increased awareness of a stimulus defines _____ . (3, p. 140)

attention

47. The orienting reflex signals the onset of attention. Pupil dilation, constriction of peripheral blood vessels, and a change in heart rate are all part of the _____ _____ . (3, p. 140)

orienting reflex

48. One of the most commonly studied aspects of attention in infancy is vision, where saccadic eye movements provide an index of visual _____ . (3, p. 140)

attention

49. The _____ eye movements of very young infants reveal that they primarily fixate on external parts of a pattern. (3, p. 140)

saccadic

50. Memory is a central feature of cognitive development, but it is relatively difficult to assess infant _____ . (4, p. 141)

memory

51. The conjugate reinforcement technique provides a means for investigating the _____ of infants. (4, p. 141)

memory

52. Investigators using the _____ _____ technique have shown that infants as young as two months can remember for up to three days. (4, p. 141)

conjugate reinforcement

53. Some theorists distinguish *memory* in the wide sense from *memory* in the strict sense. The learning of adaptive responses or skills represents the use of *memory* in the _____ sense. (4, p. 142)

wide

54. On the other hand, the conscious recollection of past events is referred to as *memory* in the _____ sense. (4, p. 142)

strict

55. It is fairly clear that memory in the wide sense is present soon after birth, but memory in the _____ sense develops somewhat later. (4, p. 142)

strict

56. It is hypothesized that memory in the strict sense develops later because it must wait for the development of certain brain structures, or the development of _____ of knowledge called schemata. (4, p. 142)

structures

57. The fact that as adults we cannot recall events prior to the age of three years is referred to as infantile _____ . (4, p. 142)

amnesia

58. Cognitive development in infancy is assessed using developmental scales. The best known of these early intelligence tests is the Bayley _____ . (5, p. 142)

scales

59. Both motor and mental types of responses are assessed using the _____ _____ . (5, p. 142)

Bayley scales

60. Many argue about the definition of language. A complex set of rules used in speaking, listening, and writing defines _____ . (6, p. 145)

language

61. Using these finite sets of rules, a speaker can generate an infinite number of meaningful expressions. This is referred to as _____ generativity. (6, p. 145)

infinite

62. Moreover, language can be used to communicate about events and objects from another time and place. We reflect this fact when we say that language has the characteristic of _____ . (6, p. 145)

displacement

63. Spoken languages are made up of sounds. A phoneme is the basic unit of _____ in any language. (6, p. 146)

sound

64. English employs about thirty-six basic sounds, called _____ . (6, p. 146)

phonemes

65. Phonology is the study of the sound system. Concern with rules which govern the combinations of phonemes characterizes _____ . (6, p. 146)

phonology

66. A morpheme is a string of sounds which conveys meaning. Thus, the smallest meaningful unit of speech is called a _____ . (6, p. 146)

morpheme

67. While some morphemes are words, some words contain more than one _____ . (6, p. 146)

morpheme

68. Syntax defines rules for the combination of words. We produce acceptable phrases and sentences by following the rules of _____ . (6, p. 146)

syntax

69. A formal description of syntactic rules is called grammar. As school-aged children, we learned rules which we referred to as _____ . (6, p. 146)

grammar

70. To review, the smallest unit of sound is a _____ , while the smallest meaningful unit of language is the _____ . (6, p. 146)

phoneme, morpheme

71. Rules for the construction of phrases and sentences are referred to as _____ , while a formal description of a speaker's rules is called _____ . (6, p. 146)

syntax, grammar

72. There are many ways to express an idea. The deep structure is the technical term for the _____ we want to express. (6, p. 146)

idea

73. The sentence we utter to express the idea is called the surface structure. Thus, the deep structure is reflected in the _____ _____ . (6, p. 146)

surface structure

74. Several different surface structures can be constructed to express one _____ _____ . (6, p. 146)

deep structure

75. Semantics is another type of rule. Rules for the appropriate use of words in social contexts, and for the appropriate use of words in sentences, constitute _____ . (6, p. 146)

semantics

76. Pragmatics is the set of rules tying language expressions to situations. Rules which guide the speaker to make the expression appropriate to the social setting are called _____ . (6, p. 147)

pragmatics

77. Rules such as taking turns in conversation and using articles (*a* and *the*) appropriately, and for telling jokes that are funny, are rules of _____ . (6, p. 147)

pragmatics

78. Now that we know the rules which define language: How is language learned? The traditional behaviorist view is that language is _____ like any other behavior. (7, p. 147)

learned

79. The _____ view of language development has difficulty explaining the infinite generativity of language. (7, p. 148)

behaviorist

80. The nativist theory of _____ development asserts that there is in each person a prewired device for learning language. (8, p. 148)

language

81. Four major arguments support this _____ view of language acquisition and development. (8, p. 148)

nativist

82. First, several language universals such as phonological categories appear in all human _____ . (8, p. 148)

languages

83. Second, language functions are lateralized in the brain. In the left hemisphere, in the left superior temporal cortex specifically, we find the main _____ center for speech production. (8, p. 149)

language

84. This center was first systematically investigated and described by Pierre-Paul Broca. Hence, this main language production center is also called _____ area. (8, p. 149)

Broca's

85. Nearby, in the left frontal cortex, is the center for speech comprehension. This area, also called Wernicke's area, is in the left _____ cortex. (8, p. 149)

frontal

86. As the infant develops, the brain becomes increasingly lateralized. The increasing dominance of the left hemisphere for speaking and thinking and mathematical tasks is referred to as _____ . (8, p. 149)

lateralization

87. A third argument in favor of the nativist position involves critical periods. Puberty marks the end of a _____ _____ for acquiring the phonological rules of a dialect. (8, p. 149)

critical period

88. A fourth argument involves language in nonhuman species. Communication systems found in other species of animals do not approach the _____ of humans. (8, p. 149)

language

89. Cognitive theorists argue that language development depends in part on certain _____ prerequisites. (9, p. 152)

cognitive

90. Indeed, these theorists contend that language development depends less on specific linguistic skills and more on general _____ abilities. (9, p. 152)

cognitive

91. Slobin has demonstrated that children all over the world learn _____ in about the same stages. (9, p. 153)

language

92. The _____ theory of language development is also supported by evolutionary evidence. (9, p. 154)

cognitive

93. From an _____ perspective, cognition is much older than language. (9, p. 154)

evolutionary

94. Children do not learn language in silence. Children require exposure to the _____ of others. (10, p. 154)

language

95. At about six or seven months of age, the baby begins to babble. A string of consonant and vowel phonemes is called _____ . (10, p. 155)

babbling

96. Near the child's first birthday, the first words are spoken. During this stage, fewer phonemes are used than in the previous stage of _____ . (10, p. 155)

babbling

97. The term *holophrase* describes the one-word stage. The fact that the single word may express an entire sentence or phrase is captured in the term _____ . (10, p. 156)

holophrase

98. These single words are often rich in information value, and the child uses pitch, stress, and contextual cues to make the _____ understood. (10, p. 156)

holophrase

99. A debate exists over how children attach meanings to holophrases. According to the holophrase hypothesis, the single word or _____ implies a whole sentence, which the child has mentally constructed. (10, p. 156)

holophrase

100. In contrast there is the hypothesis which suggests that the one-word utterance is a thought which corresponds to just one _____ . (10, p. 156)

word

101. Eve Clark has suggested that we distinguish between words and concepts. Beginning at about age nine months, the child begins to acquire _____ . (10, p. 156)

concepts

102. The child may sometimes choose the wrong word to express a newly formed _____ . (10, p. 156)

concept

103. Children may overextend or underextend the meanings of nouns. Using the word *daddy* to refer to all adult males is an example of _____ . (10, p. 156)

overextension

104. Less obvious limitations in which the child does not use a known word to refer to all members of a category, are called _____ . (10, p. 156)

underextensions

105. By the time children are eighteen to twenty-four months old, they are forming two-_____ statements. (10, p. 157)

word

106. Language at this stage has been called _____ speech, because articles, auxiliary verbs, and other unessential words are eliminated. (10, p. 157)

telegraphic

107. It is unclear how much syntactical knowledge can be attributed to children using _____ speech. (10, p. 157)

telegraphic

You judge. Now done. Review objectives. Ace test.

Self Test

1. In classical conditioning (1, p. 130)
   a. responses which are reinforced occur more frequently
   b. reflexes are modified by pairing a neutral stimulus with the unconditioned stimulus
   c. the CS elicits the UCS
   d. affective responses are immune to change

2. Operant conditioning could be used to (1, p. 130)
   a. teach a child to walk
   b. produce a fear of sidewalks where none existed before
   c. develop a habit of picking up toys before bedtime
   d. accelerate cognitive development

3. A scheme which is based on the infant's attempt to reproduce an interesting or pleasurable event, which is based in the infant's own body, is called (2, p. 135)
   a. a habit
   b. a primary circular reaction
   c. a secondary circular reaction
   d. coordination of secondary reactions

4. According to Piaget, the infant begins to show clear patterns of search for missing objects during substage (2, p. 135)
   a. 1
   b. 2
   c. 3
   d. 4

5. The basic sounds of any language are called (6, p. 146)
   a. phonemes
   b. morphemes
   c. syntax
   d. consonants

6. The basic idea or thought expressed in a sentence is the (6, p. 146)
   a. surface structure
   b. deep structure
   c. syntax
   d. formal transformation

7. Those rules which govern the appropriate use of language in terms of physical and social requirements are called (6, p. 147)
   a. basic rules
   b. syntax
   c. grammar
   d. pragmatics

8. The development of lateralization of the brain supports the _____ theory of language development. (8, p. 149)
   a. behaviorist
   b. nativist
   c. cognitive
   d. evolutionary

9. Before young children use even two-word sentences, they have usually reached the (10, p. 157)
   a. sensorimotor stage 5 or 6
   b. age of two years
   c. age of toilet training
   d. preoperational stage

10. The fact that even chimpanzees, very intelligent animals, do not develop real language supports the
   _____ theory of language development. (8, p. 149)
   a. behaviorist
   b. nativist
   c. lateralized
   d. anthropomorphic

Individual Learning Activity

Unfortunately, access to very young infants is usually quite limited, so wide-scale observations based on research are not easy to make. However, assuming you can obtain access to a few infants (perhaps by teaming up with a few of your classmates), the most easy and interesting thing you might do is test for object permanence.

The key here is to be sure that the infant is attending to the object (rattle or small block or what have you), and that you hide it while the infant is looking at it. While this may sound easy to you, please recall that you have the advantage of age and experience. Hide the object by putting it under a small cloth, like a washcloth. Then all you have to do is wait and see if the infant searches. Recalling Piaget's substages, what would you expect at each stage? Does the infant ignore your action? Does the infant look at the place where the object last was? Does the infant remove the cloth and discover the object? (And what is the infant's reaction to this landmark event?!) As Piaget probably would have suggested, older infants like to make a game of this.

If you have been able to obtain several observations, share your observations with classmates. Did anyone find an atypical infant? If so, how does one account for this? Is the infant different for some obvious reason? What would you recommend if you were a consultant to this family?

As you can see, much information can be gleaned from an apparently simple observation of a straightforward event. It was this very ability to ask questions about the nature of the experience which made Piaget the great investigator-theoretician he was.

Answers to the Self Test

1. b	6. b
2. c	7. d
3. b	8. b
4. c	9. a
5. a	10. b

6 Social, Emotional, and Personality Development

Preview

Parenthood brings disequilibrium and many opportunities for adjustment. In recent years, more fathers have become sensitive to the important role they play during pregnancy and child rearing. For the mother, the exhaustion of pregnancy gives way to the additional exhaustion of early motherhood, which may be compounded by the "postpartum blues." In contrast to infants, two-year-olds require parents to adopt new roles as teachers and guides, and parents must learn to juggle their roles, remaining parents, partners, and self-actualizing adults.

Hartup has characterized early theories of socialization as social mold theories, since they suggested that the child's behavior is molded by parental and other adult pressures. We now see socialization as a process which is reciprocal, and perhaps synchronized as well. Early in the mother-infant relationship, the mother assumes primary responsibility for initiating and maintaining interaction. Over time, toward the end of the second year, the relationship becomes more balanced.

It is becoming popular to consider the family from a systems approach, with divisions of labor and attachments defining individual and interactive roles. The family is a complex system. Negative interaction between husband and wife is related to negative father-infant interaction; though there is little relationship between positive husband-wife relationships and positive parent-infant interaction.

The contemporary view of socialization emphasizes transactions between a changing child and a changing social environment. Sroufe and Fleeson assert that a continuity and coherence characterize close relationships over time, and previous relationship patterns are carried forward into later relationships.

Attachment defines bonding between the infant and one or more adult caregivers, most often the mother. Bowlby, working largely from an ethological framework, theorized that mother and infant instinctively trigger each other's behavior to form a bond. Bowlby described executor responses such as clinging, following, and approaching, in which the infant is the main actor; and signaling responses, such as smiling, crying, and calling, in which the infant attempts to elicit maternal behaviors. According to Bowlby, attachment develops in four phases during the first year of life. In a major longitudinal study, Schaffer and Emerson found support for Bowlby's assertions, as did Ainsworth. In both of these later studies, there were wide individual differences among infants in the course and timing of attachment.

Ainsworth distinguishes between securely and insecurely attached infants. A securely attached infant uses the caregiver as a base from which to explore the environment. Recently, Clarke-Stewart explored situational variability, finding that physical or eye contact reduces stranger fear.

Until the 1970s, the role of the father was generally neglected. Sociologists pointed to his low status, citing weaker role expectations, lack of a biological basis for paternal behavior, and poor social preparation. In nonhuman species, paternal roles are often those of protection. Human fathers often act sensitively, and infants form attachments to both parents at about the same age. Yet babies seek out their mothers for comfort and solace, and their fathers for play.

Far more children are being placed in day care settings than ever before; with much of the day care being informal and unregulated. In poor quality day care, the stress of separation may produce significant disruption of the infant-mother attachment relationship. Infants in high quality day care show few if any differences from home reared infants in attachment behaviors. When day care is begun early in the first year of life, the infant may adopt an adaptive pattern of increased distance from the mother.

Erikson asserted that infancy is characterized by the psychosocial crisis of trust versus mistrust. The infant develops an expectancy; it learns to trust if it is cared for in a consistent, warm manner. Erikson's ideas are compatible with those of Ainsworth; trust is analogous to secure attachment.

Psychologists assess the early development of a sense of self by observing the responses of children to their mirror reflections. Infants recognize and coordinate in response to their images late in the second year of life.

Also during the second year, infants are struggling with the issue of autonomy versus shame and doubt, and mutual regulation between infant and adult is tested. The sense of autonomy parents are able to grant the toddler reflects their own sense of personal independence.

Infants at risk due to prenatal or perinatal factors often experience more difficulty in development. Rutter has listed a number of ways that earlier experience may be connected to later disorders.

Child abuse is an increasing problem in the United States, and can be best understood by examining cultural, familial, and community influences. Family violence reflects the high level of violence in the culture. In other cultures where the incidence of violence is very low, such as China, child abuse is also rare. Child abuse may result from interactions of parents, or from the dynamic interaction of parents and an unattractive or unwanted child. Community-based support systems are a key ingredient in the formula for prevention of child abuse.

Autism, often diagnosed during infancy, may persist into adulthood. It is characterized by inability to relate to other people, deficits in attachments, and speech disorders including echolalia. Autistic children are often greatly upset over minor changes in routine or environment. Autism seems to involve organic brain dysfunction as well as possible genetic influence.

Learning Objectives

1. Describe the effects of parenthood on individual parents and their relationship. (p. 165)
2. Define the process of socialization, and contrast social mold theories with the concept of reciprocal socialization. (p. 166)
3. Describe the family as a system, and the construction and maintenance of relationships. (p. 167)
4. Define *attachment* as psychologists use the term, and list and define three frequently observed attachment behaviors. (p. 170)
5. Define what Bowlby means by executor and signaling responses, and describe his four phases of the development of attachment. (p. 170)
6. Characterize longitudinal research on attachment, and describe and discuss Ainsworth's classification scheme for reflecting individual differences in attachment. (p. 171)
7. Describe the role of situational variables in the empirical measurement of attachment behaviors. (p. 173)
8. Characterize the father's role in terms of both human and nonhuman species. (p. 176)
9. Contrast high and low quality day care in terms of its effects on attachment behaviors. (p. 178)
10. Review Erikson's theory of the development of trust versus mistrust and autonomy versus shame and doubt, and show the relationship of each to parental behaviors. (p. 180)
11. Define the self and trace the beginnings of its development in infancy. (p. 181)
12. List and describe three types of problems in development, and summarize what is known about causal factors for each. (p. 183)

Key Terms

For each key term, write the definition in the space provided.

social mold theories (2, p. 166) _____

reciprocal socialization (2, p. 166) _____

molar exchanges (2, p. 166) _____

attachment (4, p. 170) _____

executor responses (5, p. 170) _____

signaling responses (5, p. 170) _____

secure attachment (6, p. 172) _____

insecure attachment (6, p. 172) _____

situational variability (7, p. 173) _____

autism (12, p. 187) _____

echolalia (12, p. 186) _____

Guided Review

1. New parents discover that the birth of an infant heralds disequilibrium in their lives, and they are required to _____ . (1, p. 165)

   adapt (or similar word)

2. In recent years, fathers have become more sensitive to their roles during pregnancy and after _____ . (1, p. 165)

   birth

3. Many mothers experience the "postpartum blues," a time of exhaustion and _____ , which may last as long as nine months. (1, p. 165)

depression

4. Both parents benefit when the father is sensitive to the mother's feelings and helps actively with the care of the _____ . (1, p. 166)

child (or baby)

5. The traditional view of socialization was that children were molded by their parents' child rearing techniques, a view that Hartup calls a _____ _____ theory. (2, p. 166)

social mold

6. A more contemporary view is that of reciprocal socialization. According to this view, child and parents _____ each other. (2, p. 166)

socialize

7. Mutual gazing or eye contact is one of the most frequently used measures of _____ _____ . (2, p. 166)

reciprocal socialization

8. Recently researchers have looked at molar exchanges. A study may focus on a host of affective responses, a _____ _____ , instead of just counting smiles. (2, p. 166)

molar exchange

9. There is no question that the behaviors of mothers and infants are connected, but there is some question about which person is driving the _____ . (2, p. 167)

relationship

10. Maccoby and Martin (1983) concluded that when the infant is very young, the _____ exerts more energy facilitating the relationship. (2, p. 167)

mother

11. Just as the relationship between mother and infant is important, so other family _____ are important in predicting the quality of the parent-infant bond. (3, p. 167)

relationships

12. Research has revealed little relationship between measures of positive husband-wife interaction and their positive _____ with the infant. (3, p. 168)

interaction

13. However, measures of negative interaction between husband and wife are strongly linked to the father's _____ action toward the infant. (3, p. 168)

negative

14. In the excitement and work revolving around the child, the parents may sometimes forget that they too have a _____ to nourish and maintain. (3, p. 168)

relationship

15. The family system will be healthier in relation to the extent that the husband can adapt and share in what have been traditionally _____ duties and tasks. (3, p. 168)

female

16. Socialization occurs in the context of relationships. Sroufe and Fleeson have formulated two postulates regarding _____ . (3, p. 168)

relationships

17. First, they postulate that continuity and coherence characterize close _____ over time. (3, p. 168)

relationships

18. Also, they assert that previous relationship patterns are carried forward to influence later _____ . (3, p. 168)

relationships

19. A key consequence of early parent-infant interactions is attachment. In psychological terms, the infant forms a relationship or bonding with one or more adult caregivers, and we call this phenomenon _____ . (4, p. 170)

attachment

20. The specific behaviors of maintaining contact and proximity, protest at separation, and stranger anxiety, form the measurable aspects of _____ . (4, p. 170)

attachment

21. Both ethological theory and psychoanalytic concepts have fostered interest in _____ . (4, p. 170)

attachment

22. According to Bowlby, infant and mother instinctively trigger the behavior in each other, forming the _____ bond. (4, p. 170)

attachment

23. Bowlby classified attachment into two main classes of activities, executor and signaling responses. Clinging, following, sucking, and physical approach constitute the former, or _____ responses. (5, p. 170)

executor

24. Smiling, crying, and calling constitute _____ responses, which elicit the reciprocal responses from the mother. (5, p. 170)

signaling

25. According to Bowlby, attachment occurs in four phases during the first year of life. During the first phase, from birth to two or three months of age, the infant forms the _____ to humans on the basis of an instinctual or unlearned bias. (5, p. 170)

attachment

26. During phase two, from three to six months, the attachment becomes focused on one person, usually the primary caregiver, who is often the _____ . (5, p. 170)

mother

27. In phase three, from six to nine months, the intensity of _____ to the mother increases, due to the increased ability of the infant to move about. (5, p. 171)

attachment

28. In the fourth phase, from nine months to one year of age, the elements of _____ become integrated into a mutual system. (5, p. 171)

attachment

29. Schaffer and Emerson conducted a major longitudinal study of attachment, and found strong support for the phases of attachment outlined by _____ . (6, p. 171)

Bowlby

30. Mary Ainsworth has also contributed several ideas to the literature on _____ . (6, p. 171)

attachment

31. Ainsworth points out that there are vast individual differences in caretaker-infant interaction which have profound consequences on the development of _____ . (6, p. 172)

attachment

32. Also, attachment relationships which result are relatively enduring in the child, according to _____ . (6, p. 172)

Ainsworth

33. Individual differences in _____ have been investigated by Ainsworth. (6, p. 172)

attachment

34. Ainsworth distinguishes between infants who are securely attached and those who are not. Among those who are insecurely _____ , she further distinguishes between those who avoid and those who resist the caregiver. (6, p. 172)

attached

35. Situational variables are also important determinants of the expression of _____ .
(7, p. 173)

attachment

36. The fact that an infant shows less distress in a strange situation when sitting on mother's lap than when sitting on a table, is an example of the effect of a _____ variable. (7, p. 173)

situational

37. The nature of the behavior of the stranger in the experiment, whether the stranger is nice or nasty, is another _____ _____ to consider. (7, p. 173)

situational variable

38. The father's role in the social development of the child is still not very clear. In fact, until the 1970s, the role of the _____ was generally neglected. (8, p. 176)

father

39. Family sociologists believe the father has a low status in the family for three reasons. First, it is believed that the _____ role is much weaker than the mother's. (8, p. 176)

father's

40. Second, there is no biological basis for the relationship between father and _____ .
(8, p. 176)

child

41. Third, the _____ is poorly prepared, socially and culturally, for his parental role.
(8, p. 176)

father

42. In nonhuman species, the father's function after procreation involves the protection of mother and _____ . (8, p. 176)

child (or offspring)

43. But many fathers do act sensitively toward their infants, and infants form _____ to both mothers and fathers. (8, p. 177)

attachments

44. Mothers and fathers do play different roles, however. Infants who are wet, tired, or hungry tend to prefer the _____ . (8, p. 177)

mother

45. Infants tend to seek out their fathers for _____ , but under stressful conditions still prefer the mother. (8, p. 177)

play

46. Many infants and young children are cared for in day care settings, much of which is informal and unregulated. It is important to examine the issue of the effects of _____ _____ on attachment and infant development. (9, p. 178)

day care

47. One investigation found significant disruption of the infant-mother attachment for infants in low quality _____ _____ . (9, p. 178)

day care

48. When infants in high quality day care were compared to home reared infants, few if any _____ were found. (9, p. 179)

differences

49. Sometimes the quality of the infant-mother attachment is affected by _____ _____ . (9, p. 179)

day care

50. In many instances, these involve greater avoidance or independence from the _____ , and are more pronounced when day care begins in the first year of life. (9, p. 179)

mother

51. For many children, the pattern of increased distance from the mother is an adaptive pattern to the circumstances of being away from the _____ a large part of the day. (9, p. 179)

mother

52. Erikson sees infancy as a time for the development of basic trust. Infants who are cared for in a consistent, warm manner will develop an expectancy Erikson refers to as _____ . (10, p. 180)

trust

53. Erikson's ideas coincide with those of Ainsworth; the infant who is _____ attached develops trust. (10, p. 181)

securely

54. The development of expectancies such as trust demonstrates the beginning of the sense of self. The sense of who one is and what makes one different from everyone else is the sense of _____ . (11, p. 181)

self

55. Children begin to develop a sense of _____ by learning to distinguish themselves from others. (11, p. 181)

self

56. Human infants can recognize their reflection in a _____ , a typical test for self-recognition, by eighteen months of age. (11, p. 181)

mirror

57. The second stage of Erikson's theory of development involves the struggle between autonomy versus shame or doubt. Erikson believes that if a child does not develop a sense of independence, or free will, during the second year of life, he may be saddled with a propensity for feelings of _____ and _____ . (10, p. 182)

shame, doubt

58. Erikson contends that a child's sense of autonomy is a reflection of the parents' dignity as _____ beings. (10, p. 182)

autonomous

59. According to Erikson, parents who are frustrated in marriage, work, or citizenship are more likely to have a child with a lasting sense of _____ or _____ . (10, p. 182)

shame, doubt (either order)

60. In actual research on independence, Reingold and Eckerman placed mothers and their infants in a back yard environment and found a positive relationship between the age of the child and the distance the child traveled from the _____ . (10, p. 182)

mother

61. Koop has pointed out that a variety of biological risk factors can impinge on the organism at the time of conception or during prenatal, perinatal, or _____ life. (12, p. 183)

postnatal

62. Rutter has listed a number of ways in which earlier experience might be connected to later disorder. First, says Rutter, experience may produce a _____ immediately, which then persists. (12, p. 184)

disorder

63. Second, _____ may create bodily changes which affect later functioning. (12, p. 184)

experience

64. Third, experience may alter patterns of behavior, which later take on the form of a _____ . (12, p. 184)

disorder

65. Fourth, early experiences can alter family relationships which in turn can lead, over time, to a
_____ . (12, p. 184)

disorder

66. Fifth, sensitivities to stress or coping strategies are changed, and later predispose the person to a
_____ , or, by the same token, insulate a person from stress. (12, p. 184)

disorder

67. Sixth, early experiences may alter the child's self-concept or attitudes, which in turn affect later
_____ . (12, p. 184)

behavior

68. Last, experience may influence behavior by affecting the selection of environment or restricting or
_____ _____ opportunities. (12, p. 184)

opening up

69. One of the most serious problems in the United States is a form of violence toward children which we call
_____ . (12, p. 184)

child abuse

70. Parents who abuse children are rarely psychotic; most are responding to a pattern of cultural, familial, and
community _____ . (12, p. 184)

influences (or similar word)

71. The extent of child abuse in our culture reflects the general level of violence. In China, where there is relatively
little violence, _____ _____ is rare. (12, p. 184)

child abuse

72. Many parents who abuse their children were themselves as children _____ . (12, p. 185)

abused

73. Very often the children who are abused are unattractive or resulted from an unwanted _____ .
(12, p. 185)

pregnancy

74. Sometimes parents displace their violence from interpersonal frustrations, and _____ the
child. (12, p. 185)

abuse

75. A very serious emotional problem of infancy is autism. The inability to relate to others, and the resulting deficits
in attachment, characterize the _____ child. (12, p. 186)

autistic

76. Speech problems, particularly echolalia, are also associated with ＿＿＿＿＿＿＿＿＿＿ . (12, p. 186)

autism

77. The rote repetition of statements by others defines the language disorder termed ＿＿＿＿＿＿＿＿＿ .
(12, p. 186)

echolalia

78. Contrary to earlier theories which blamed the mother, we now believe that ＿＿＿＿＿＿＿＿ involves
organic brain dysfunction and perhaps reflects genetic ties as well. (12, p. 186)

autism

Self Test

1. The current view of socialization could be expressed in terms of (2, p. 166)
   a. the effects of parents on their children
   b. the responsibility of parenthood for child rearing
   c. children's attachments to their parents
   d. relationships

2. The notion of molar exchanges carries with it the idea that the researcher could just as easily measure or record
   (2, p. 166)
   a. a subcomponent of the molar exchange
   b. a number of types of molar exchanges
   c. any other aspects of teeth eruption
   d. related genetically programmed elements

3. Negative social interaction between husband and wife is a predictor of (3, p. 168)
   a. child abuse
   b. negative affect expressed by the father toward the infant
   c. negative affect expressed by both parents toward the infant
   d. divorce

4. According to Bowlby, clinging, following, sucking, and physical approach are called (5, p. 170)
   a. learned patterns
   b. executor responses
   c. signaling responses
   d. attachment responses

5. Visiting a day care center, you hear an aid describe a child as insecurely attached. You are not surprised when
   the child (6, p. 172)
   a. runs to greet its mother with a hug
   b. periodically comes over to the aid to touch her
   c. plays quietly with the other children, oblivious to adults
   d. cries as soon as she notices you are in the room

6. One reason that fathers may have been neglected in the past by infancy researchers may well have been because
   fathers (8, p. 176)
   a. know nothing about infants
   b. are too rough to be allowed to handle infants
   c. have had no training for parenthood
   d. have a biological mandate to protect the infant, not play with it

7. Having reviewed all the evidence, a reasonable person could accurately claim that high quality day care (9, p. 179)
    a. is not affordable by or available to most Americans
    b. does no more good for infants than rearing them at home
    c. contributes to parental distancing from the infant, and therefore is dangerous to attachment behaviors
    d. is not significantly better for infants than low quality day care in the second year of life

8. If Erikson and Ainsworth were speaking, Ainsworth might very well say: Dr. Erikson, I believe that we (10, p. 181)
    a. disagree about the basic tasks of infancy because we are looking at infants in different cultures
    b. are examining the same variables, calling them attachment and autonomy
    c. are confusing autonomy with independence
    d. are both looking at the same phenomenon; i.e. trusting infants are securely attached

9. According to Erikson, there is a connection between the development of autonomy in the infant and the status of the relationship between the parents. Given this information, it is not sensible for parents to (10, p. 182)
    a. share tasks, since it confuses the infant
    b. remain together unhappily for the sake of the child
    c. encourage the child to excel in areas they did not
    d. demonstrate their own independence to the child

10. When shown a mirror, a typical twenty-month-old infant will (11, p. 181)
    a. recognize his reflection and reach for it
    b. cry in surprise and dismay
    c. not respond to it at all
    d. seek out mother for consultation and emotional refueling

Individual Learning Activity

For most college and university students, extensive studies of attachment behaviors, or independence, are not feasible. You will be relieved to know we are not going to ask you to go out and observe infants as part of this chapter's work.

However, attachment and independence are issues of great concern to parents of infants, and these parents are frequently confused about the meaning of the infant's behavior. You can serve an important role here, in allaying fears, clarifying issues, and reducing uncertainty. (If that doesn't appeal to you, how about expanding truth, mediating reality, assuring justice and the rights of infants, and perpetuating the American tradition?)

Your task is to prepare a set of guidelines for parents of infants, specifically oriented to the issues of attachment and independence. Your guidelines should (1) explain the development of each phenomenon, (2) describe appropriate infant behavior at each typical age level (in accord with prominent theories as well as empirical evidence), (3) suggest games or activities the parents might play or do with the infant to encourage proper development, and (4) try to anticipate and respond to, some questions you think parents might have about the child's behavior.

I would suggest that you work on this assignment in a group of four or five, because the cross-fertilization of ideas among you should prove valuable on this topic. In fact, this very type of cross-fertilization often produces testable hypotheses which result in significant new advances in our knowledge and understanding of human development.

Answers to the Self Test

1. d	6. c
2. a	7. b
3. b	8. d
4. b	9. b
5. d	10. a

7 Physical and Cognitive Development

Preview

Physical development slows in early childhood, with average gains of two and one-half inches in height and five to seven pounds per year. Both boys and girls slim down as their trunks become longer, and body fat shows a steady decline. The heart rate slows and steadies, but many body systems remain immature and susceptible to injury. Much of the considerable variation in height is due to the effects of ethnic origin and nutrition. Growth problems may result from congenital, physical, or emotional difficulties, as is the case in deprivation dwarfism. Gross motor skills improve markedly and fine motor skills improve slightly. Handedness appears between ages two and five, it is probably determined by genetic or prenatal forces, and is unrelated to competence.

The stage of preoperational thought extends from age two through seven, and consists of substages of symbolic functions and intuitive thought. Preoperational thought is characterized by a number of limitations, including egocentrism and animism.

During the early childhood years, there are major changes in attention, with the ability to attend to a stimulus increasing with age. After the age of six or seven, cognitive control of attention emerges, and children are more reflective. Preschool children more often attend to salient features than relevant features in problem solving tasks. Low achieving students are often deficient in attentional skills.

Short-term memory can retain information for twenty to thirty seconds, longer with rehearsal. Compared to the ease of short-term retention, encoding for long-term retention is more difficult. Based on memory span, it appears that short-term memory increases during early childhood. Age differences in memory span appear to be due to strategies such as rehearsal, and the speed and efficiency of information processing. Task analysis of problem solving involves strategies for teaching children to work more efficiently, in contrast to the Piagetian position that cognitive development occurs in fixed stages and is not subject to acceleration.

Language continues to develop during this period, as reflected in the increasing mean length of utterance (MLU), and including accomplishments in phonology, morphology, syntax, semantics, and pragmatics.

Most preschool education is child centered, and typically provides benefits in social interaction with peers and social competence, at the sacrifice of cooperation with adults. Projects Head Start and Follow Through are examples of large scale compensatory education programs. While many of the benefits provided to young children by Head Start appeared to wash out after a few years, long term studies indicate some lasting benefits, particularly for boys. Project Follow Through, with planned variations, is providing important information about how specific types of interventions influence specific cognitive and social aspects of human development.

Learning Objectives

1. Describe physical development, including individual variations and problems in growth, during early childhood. (p. 196)
2. Trace the course of gross and fine motor development, and handedness, in early childhood. (p. 197)
3. Describe preoperational thought, the two phases of the preoperational stage, and two major limitations present at this stage. (p. 202)
4. Define the process of attention, and describe how it changes during the early childhood years. (p. 207)
5. Distinguish between short-term and long-term memory, and detail the use of the memory span technique to identify changes in memory functions. (p. 208)
6. Describe the information processing approach to cognitive development, and provide an example of task analysis. (p. 209)
7. Describe the role of MLU in assessing language development, and list the changes in phonology, morphology, syntax, semantics, and pragmatics which occur during early childhood. (p. 210)

8. List at least five positive and three negative behavioral outcomes of preschool education. (p. 214)
9. Define compensatory education, and summarize the design and known effects of Projects Head Start and Follow Through. (p. 214)

Key Terms

For each key term, write the definition in the space provided.

deprivation dwarfism (1, p. 197) _____

handedness (2, p. 198) _____

operations (3, p. 202) _____

symbolic function substage (3, p. 202) _____

intuitive thought (3, p. 202) _____

egocentrism (3, p. 203) _____

animism (3, p. 205) _____

short-term memory (5, p. 208) _____

memory span task (5, p. 208) _____

class inclusion reasoning (6, p. 209) _____

mean length of utterance (MLU) (7, p. 210) _____

overgeneralizations (7, p. 211) _____

child-centered (8, p. 214) _____

compensatory education (9, p. 214) _____

Project Head Start (9, p. 214) _____

Project Follow Through (9, p. 214) _____

Guided Review

1. This chapter deals with physical and cognitive development in early childhood. Physical growth slows markedly in _____ _____ . (1, p. 196)

   early childhood

2. The average child grows two and one-half inches and gains between five and seven pounds each year, during _____ _____ . (1, p. 196)

   early childhood

3. As trunks become longer, both boys and girls become _____ in appearance. (1, p. 196)

   slimmer

4. There is considerable variation in height during early childhood, most of it due to ethnic origin and _____ . (1, p. 196)

   nutrition

5. Some children experience growth problems. Malnutrition and chronic infections can severely stunt _____ . (1, p. 197)

   growth

6. Some psychologists believe that emotional problems can also stunt growth. Deprivation dwarfism is a type of growth retardation produced by _____ problems. (1, p. 197)

emotional

7. While physical growth _____ , gross motor coordination improves noticeably. (1, p. 198)

slows

8. With rapid development of large muscles, daily forms of _____ are recommended. (2, p. 198)

exercise

9. At the same time, fine motor skills are improving more slowly. One _____ _____ skill which children should practice frequently is scribbling. (2, p. 197)

fine motor

10. The term *handedness* refers to the hand the child prefers to use. Between ages two and five years, it is increasingly easy to detect _____ . (2, p. 198)

handedness

11. Only about one in ten children is _____-handed, a condition which parents and teachers used to try to alter. (2, p. 198)

left

12. In terms of Piaget's cognitive theory, the period of _____ _____ involves the preoperational stage. (3, p. 202)

early childhood

13. During the preoperational stage, thought is not governed by operations. Internalized sets of actions which permit the person to do mentally what before was done physically, are called _____ . (3, p. 202)

operations

14. It is convenient to divide the preoperational stage into two substages. The first, or symbolic function _____ , extends roughly from age two to age four years. (3, p. 202)

substage

15. The child can use mental representations in lieu of physical objects or people during the _____ _____ substage. (3, p. 202)

symbolic function

16. The second substage is called intuitive thought. The child begins to reason and asks many questions during the _____ _____ substage. (3, p. 202)

intuitive thought

17. Thinking at this time is called _____ , because children are very sure of their knowledge but unaware of its source or derivation. (3, p. 202)

intuitive

18. Preoperational thought is characterized by egocentrism. The child's inability to distinguish easily between his or her own perspective and that of another person is referred to as _____ . (3, p. 203)

egocentrism

19. Another aspect of preoperational thought is animism. Attributing human qualities to inanimate objects, such as trees and cars, is called _____ . (3, p. 205)

animism

20. Noticing an event, or stimulus, in the environment constitutes attention. There are great changes in the child's ability to pay _____ during the early childhood years. (4, p. 207)

attention

21. As children get older, their span of _____ increases, and the control of attention becomes more cognitive. (4, p. 207)

attention

22. Preschool children are more attentive to salient features of a stimulus. Those features which stand out or attract attention are called _____ . (4, p. 208)

salient

23. Low-achieving students are often those who are deficient in _____ skills. (3, p. 208)

attentional

24. There are several processes involved in memory. The ability to retain information for up to twenty or thirty seconds is a feature of short-term _____ . (5, p. 208)

memory

25. With appropriate rehearsal, the duration of information in _____ memory can be increased considerably. (5, p. 208)

short-term

26. Compared to the use of short-term memory, encoding information in and retrieving information from _____ memory is more difficult. (5, p. 208)

long-term

27. One task used to assess the function of short-term _____ is the memory span task. (5, p. 208)

memory

28. Using the _____ _____ task, researchers have shown consistent increases in short-term memory during early childhood. (5, p. 208)

memory span

29. Research with young adults suggests that performance on the _____ _____ task correlates well with performance on the SAT. (5, p. 208)

memory span

30. Most of the age differences in memory span performance are related to the speed and efficiency of information processing. The speed of _____ is seen as an important aspect of the child's cognitive abilities. (6, p. 209)

processing

31. A major emphasis in information _____ is task analysis, to identify the components of the task in detail. (6, p. 209)

processing

32. Many of the errors and limitations of preoperational thinkers can be better explained if the psychologist performs a _____ _____ on the problem presented to the child. (6, p. 209)

task analysis

33. One result of such task analysis is to suggest appropriate strategies for teaching children the essential skills they need to be successful on a given _____ . (6, p. 210)

task

34. This is an important distinction between Piaget's perspective and that of information _____ . (6, p. 210)

processing

35. Piaget responds to the child's inability to complete a task by pointing to his cognitive immaturity; the information processing view focuses on the task requirements and considers the complexity of the task for the _____ . (6, p. 210)

child

36. During the years of _____ childhood, language development continues. (7, p. 210)

early

37. Roger Brown has developed a technique for assessing language development: the mean length of utterance, or _____ . (8, p. 210)

MLU

38. In the area of phonology, some preschool children have difficulty pronouncing consonant clusters, and some of the _____ rules for word endings are not yet mastered. (7, p. 211)

phonological

39. Morphological rules are also learned rapidly during early childhood, as is easily seen in evidence from overgeneralizations. That the child really does learn and apply *rules,* and not just examples, is clear when one listens to _____ . (7, p. 211)

overgeneralizations

40. Preschool children also learn rules of syntax rapidly. Learning to ask questions, including the inversion of the secondary verb, demonstrates the development of _____ . (7, p. 211)

syntax

41. In the area of semantics, we find the child's knowledge of meanings advancing well also. Speaking vocabulary increases dramatically, reflecting the development of _____ . (7, p. 212)

semantics

42. Pragmatics also reflect great development. Rules of conversation, such as taking turns, are referred to as _____ . (7, p. 212)

pragmatics

43. That four-year-old children speak differently to an adult or to a younger child than they do to same-age peers demonstrates a grasp of the rules of _____ . (7, p. 213)

pragmatics

44. Most organized preschool education is called child-centered. The emphasis is on the individual _____ , and the goal is to make learning a fun-filled adventure. (8, p. 214)

child

45. There are many advantages as well as some disadvantages for children involved in preschool _____ . (8, p. 214)

education

46. Increases in social competence, independence, verbal expressiveness, and leadership are all associated with _____ education. (8, p. 214)

preschool

47. However, there are also some negative behaviors associated with preschool _____ , including less politeness, increased aggression, and less compliance with teacher demands. (8, p. 214)

education

48. Beginning in the 1960's, the United States government sought to break the cycle of poverty and poor education by funding _____ education, including Project Head Start and Project Follow Through. (9, p. 214)

compensatory

49. It soon became apparent that some of the Head Start centers were more successful than others, so Project _____ _____ was established, involving planned variation. (9, p. 214)

Follow Through

50. The long term effects of Project Head Start have involved sex differences. The long-term benefits, by the time early adulthood arrives, favor _____ . (9, p. 215)

males

51. Some of the reasons the benefits did not last for the females may have to do with the structure of the elementary classroom, where verbal skills, inquisitiveness, and self-confidence are not encouraged in young _____ . (9, p. 215)

females (or girls)

52. Project Follow Through, because it involves _____ _____ , can provide much more detailed information on the particular aspects of preschool compensatory education most likely to benefit children. (9, p. 214)

planned variation

Please be sure to plan some time to review the learning objectives, then give the self test your best effort.

Self Test

1. During early childhood, there is considerable gain in (1, p. 197)
   a. physical size
   b. gross motor coordination
   c. fine motor coordination
   d. weight

2. The child's inability to distinguish his perspective from that of another is termed (3, p. 203)
   a. centration
   b. egocentrism
   c. irreversibility
   d. animism

3. The class inclusion problem is a clear example of the preoperational child's inability to (3, p. 202)
   a. decentrate
   b. use reversals
   c. conserve
   d. reason hierarchically

4. The attribution of human qualities to inanimate objects during early childhood is called (3, p. 205)
   a. animism
   b. symptomatic of cognitive defects
   c. egocentrism
   d. lack of conservation

5. The emergence of cognitive control over attention leads to the observation that older preoperational children (4, p. 207)
   a. are less impulsive
   b. attend more to salience than to relevance
   c. enjoy class inclusion problems
   d. are less capable of task analysis

6. Contrasted with Piaget's approach to cognitive development, the information processing approach stresses (6, p. 209)
   a. the speed of mental activity
   b. increases in the attention span
   c. task analysis
   d. class inclusion reasoning

7. According to Roger Brown, language development can be easily assessed by simply calculating the mean number of (7, p. 210)
   a. phonological rules the child applies
   b. syntax errors per sentence
   c. morphemes in each statement
   d. children who can accomplish a given skill

8. The use of overgeneralizations by children demonstrates conclusively that (7, p. 211)
   a. rules are being learned
   b. behavioral principles of language development are adequate
   c. language cannot develop beyond the critical period
   d. phonological rules are more important than syntactical rules

9. Preschool children speak differently to peers and to parents, demonstrating their understanding of (7, p. 213)
   a. morphology
   b. semantics
   c. phonology
   d. pragmatics

10. Longitudinal evaluation of Head Start children showed that (9, p. 215)
    a. boys fared better than girls
    b. all gains were washed out after three years
    c. planned variation was the key to Head Start successes
    d. the Head Start program was a waste of funds

Individual Learning Activity

Children in the preoperational stage are identified primarily by the limits of their reasoning abilities, as you have by now realized. This seems a rather awkward way to describe a stage of cognitive development, and the listing and identification of limitations appropriate to this stage is hardly an adequate explanation of the quirks in the child's reasoning. For example, it is astounding to most parents to see their six- or seven-year-old child respond to a class inclusion problem in a way which they believe is clearly "wrong," and then be unable to teach the child the "correct" way to solve the problem.

   Your task here is to resolve this dilemma in two stages. Along the way, you will gain a deeper appreciation of the contrast between Piaget's perspective on cognitive development, and that of the information processing view.

First, take a few minutes to consider the key limitations of the preoperational stage: egocentrism, animism, failure to conserve, and the inability to use hierarchical classifications. Using this list, create at least two problems or questions which you think will display each of these limits. For example, you may use the classic class inclusion test ("Are there more nickels or more coins?") to demonstrate the inability to reason hierarchically. If you have the opportunity, try out a few of your questions on a child in the preoperational stage. You will probably be as delighted with the child's responses as the parents will be concerned about their child's "erroneous" thinking. Of course, if you actually do this, be sure to reassure the parents that the child's cognitive functions are "normal" and appropriate to his or her age.

Now the good part. Do a task analysis on each test or problem which you have posed. This can be done easily: just think out loud as you solve the problem. Breaking down the problem into the smallest possible steps, you can very likely see where the errors have occurred, and will be in a much better position to describe the limits of the child's reasoning at this age.

To truly demonstrate your success in the second part of this exercise, see if you can reword your problems (be creative; don't be afraid to give very detailed directions!) so that the child would have a greater chance of solving the problems. Can you do it? Of course, if you can, test your new problems on another child, or on the same one. Did your task analysis enable you to word the problem in such a way that you increased the likelihood of success? Can you think of ways to apply this type of task analysis in teaching? Parenting? Management? Now you are beginning to see some of the advantages of the information processing perspective. Be patient; there's more to come.

Answers to Self Test

1. b	6. c
2. b	7. c
3. d	8. a
4. a	9. d
5. a	10. a

---

8 Social, Emotional, and Personality Development

Preview

Parenting has long been a subject of both debate and research. In the 1930s, Watson cautioned parents against being affectionate with their children. In 1971 Baumrind found that parents should be neither punitive nor aloof, but should develop and enforce rules. Authoritarian parents, who are restrictive and punitive, have children who are anxious about social comparisons, fail to initiate activity, and interact ineffectually. Authoritative parents encourage independence and demonstrate warmth, and have socially competent, self-reliant and responsible children. Parents who are permissive, indulgent, and undemanding have impulsive, aggressive children. Parents who are permissive and indifferent do not control their children's negative behaviors so they have children who lack self-control.

As the child matures, the focus of the parent-child interaction moves from routine caretaking to playful exchanges to discipline. Discipline is taught first by physical manipulation and later by reasoning, moral exhortation, or the withholding of privileges.

Competition is the keynote of sibling relationships, coupled with concerns about fair treatment. Children interact more positively with parents than with their siblings. In some instances, however, siblings are a stronger socializing force than parents; this is particularly true in areas such as dealing with difficult teachers, discussing taboo subjects, and dealing with peers. Siblings are valuable sources of support for children in therapy.

Mothers may respond to each child differently, which could account for birth order effects. Firstborns are more achievement oriented and affiliative, while middle children are reputed to be more neglected.

The variety of family patterns is increasing as more mothers are employed and more parents experience divorce and remarriage. Most American fathers spend less time with their families than at any other time in history. Boys who experience full-time mothering during the preschool years are more competent intellectually but more fearful and compliant as adolescents.

The effects of divorce on the child are mediated by such factors as the relationship with the noncustodial parent, the availability of support services, and the ongoing relationship with the custodial parent. Children in single-parent families fare better than those in conflict-ridden nuclear families. Parenting suffers in the first year after divorce, but it usually recovers in the second year. Competent support systems are particularly important for low-income families, and for parents with infants and preschool children. Divorce may upset the attachment bond of infancy; older children may blame themselves for the divorce, or hold unrealistic expectations of reconciliation. Children who live with the parent of the same sex develop greater social competence than those living with the opposite-sex parent.

At present trends, more than 25 percent of all children in the 1990s will live with a stepparent before the age of eighteen. The stepparent role is ambiguous, and often must be shared with the biological parent. Children in complex stepfamilies, blended from two earlier families, have more adjustment problems than children in simple stepfamilies, where all the children derive from only one prior family.

Children spend a great deal of time with peers, children of similar age or behavioral level. Mixed-age groups often produce more altruistic behaviors than same-age groups, who are more likely to engage in aggression. The peer group provides information and comparison about the world outside the family. Both animal and human research suggests that peers are instrumental in social competence and the recovery from isolation and depression.

Peers also provide an opportunity for rough-and-tumble play, while parents remain preferred in times of stress. These different socioemotional responses are made early, but realized later. A secure early attachment to the mother may promote positive peer relations.

Play serves many functions: affiliation, tension release, cognitive advances, and exploration. Play therapy also permits symbolic expression of emotional problems. Parten has identified patterns of unoccupied, solitary, onlooker, parallel, associative, and cooperative play. Barnes has recently confirmed Parten's observations regarding developmental changes in play. The play of preschoolers may involve rituals, sometimes referred to as turns and rounds. Pretend play includes the transformation of the physical environment into a symbol, and permits children to try out many roles.

Many children spend more time watching television than they do with their parents. Television has been charged with reducing achievement test scores, distracting children from their homework, promoting passivity, deceiving viewers, and promoting violence. Television also opens up a wider world to the child. Children increase their use of television and other pictorial media until about age twelve, after which their use of it declines. Television can influence a spectrum of behavior ranging from aggression to prosocial behaviors. Children whose parents are well educated and of high occupational status, as well as those children who attend nursery school, watch less television than the average. Television commercials have been implicated in children's preferences for snacks high in sugar content.

The self begins to develop early, with three-year-olds aware of a private self. Sex roles are those behaviors defined as sex-appropriate, while the extent to which a child adopts a sex role defines the sexual or gender identity. Historically, the well-adjusted child has been defined as accepting a sex-appropriate sex role. More recently, androgyny, the inclusion of valued attributes of both male and female sex roles, is preferred. While Bem and Spence promote androgyny, Katz promotes conformity to traditional sex roles. Psychoanalytic theory asserts that biological influences dictate sex roles, while Kohlberg points to the importance of cognitive factors. Cultural and other environmental influences also make sex or gender an important component of life. Parents, particularly fathers, and teachers are also important contributors to the development of the child's sex role.

Moral development is indicated by how children reason about moral issues, the behavioral decisions they make in response to moral questions, and their feelings about their moral decisions. Piaget has described moral realism and moral autonomy as distinctly different stages. The study of moral behavior has been strongly influenced by social learning theory. Psychoanalytic theory holds that guilt develops as hostility is turned inward as a result of identification with parents who withhold love as a disciplinary technique. In addition to guilt, the study of moral feelings has focused on empathy, the ability to understand the feelings or ideas of another person. Altruism, which is based on empathy, increases as children develop, as do role-taking and perspective-taking skills. The development of altruistic behaviors depends heavily on parent models and parental nurturance.

Learning Objectives

1. Trace interest in parenting, and describe authoritarian, authoritative, permissive-indulgent, and permissive-indifferent parenting styles, and the social behaviors of children associated with each. (p. 223)
2. Describe the nature and development of sibling relationships, and contrast them to parent-child relationships. (p. 225)
3. Trace changes in the pattern of the American family, and list and describe the effects of working mothers and of divorce on children. (p. 226)
4. List and describe at least two types of stepparent families, and show how each affects the development of the child, including relationships with each parent and stepparent. (p. 230)
5. Contrast family and peer relationships, and list and describe three important functions of peers. (p. 232)
6. List and describe three functions of play, define unoccupied, solitary, onlooker, parallel, associative, and cooperative play, and describe the development and effects of pretend play. (p. 234)
7. Describe the involvement of television in the lives of children, and identify three effects of television on children's behavior. (p. 238)
8. Trace the early development of the self, emphasizing the nature and development of sex roles and gender identity, with special attention to androgyny. (p. 244)
9. Identify three components of moral development, and review Piaget's model of the development of moral reasoning. (p. 250)
10. Describe the connection between guilt and empathy, and trace the development of altruism, role-taking, and perspective-taking skills. (p. 251)

Key Terms

For each key term, write the definition in the space provided.

authoritarian parenting (1, p. 223) _____

authoritative parenting (1, p. 223) _____

permissive-indulgent pattern (1, p. 224) _____

permissive-indifferent pattern (1, p. 224) _____

siblings (2, p. 225) _____

complex stepfamily (4, p. 230) _____

simple stepfamily (4, p. 230) _____

peers (5, p. 232) _____

play therapy (6, p. 234) _____

unoccupied play (6, p. 235) _____

solitary play (6, p. 235) _____

onlooker play (6, p. 235) _____

parallel play (6, p. 235) _____

associative play (6, p. 235) _____

cooperative play (6, p. 235) _____

ritual (6, p. 236) _____

pretend play (6, p. 237) _____

sex roles (8, p. 244) _____

sexual (or gender) identity (8, p. 244) _____

androgyny (8, p. 245) _____

moral development (9, p. 250) _____

moral reasoning (9, p. 250) _____

moral realism (9, p. 250) _____

moral autonomy (9, p. 250) _____

empathy (10, p. 251) _____

guilt (10, p. 251) _____

role-taking (10, p. 252) _____

perspective-taking skills (10, p. 252) _____

Guided Review

1. For many years, people have debated how parents should rear their children. Behind these debates is the assumption that what parents do determines what _____ do. (1, p. 223)

   children

2. Experts have for years been interested in developing theories about the patterns or dimensions of _____ . (1, p. 223)

   parenting

3. In the 1930s, behaviorist John Watson warned parents not to be affectionate with their _____ . (1, p. 223)

   children

4. More recently, Diana Baumrind has emphasized three styles of parenting: authoritarian, authoritative, and laissez-faire are the three categories proposed by _____ . (1, p. 223)

   Baumrind

5. Authoritarian parents are restrictive, have a punitive orientation, respect work and effort, exhort the child to follow directions, and place many limits and controls on the child. Children whose parents are _____ are very anxious, fail to initiate activities, and have trouble with social interactions. (1, p. 223)

   authoritarian

6. Authoritative parents encourage their children to be independent, but still place limits, demands, and controls on the child's actions. In addition, _____ parents are very warm and nurturant. (1, p. 223)

   authoritative

7. Children high in social competence, self reliance, and social responsibility are often the products of _____ parenting. (1, p. 223)

   authoritative

8. Eleanor Maccoby and John Martin have configured parenting styles on a model involving dimensions of demanding-undemanding and accepting-_____ parenting. (1, p. 224)

   rejecting

9. On Maccoby and Martin's model, the equivalent of _____'s authoritative parent is referred to as authoritative-reciprocal. (1, p. 224)

Baumrind

10. Other developmental psychologists have pointed out that permissive parenting occurs in at least two patterns. Both very indulgent and very indifferent parents can be classified as laissez-faire or _____. (1, p. 224)

permissive

11. Permissive-indulgent parents are undemanding but accepting and responsive. The children of such _____ parents are impulsive, aggressive, lack independence, and are unable to assume responsibility. (1, p. 224)

permissive-indulgent

12. The permissive-indifferent pattern also has negative effects on children. The assumption that they can get away with anything, and a strong disregard for rules and regulations are typical of the child of _____ _____ parents. (1, p. 224)

permissive-indifferent

13. The most competent style of parenting is neither permissive nor authoritarian, but is the one Maccoby and Martin refer to as _____ . (1, p. 224)

authoritative-reciprocal

14. The parent's behavior changes as the child ages, of course. During the first year, parents move from basic caretaking to playing with the _____ . (1, p. 224)

child

15. Also, as the child grows older, discipline changes from physical manipulation to reasoning and the giving or withholding of special privileges as befits the age of the _____ . (1, p. 225)

child

16. Most children have at least one sibling. A generic word that applies equally well to a brother or sister is _____ . (2, p. 225)

sibling

17. Competition and concerns about being treated fairly and equally by parents are the major sources of concern for _____ . (2, p. 225)

siblings

18. Children relate more positively to their parents than they do to their _____ . (2, p. 225)

siblings

19. In some instances, however, such as dealing with peers, coping with difficult teachers, or discussing taboo topics, the socialization of siblings is more powerful than that of _____ . (2, p. 225)

parents

20. Miller and Cantwell have found that in therapeutic relationships the involvement of a _____ as therapist makes the effort far more successful. (2, p. 225)

sibling

21. It would appear that some of the observed birth order effects may be brought about by different treatment of each child by the _____ . (2, p. 226)

mother

22. First-born children are more achievement-oriented, affiliative, and compliant, perhaps because they received more attention from the _____ . (2, p. 226)

mother

23. After the birth of another child, the mother and _____ exchanged affection less often and were more neutral toward each other. (2, p. 226)

firstborn

24. The conflict between _____ appears to begin in the second year of life. (2, p. 226)

siblings

25. A longitudinal study of dyadic pairs of _____ showed that during the preschool years the older siblings expressed more concern about social rules. (2, p. 226)

siblings

26. Many changes occur in the structure of families. One recent change has involved mothers being _____ away from home. (3, p. 226)

employed

27. In addition, almost half of the children born during the 1970s will spend some of their childhood in a family with only one _____ . (3, p. 226)

parent

28. Research has not confirmed many of the fears surrounding the phenomenon of _____ mothers. (3, p. 227)

working

29. It is not clear, in fact, that _____ mothers give less time to their children than do mothers who are not employed. (3, p. 227)

working

30. However, Moore (1975) conducted one study in which boys who had full-time mothers during the preschool years were more competent intellectually, but also more ready to conform, fearful, and inhibited as adolescents, compared to boys whose mothers _____ away from home. (3, p. 227)

worked

31. So the evidence on the effects of working mothers is still unclear. The interest in situations where parental contact may be reduced has led researchers to also examine single-_____ families. (3, p. 226)

parent

32. Probably the most common cause of single-_____ families is divorce. (3, p. 228)

parent

33. Santrock and Tracy (1978) showed that boys from homes disrupted by _____ were treated differently by teachers. (3, p. 228)

divorce

34. The teachers rated the boys whose parents they believed were _____ more negatively in terms of happiness, emotional adjustment, and ability to cope with stress. (3, p. 228)

divorced

35. This study showed that divorce may have indirect effects. The more _____ effects are influenced by family conflict, the child's relationship with both parents, and the availability of support systems. (3, p. 228)

direct

36. Parental conflict has a deleterious effect on _____ . (3, p. 228)

children

37. Children in single-parent families function better than children in conflict-ridden nuclear _____ . (3, p. 228)

families

38. While divorce may provide an escape from conflict, the year immediately following the divorce is usually marked by an increase in _____ . (3, p. 228)

conflict

39. During this year, children (particularly boys) from divorced families show more adjustment patterns than children in homes in which both _____ are present. (3, p. 228)

parents

40. In this first year after divorce, the quality of parenting suffers. During the second year, the quality of _____ improves. (3, p. 228)

parenting

41. Young children often do not understand why their parents are getting a _____ , so they may blame themselves, and have unrealistic hopes for reconciliation. (3, p. 229)

divorce

42. Children who live with a parent of the same sex are typically more competent socially than those children who live with the parent of the opposite _____ . (3, p. 229)

sex

43. If present trends continue, by the 1990s about 25 percent of all _____ will be part of a stepfamily before they reach age eighteen. (4, p. 229)

children

44. The roles of the stepparent are ambiguous, because they are shared with the child's _____ parent. (4, p. 229)

biological (or natural)

45. Also, because the children are present from the outset, there is little time or privacy for the development of a relationship between the husband and _____ in a stepfamily. (4, p. 230)

wife

46. We know that children show more adjustment problems when they are in a complex stepfamily than when they are in a simple _____ . (4, p. 230)

stepfamily

47. A family in which both parents have brought their children from a previous marriage is called a _____ stepfamily. (4, p. 230)

complex

48. In contrast, when only one of the newly remarried adults brings children from a previous marriage, the new family is called a _____ stepfamily. (4, p. 230)

simple

49. In general, relationships in the _____ are less positive than those in the intact family. (4, p. 230)

stepfamily

50. Peers are important elements in a child's social development. Children of about the same age, or children who interact at about the same behavioral level, are called _____ . (5, p. 232)

peers

51. Social contacts and aggressive displays are most frequently found among _____ . (5, p. 232)

peers

52. Mixed-age groups produce more dominant and altruistic behaviors than do groups of _____ . (5, p. 232)

peers

53. One important function of the _____ group is feedback about abilities, a form of social comparison. (5, p. 232)

peer

54. Suomi, Harlow, and Domek (1970) trained monkeys to counteract the effects of social isolation, and found the isolated monkeys were most likely to recover when assigned to their slightly younger _____ . (5, p. 233)

peers (monkeys is almost correct!)

55. Willard Hartup has gathered some early evidence from a nursery school setting which suggests that Harlow's technique works as well with young children as it did with _____ . (5, p. 233)

monkeys

56. As childhood continues, the frequency of interaction with peers increases, but the proportion of aggressive exchanges to friendly interactions _____ , especially among middle-class boys. (5, p. 233)

decreases

57. Some parents may fear that the child has attempted to replace their influence with the influence of _____ , but such is not the case. (5, p. 234)

peers

58. In times of stress, children still prefer to approach their _____ rather than peers. (5, p. 234)

parents

59. As children get older, their _____ with associates (parents and peers) become more differentiated. (5, p. 234)

interactions

60. Dominance and nurturance are directed from adults to children, but appeals and submissions are directed primarily from _____ to adults. (5, p. 234)

children

61. Most peer interactions take the form of play. Affiliation with peers, tension release, advances in cognitive development, and exploration are all valid functions of _____ . (6, p. 234)

play

62. Both Freud and Erikson contend that tension release is the major function of _____ . (6, p. 234)

play

63. Some therapists also believe that children can express emotional problems and their solutions symbolically, and use play _____ as a technique. (6, p. 234)

therapy

64. By contrast, Piaget sees play as a chance to use and exercise newly developing _____ abilities, and Berlyne sees play as satisfying curiosity and exploration needs. (6, p. 234)

cognitive

65. Mildred Parten (1932) developed a taxonomy (a system of classification) of _____ which is still used. (6, p. 235)

play

66. A technical term for a system of classification is _____ . (6, p. 235)

taxonomy

67. One of Parten's categories is called unoccupied play. When the child is not engaging in play, but is simply looking around the room or engaged in random movements, he is engaging in _____ play. (6, p. 235)

unoccupied

68. Solitary play is common among two- and three-year-olds. When the child plays alone and independently of those around him, the play is called _____ . (6, p. 235)

solitary

69. Onlooker play is just what it sounds like. The child who watches other children playing is said to be an _____ . (6, p. 235)

onlooker

70. Parallel play is more common among younger preschoolers. Playing by oneself but with toys and actions that mimic the play of others nearby is called _____ play. (6, p. 235)

parallel

71. Associative play involves social interaction. However, no organization or plan is involved in _____ play. (6, p. 235)

associative

72. The last category is cooperative play. A sense of group identity is present and activity is organized in _____ play. (6, p. 235)

cooperative

73. Using these categories developed by _____ , Barnes (1971) discovered that the children he observed did not engage in as much cooperative or associative play as the children did in the 1930s. (6, p. 235)

Parten

74. Peer interaction among preschoolers often involves rituals. A form of play which involves controlled repetition may be referred to as a _____ . (6, p. 236)

ritual

75. Catherine Garvey calls these interchanges turns and rounds. The part accomplished by each child is called a turn, while the sequence of turns for all children is called a _____ . (6, p. 236)

round

76. Some play is pretend. Transforming the physical environment into a symbol is the key to _____ play. (6, p. 237)

pretend

77. Beginning at about eighteen months, _____ play peaks between five and six years of age, then declines. (6, p. 237)

pretend

78. Besides engaging in play, children also watch television. Many experts believe that children should watch far less _____ . (7, p. 238)

television

79. Many believe that _____ can cause the child to become a passive learner, and that it presents an unreal image of life. (7, p. 239)

television

80. In addition, most television shows depict acts of _____ . (7, p. 240)

violence

81. The frequency of _____ is highest on Saturday morning cartoon shows, which are presented primarily for _____ . (7, p. 240)

violence, children

82. Bandura has shown that children imitate acts of _____ they have seen on television. (7, p. 240)

violence

83. Some programs are prosocial. Sesame Street is a program which contains many _____ episodes. (7, p. 241)

prosocial

84. The children of well-educated parents, or those children involved in preschool education, watch less _____ than their age-mates watch. (7, p. 241)

television

85. Besides watching the programs, children also watch the intermittent, rapid, brief _____ . (7, p. 241)

commercials

86. Unfortunately, many of the commercials advertise food for children, much of it heavily laced with _____ . (7, p. 241)

sugar

87. It has been shown that the snack preferences of children can be manipulated by controlling the content of the television _____ they watch. (7, p. 241)

commercials

88. Toward the end of the second year of life, children begin to develop their sense of who they are, their sense of _____ . (8, p. 244)

self

89. As we develop a sense of who we are, our gender or sex is an important part of that definition. This gender identity and the sex roles we learn manifest it are an important part of our definitions of _____ . (8, p. 244)

self

90. The behaviors expected of people based on their sex are called the _____ . (8, p. 244)

sex roles

91. The extent to which an individual takes on as part of the personality the behaviors and attitudes associated with either the male or female sex role is called the _____ identity. (8, p. 244)

gender (or sexual)

92. Reaction against the arbitrary and sometimes extreme demands of _____ roles has led to the development of the concept of androgyny. (8, p. 245)

sex

93. The expression of both masculine and feminine characteristics which are valued by society is called _____ . (8, p. 245)

androgyny

94. According to both Bem and Spence, children who are _____ can more easily adapt to a wider range of social situations. (8, p. 245)

androgynous

95. Psychoanalytic theory has long held that sex roles are the reflection of biological and instinctual forces. Erikson says that because of their external genital structures, _____ are more intrusive and aggressive. (8, p. 247)

males

96. In addition to biological factors, cognitive elements are also important in determining _____ _____ . (8, p. 248)

sex roles

97. Kohlberg points out that a child must have the ability to classify objects and behavior before adherence to the _____ _____ can occur. (8, p. 248)

sex roles

98. Children have a firm concept of their own gender by about age 6, according to _____ . (8, p. 248)

Kohlberg

99. Parents are also involved in the development of _____ _____ . (8, p. 248)

sex roles

100. Fathers are particularly implicated in studies of sex-typing. Fathers are more likely to act differently toward children based on their _____ than mothers are. (8, p. 249)

sex

101. In father-absent homes, _____ show a more feminine pattern of behavior. (8, p. 249)

boys

102. Parents often play more actively with _____ than with girls, and respond more positively to their physical activity. (8, p. 249)

boys

103. Boys are also permitted more freedom than _____ . (8, p. 249)

girls

104. In addition to _____ , teachers and peers are involved in sex-typing. (8, p. 249)

parents

105. Female teachers are more likely to reward _____ behavior by both girls and boys. (8, p. 250)

feminine (or female)

106. In addition to the development of _____ roles, children also experience moral development. (9, p. 250)

sex

107. The rules and conventions about what people SHOULD do in their interactions with others form the basis for _____ development. (9, p. 250)

moral

108. There are three domains or aspects of _____ _____ : thought, action, and feelings. (9, p. 250)

moral development

109. The first has to do with moral reasoning. How children reason or think about moral issues constitutes the domain called _____ _____ . (9, p. 250)

moral reasoning

110. A second domain is moral behavior. How children actually behave in the face of ethical issues is the variable we call _____ _____ . (9, p. 251)

moral behavior

111. The third domain is moral feelings. A sense of guilt or pride after making a decision or taking action is referred to as _____ _____ . (9, p. 251)

moral feelings

112. Piaget offers a theoretical perspective on _____ development. (9, p. 250)

moral

113. Piaget suggests two different modes of moral thought or reasoning. The first is moral realism. The young child, from four to seven years old, judges the goodness of an action by its consequences, reflecting _____ _____ . (9, p. 250)

moral realism

114. A belief that rules are unchangeable, and a belief in imminent justice, are also features of _____ _____ . (9, p. 251)

moral realism

115. A more advanced stage is moral autonomy. Children over ten years old consider the intention of the person in determining the rightness of actions, reflecting _____ _____ . (9, p. 251)

moral autonomy

116. Rules are changeable but convenient, and punishment is socially mediated and not inevitable for the child in the stage of _____ _____ . (9, p. 251)

moral autonomy

117. Social learning theory has had the most impact on the study of moral behavior. Emphasis on reinforcement, punishment, and imitation marks _____ _____ theory. (9, p. 251)

social learning

118. In terms of moral development, the laws of reinforcement and punishment do shape moral _____ . (9, p. 251)

behavior

119. The study of moral feelings has emphasized guilt. In psychoanalytic theory, guilt is viewed as hostility turned inward, resulting from identification with parents who withdraw their love when the child does something _____ . (9, p. 251)

wrong

120. Guilt is a weapon used by superego to force ego to make decisions which are socially acceptable or _____ . (9, p. 251)

moral

121. People should act properly to avoid feelings of _____ and the anxiety associated with it. (9, p. 251)

guilt

122. Erikson refers to early childhood as the stage of initiative vs. _____ . (9, p. 251)

guilt

123. The positive side of moral development is altruism. Sharing possessions, contributing to worthy causes, and helping people in distress are examples of _____ . (10, p. 252)

altruism

124. As children grow, altruism increases. Empathy is viewed as a critical element in the development of _____ . (10, p. 252)

altruism

125. Role-taking and perspective-taking are also important to the development of _____ . (10, p. 252)

altruism

126. Children who have well-developed role-taking skills are more likely to display _____ . (10, p. 253)

altruism

127. Parents are also important. Parental nurturance, assignment of responsibility, maturity demands, and inductive discipline all promote _____ in both boys and girls. (10, p. 254)

altruism

Well done!! We have come to the end of this unit. Please take a few minutes to look over the learning objectives, then do your very best on the self test.

Self Test

1. Preschool aged children relate to their siblings as though they believe that (2, p. 225)
   a. the other child has been treated better by the parents
   b. parental authority is absolute
   c. the parents will love them more if they can get rid of the other child
   d. parents have no favorites among their children

2. Research evidence confirms that (3, p. 227)
   a. preschoolers are damaged by mother working away from home
   b. working mothers spend less than half the time with their children that full-time mothers do
   c. most full-time mothers feel guilty because they are not employed
   d. employed mothers spend just as much time with their preschoolers as mothers who are homemakers

3. In the year immediately following a divorce, (3, p. 228)
   a. conflict decreases sharply
   b. conflict increases
   c. boys show fewer adjustment problems than girls
   d. the quality of parenting improves

4. Support systems for divorced families (3, p. 228)
   a. are not helpful in reducing problems
   b. are less important for small families than large
   c. are more important for low-income families
   d. seem to complicate and intensify conflicts

5. A high degree of psychological control by parents, as is seen in authoritarian parenting styles, promotes (1, p. 223)
   a. independent behavior
   b. dependent and regressive behavior
   c. inhibited, shy behavior
   d. impulsive behavior

6. Parents who are cold and hostile (1, p. 223)
   a. should be executed at sunrise
   b. have very inhibited, shy children
   c. have children who cry and suck their thumbs
   d. have children who are violent and hostile

7. What type of parenting teaches the child to be independent, socially competent, self reliant, and responsible? (1, p. 223)
   a. permissive
   b. authoritarian
   c. authoritative
   d. laissez-faire

8. Violence on television (7, p. 240)
   a. teaches children to be careful
   b. is a true reflection of modern life
   c. has no effect on the viewer
   d. promotes violence in child viewers

9. Compared to the relationship between a child and stepmother, the relationship between a child and stepfather is likely to be more (4, p. 231)
   a. distant
   b. abrasive
   c. affectionate than with the biological father
   d. mutual in terms of self-disclosure

10. In terms of the development of sex-roles, (8, p. 249)
    a. fathers are only important for girls
    b. fathers are important for both boys and girls
    c. mothers are more important than fathers
    d. parents have no lasting impact on children

Individual Learning Activity

The concept of androgyny is appealing to most of us. It encourages us to be all that we are capable of being by freeing us from the bonds of social sex roles, with their impossible stereotypes and outrageous demands to conform. A key to the concept of androgyny is the notion that the androgynous person expresses those attributes which are valued in each sex role.

This suggests that attributes are not only sex-specific in preference or appropriateness; but also that, within sex roles, attributes vary in desirability. For example, the feminine role includes expectations of emotional displays, sensitivity to the feelings of others, the avoidance of vulgarity, and difficulty in making decisions. Can you see that some of these are desirable and some are less desirable? Good.

Your task is to first collect descriptive words and phrases to differentiate the sex roles. Simply ask your friends what boys are like and what girls are like, and see how many adjectives and phrases you can get. Then, place them in a list and ask a few dozen (if you can) people to rate them in terms of their desirability, without specifying sex. Using the same list, have a few dozen people indicate whether each is more appropriate to men or to women. At this point, some will wash out as undifferentiated, that is, appropriate to either sex.

Using these ratings, you can make a two-by-two matrix with desirability on one axis and sex on the other. At this point, it is easy to develop a description of an androgynous person, so you may as well do so. Try writing a thumbnail sketch of this person, and then change the name and gender and see if it still sounds right. If it does, you have done an excellent job.

Answers to the Self Test

1. a
2. d
3. b
4. c
5. b

6. d
7. c
8. d
9. a
10. b

Section IV   Middle and Late Childhood

---

9   Physical and Cognitive Development

Preview

The period of middle and late childhood involves slow, consistent growth. During the elementary years, children grow an average of two to three inches and gain from three to five pounds per year. Their legs become longer and their trunks slimmer, and they are steadier on their feet. Fat tissue tends to develop more rapidly than muscle tissue, and endomorphic, mesomorphic, and ectomorphic body shapes become differentiated.

Motor behavior becomes much smoother and more coordinated, and sensory mechanisms continue to mature. Early farsightedness is overcome, binocular vision becomes well-developed, and hearing acuity increases. The frequency of illnesses, particularly respiratory and gastrointestinal disorders, decreases.

When asked about their health, elementary school children understand that good health requires almost constant attention and effort. As they grow older, children define health in more global and abstract terms.

Involvement in sports involves risks of injury, particularly in football. But vigorous exercise for healthy children, if not carried to extremes, is beneficial and provides a sound base for later stamina.

According to Piaget, the middle and late childhood years are characterized by the stage of concrete operational thought. The child in this stage is less egocentric, does not show animistic thought, reveals conservation skills, and displays decentered and reversible thought patterns. An operation may be thought of as a mental action or representation, and a concrete operation involves real, concrete objects.

The concrete operational thinker has the ability to classify or divide objects into sets and subsets, and to consider the interrelationships between classes. Yet, the child requires that the objects or events be present in order to think about them. Piaget's ideas about this stage have prompted numerous educational projects and programs, since his theory provides information and strategies not found elsewhere in the professional literature of developmental psychology.

While Piaget was certainly a genius in the sense that he showed us where and how to examine cognitive development in children, his perspective is questioned by four types of research findings: (1) the abilities he assembled in his unitary stages do not always emerge in synchrony; (2) very small changes in Piaget's procedures have significant effects on the child's responses; (3) children can be trained to respond at more advanced levels; and (4) younger children can do more and older children often do less than Piaget's stages would predict.

Intelligence and IQ are often equated. Binet and Simon devised the first intelligence test in 1905. They found that higher mental abilities were better predictors of success in school than were such lower abilities as reaction time. Binet was concerned with general intelligence (g), and developed the concept of mental age to describe the child's level of intellectual functioning. In standardizing the Binet test, it has been found that scores are normally distributed, with a mean of 100 and a standard deviation of 16. In the 1972 sample, preschool children attained an average score of 110, perhaps because of the increased stimulation of television and higher levels of education of their parents.

While the Binet depends heavily on verbal skills, the Wechsler scales are divided into verbal and nonverbal (performance) categories, which are further subdivided. The factor analytic approach emphasizes specific components of intelligence, but it uses complex mathematical formulas. Spearman originally proposed a two-factor theory, and Thurstone proposed an elaborate multiple-factor theory.

Cattell has proposed that there are two types of intelligence; fluid and crystallized. Fluid intelligence focuses on adaptability and capacity to perceive and integrate things; it is independent of education and experience. Crystallized intelligence results from education and experience, and involves skills, abilities, and understanding.

Guilford proposed that the structure of the intellect is composed of 120 combinations of five operations, four contents, and six products.

All efforts to measure any construct must address the issue of validity, the extent to which a test measures what it claims to measure. Criterion validity is the extent to which the test score predicts another measure. Intelligence tests are good predictors of school grades, and not bad at predicting occupational success.

David McClelland has suggested testing for competence, and recommends criterion sampling, measuring changes in what a person has learned, and publicizing the strategies to improve the characteristic tested. Culture-fair tests seek to replace traditional standardized intelligence tests, to avoid cultural bias. Two strategies have been applied to the development of culture-fair tests: (1) removing all the verbal items, and (2) using items familiar to all the people for whom the test is intended. A recently developed test, the Kaufman Assessment Battery for Children, is less verbal than the Binet, has been standardized using a more representative sample, and includes an achievement section.

Mercer contends that intelligence tests should be supplemented with measures of social competence, and has authored SOMPA, which includes assessment of (1) verbal and nonverbal intelligence, (2) social and economic background, (3) social adjustment to school, and (4) physical health.

The prevailing view of experts is that intelligence and creativity are not the same thing. Guilford distinguished between convergent and divergent thinking, with the latter supposedly related to creativity.

IQ is not a stable variable, as many believe, and may change as much as thirty points between age two and seventeen.

During middle childhood, both attention and memory show improvement. Long-term memory depends on control processes, including rehearsal, organization, elaboration, imagery, and retrieval or search processes. Maintenance rehearsal is simple rote repetition, while elaborative rehearsal may include organizational, elaborative, and imaginative activities. As children get older, they rehearse more and are more likely to use elaborative rehearsal. The use of organizational processing and semantic elaboration also increases with age. By age seven or eight, children can also use mental imagery, but not very well yet. There are also developmental differences in retrieval activities.

Knowledge already possessed contributes to most memory tasks. Metamemory is knowledge about one's own memory, and increases during the middle childhood years.

An inference is an unstated relationship between two events, and may be logical or depend on prior knowledge, which may take the form of scripts or semantic networks.

Sternberg has proposed an information-processing view of intelligence. In this view, the basic concept is the component, which can be classified by function and level. The five types of components are: metacomponents, performance components, acquisition or storage components, retention or retrieval components, and transfer components.

Children learn to read during the elementary school years. Our alphabetic writing system developed from the Egyptian system, which originated around 3500 B.C. Rozin and Gleitman have developed a method for teaching reading, which involves five stages: (1) semasiographic, (2) logographic, (3) phoneticization, (4) syllabary, and (5) alphabet. First grade students can learn the first four stages easily while the fifth stage causes more problems. The motivational aspect of the five-stage method may be its strongest feature. Many current techniques of reading instruction involve both whole-word and phonic methods; using the ABC method is considered archaic. While some experts discourage it, speech coding might contribute to short-term memory for words, and may serve an important rehearsal function.

Learning Objectives

1. Describe middle and late childhood growth and distinguish endomorphic, mesomorphic, and ectomorphic body builds. (p. 261)
2. Summarize the sensory and motor development of middle and late childhood. (p. 262)
3. Comment on the advisability of children playing competitive sports. (p. 262)
4. Define the stage of concrete operations, including at least two changes involved in this stage. (p. 264)
5. List four major limitations of Piaget's theory. (p. 265)
6. Describe the psychometric approach to intelligence, and trace the development and standardization of the Binet test. (p. 269)
7. Contrast the ideas of Binet and Wechsler and the factor analytic approaches of the Spearman, Thurstone, Cattel-Horn, and Guilford views. (p. 269)
8. Discuss the issue of validity, and describe the efforts to develop a culture-fair intelligence test. (p. 274)
9. Describe efforts to define and measure social intelligence and creativity. (p. 278)
10. Detail the information processing approach to middle and late childhood, and list and describe how children this age use five control processes. (p. 281)
11. Explain the role of scripts and semantic networks in the child's developing ability to draw inferences. (p. 285)
12. Recount Sternberg's componential view of intelligence. (p. 286)
13. Trace the development of our modern alphabetic writing system, and describe techniques for teaching reading. (p. 288)

Key Terms

For each term, write the definition in the space provided.

endomorphic (1, p. 261) —————————————————————————————

mesomorphic (1, p. 261) —————————————————————————————

ectomorphs (1, p. 261) —————————————————————————————

operations (Piaget) (4, p. 264) ————————————————————————

concrete operation (4, p. 264) ————————————————————————

psychometric (6, p. 269) ————————————————————————————

psychometricians (6, p. 269) ———————————————————————————

g (6, p. 272) ——————————————————————————————————————

mental age (MA) (6, p. 269) ——————————————————————————

normal distribution (6, p. 270) ————————————————————————

mean (6, p. 270) —————————————————————————————————————

standard deviation (6, p. 270) —————————————————————————

factor analytic approach (7, p. 272) ———————————————————————

two-factor theory (7, p. 272) ——————————————————————————

multiple-factor theory (7, p. 272) ————————————————————————

fluid intelligence (7, p. 272) ——————————————————————————

crystallized intelligence (7, p. 272) ————————————————————————

structure of intellect (7, p. 272) ——————————————————————————

operations (Guilford) (7, p. 273) ——————————————————————————

contents (7, p. 273) ————————————————————————————————

products (7, p. 273) ————————————————————————————————

validity (8, p. 274) ——————————————————————————————————

criterion validity (8, p. 274) —————————————————————————————

criterion sampling (8, p. 275) _____

culture-fair tests (8, p. 275) _____

SOMPA (9, p. 278) _____

divergent thinking (9, p. 278) _____

convergent thinking (9, p. 278) _____

control processes (10, p. 281) _____

rehearsal (10, p. 281) _____

maintenance rehearsal (10, p. 281) _____

elaborative rehearsal (10, p. 281) _____

organizational processing (10, p. 282) _____

semantic elaboration (10, p. 282) _____

mental imagery (10, p. 282) _____

retrieval (10, p. 282) _____

metamemory (10, p. 283) _____

inference (11, p. 284) _____

scripts (11, p. 285) _____

semantic networks (11, p. 285) _____

componential analysis (12, p. 286) _____

component (12, p. 286) _____

metacomponents (12, p. 286) _____

performance components (12, p. 286) _____

acquisition (or storage) components (12, p. 286) _____

retention (or retrieval) components (12, p. 286) _____

transfer components (12, p. 286) _____

alphabetic system (13, p. 288) _____

syllabic (13, p. 288) _____

logographic (13, p. 288) _____

ABC method (13, p. 290) _____

whole-word method (13, p. 290) _____

phonics method (13, p. 290) _____

Guided Review

1. Middle and late childhood are characterized by slow and consistent growth. Children's legs become longer and their trunks slimmer in _____ and _____ childhood. (1, p. 261)

   middle, late

2. Fat tissue tends to develop more rapidly than muscle in _____ and _____ childhood. (1, p. 261)

   middle, late

3. Children who have noticeably more _____ than muscle are called endomorphs, while children who are more muscular are called mesomorphs. (1, p. 261)

   fat

4. Children who have a predominance of neither fat nor _____ are called ectomorphs. (1, p. 261)

muscle

5. During this time, motor development is smoother, and coordination _____ . (2, p. 262)

improves

6. During middle and late _____ , sensory mechanisms continue to mature. (2, p. 262)

childhood

7. Early farsightedness is overcome, binocular _____ becomes well established, and hearing acuity _____ . (2, p. 262)

vision, improves or increases

8. Some children at this age are encouraged to play competitive sports. Of all the _____ children play, football involves the most injuries. (3, p. 263)

sports

9. It appears that playing sports, if the child's cardiovascular system is sound, may be a beneficial form of _____ . (3, p. 263)

exercise

10. However, parents must be careful not to demand too much in the way of athletic performance from the _____ . (3, p. 263)

child

11. According to Piaget's theory, the stage of concrete operations spans ages seven to eleven. The flaws associated with the preoperational stage disappear during the stage of _____ _____ . (4, p. 264)

concrete operations

12. The shift from egocentrism to relativism is a major change which occurs during the stage of _____ _____ . (4, p. 263)

concrete operations

13. As the child gives up _____ , he is able to decenter, to operate dealing with two or more aspects of a problem at the same time. (4, p. 264)

egocentrism

14. Another change is reversibility. As the child becomes able to _____ actions, he can coordinate several characteristics rather than focusing on a single property of an object. (4, p. 264)

reverse

15. Performing mental arithmetic, imagining a game of ping-pong, or mentally shifting marbles between cups are examples of the products of _____ . (4, p. 264)

reversibility

16. But the stage of _____ _____ is not without limitations. (4, p. 264)

concrete operations

17. One such _____ is the fact that the child needs to have objects on hand in order to think about them. (4, p. 264)

limitation

18. An important skill of middle and late childhood, the stage of _____ _____ , is the arrangement of objects and events into sets and subsets, and the definition of their relationships. (4, p. 264)

concrete operations

19. As we evaluate _____ theory, we find he was a brilliant observer of children. (5, p. 265)

Piaget's

20. _____ has also given us many good ideas about what to look for in development. (5, p. 265)

Piaget

21. A third major contribution is _____ emphasis on the qualitative nature of mental life. (5, p. 265)

Piaget's

22. It is clear that the entire study of cognitive development owes its existence to the monumental contributions of _____ . (5, p. 265)

Piaget

23. Yet, many psychologists are proposing changes in the theory of cognitive _____ . (5, p. 265)

development

24. There are, in fact, four problems with _____ theory. (5, p. 265)

Piaget's

25. First, Piaget conceived of his _____ as unitary structures of thought, and predicted that the major characteristics of each stage would emerge in synchrony. (5, p. 265)

stages

26. Yet, researchers have shown that many aspects of concrete operations do not appear in _____ . (5, p. 266)

synchrony

27. Second, very small changes in the way the tasks designed by _____ are presented can cause major changes in the way the child responds. (5, p. 266)

Piaget

28. Third, contrary to Piaget's claims, young _____ can be trained to respond correctly to tasks at a stage higher than they are. (5, p. 266)

children

29. Fourth, recent studies have shown that the timing of the stages is not always as Piaget asserted; many children develop abilities _____ and in a more prolonged manner than Piaget predicted. (5, p. 266)

earlier

30. But Piaget's is not the only approach to intelligence. In fact, in our casual discussions, we often equate IQ with _____ . (6, p. 269)

intelligence

31. The first test of _____ was devised by Binet and Simon in 1905. (6, p. 269)

intelligence

32. The _____ test yields a mental age score (MA), which reflects the number of items the individual answered correctly in relation to the average number correct for a child of a given age. (6, p. 269)

Binet

33. If a child answers correctly the number of items the average ten-year-old answers correctly, the child has a _____ _____ of _____ . (6, p. 269)

mental age, 10

34. The current version of the Binet is called the Stanford-Binet, because revisions were made at _____ University. (6, p. 270)

Stanford

35. In the course of administering the test to large numbers of people, it has been discovered that the scores approximate the normal distribution. The technical term for the bell-shaped curve is the _____ _____ . (6, p. 270)

normal distribution

36. The distribution of intelligence has a mean or average score of 100. Another word for average is
_____ . (6, p. 270)

mean

37. The standard deviation is a measure of how much the scores vary within the population. On the Binet, the
_____ _____ is 16. (6, p. 270)

standard deviation

38. The _____-Binet includes both verbal and nonverbal items, and produces an overall score
which indicates IQ, or general level of functioning of the person's _____ . (6, p. 271)

Stanford, intelligence

39. Another popular _____ test is the Wechsler Intelligence Scale for Children (WISC).
(7, p. 271)

intelligence

40. Wechsler defines _____ as "the global capacity of the individual to act purposefully, to
think rationally, and to deal effectively with the environment." (7, p. 271)

intelligence

41. Thus, _____ stresses the global nature of intelligence. (7, p. 271)

Wechsler

42. For very young children, there is the _____ Preschool and Primary Scale of Intelligence
(WPPSI). (7, p. 272)

Wechsler

43. Many psychologists prefer the _____ scales because they are divided into subtests and into
verbal and performance categories. (7, p. 271)

Wechsler

44. Thus, psychologists may be able to get more specific information about intellectual strengths and weaknesses
from the _____ Scales than from the _____ Test. (7, p. 271)

Wechsler, Stanford-Binet

45. In contrast to the Wechsler and Binet tests, the factor-analytic approach uses a mathematical analysis of large
numbers of scores to determine the basic elements which make up _____ . (7, p. 272)

intelligence

46. Spearman was the first to propose a _____ approach, with his two-factor theory.
(7, p. 272)

factor-analytic

47. Intelligence was composed of a general (g) factor and a specific (s) factor, according to _____.
(7, p. 272)

Spearman

48. Thurstone proposed a more elaborate model of _____. (7, p. 272)

intelligence

49. A number of specific factors, rather than one general factor, make up intelligence, according to _____.
(7, p. 272)

Thurstone

50. Cattell proposed that two forms of intelligence exist. Fluid and crystallized intelligence operate together to influence primary mental abilities, according to _____. (7, p. 272)

Cattell

51. Fluid intelligence refers to adaptability and capacity to perceive things and integrate them mentally. As such, _____ _____ seems to be independent of formal education and experience. (7, p. 272)

fluid intelligence

52. Crystallized intelligence is determined by schooling and other environmental experiences. Skills, abilities, and understanding gained through instruction and observation make up _____ intelligence.
(7, p. 272)

crystallized

53. Guilford developed the structure of intellect model of intelligence. Three major dimensions: operations, contents, and products, make up the _____ _____ _____ model proposed by _____ . (7, p. 272)

structure of intellect, Guilford

54. Each dimension has a different number of categories, so that 120 factors in all comprise the _____ _____ _____ model. (7, p. 272)

structure of intellect

55. Spearman, Thurstone, Cattel, and Guilford are all proponents of the _____ approach to defining and measuring _____ . (7, p. 272)

factor-analytic, intelligence

56. Many critics of intelligence tests believe that they are not valid. The extent to which a test measures what it claims to measure is termed its _____ . (8, p. 274)

validity

57. One type of validity is criterion validity, the extent to which one test predicts scores or behavior on some other _____ or measure. (8, p. 274)

criterion

58. Scores on intelligence tests are pretty good at _____ school grades. (8, p. 274)

predicting

59. Several attempts have been made to replace or supplement traditional _____ tests. (8, p. 274)

intelligence

60. McClelland has recommended assessing competence, and has provided three specific _____ to those who design tests. (8, p. 275)

recommendations

61. First, McClelland recommends criterion sampling. This means simply assessing the _____ or requirements for success in the area the test is trying to measure. (8, p. 275)

criteria

62. Second, McClelland recommends measuring changes in what a person has _____ , rather than measuring an absolute value. (8, p. 275)

learned

63. McClelland's third recommendation is most controversial. He wants test designers to publish techniques for improving on the characteristic the test is designed to _____ . (8, p. 275)

measure

64. One frequent criticism of intelligence tests is that they reflect a cultural bias. Many efforts have been made to produce a test which is _____-fair. (8, p. 275)

culture

65. A widely used culture-fair test is the Raven Progressive Matrices Test. The person must select the correct element to complete each of sixty designs in the _____ _____ _____ Test. (8, p. 276)

Raven Progressive Matrices

66. Efforts to develop culture-free tests have not been very successful. Dove presented his "Chitling Test" to remind us of the need for a _____ intelligence test. (8, p. 277)

culture-free

67. A related issue involves the development of tests of social intelligence. Mercer suggests that we test _____ skills as well as mental ones. (9, p. 278)

social

68. Mercer's test is the System of Multicultural Pluralistic Assessment, abbreviated as _____. (9, p. 278)

SOMPA

69. A traditional intelligence test, an assessment of social and economic family background, a measure of social adjustment in school, and a physical exam make up the _____. (9, p. 278)

SOMPA

70. It is important to note that creativity and intelligence are not the same, although _____ thinking is part of Guilford's model of intelligence. (9, p. 278)

creative

71. Guilford refers to creative thinking as divergent thinking. A form of thinking that produces many different answers to a single question is called _____ thinking. (9, p. 278)

divergent

72. In contrast, a form of thinking which works toward only one "correct" answer is called _____. (9, p. 278)

convergent

73. Many people believe that a person's IQ is somehow fixed and invariant, but research shows that scores on _____ tests vary considerably over time. (9, p. 279)

intelligence

74. In sharp contrast to the Piagetian and psychometric approaches to _____, we find the information processing perspective. (10, p. 281)

intelligence

75. In the information processing view, cognitive activity is synonymous with the processing of _____. (10, p. 281)

information

76. One of the key elements in the information processing view is memory. Studies have shown that there are age-related changes in _____ during middle and late childhood. (10, p. 281)

memory

77. Long-term _____ depends heavily on learning activities called control processes. (10, p. 281)

memory

78. One such _____ _____ is rehearsal. (10, p. 281)

control process

79. If we just repeat something over and over again, we are using maintenance _____ . (10, p. 281)

rehearsal

80. On the other hand, if we make an association between what we are trying to learn and something we already know, we are using elaborative _____ . (10, p. 281)

rehearsal

81. As children age, they are more likely to spontaneously use rehearsal; and they are more likely to use _____ rehearsal, which is more effective. (10, p. 281)

elaborative

82. Long-term memory is also aided by organization, and children use increasing levels of _____ processing during middle and late childhood. (10, p. 282)

organizational

83. Another type of control process is semantic elaboration, which is designed to encode information in terms of its _____ . (10, p. 282)

meaning

84. Mental imagery is yet another control process. By the age of seven or eight, children can use _____ strategies, but not with rapid presentation or difficult tasks. (10, p. 282)

imagery

85. Control processes involve more than the time of learning; they also involve retrieval activities. Children who use imagery when recalling information are more likely to be able to _____ it. (10, p. 282)

retrieve

86. Memory is important because it stores what we have learned; prior knowledge contributes to most _____ tasks. (10, p. 283)

memory

87. One type of memory knowledge is metamemory, which is loosely defined as knowledge about one's own _____ . (10, p. 283)

memory

118

88. We use memory in many ways. Drawing inferences is one way we make connections between events stored in _____ . (11, p. 284)

memory

89. Some inferences are logical. We need no prior knowledge or direct experience to understand a _____ inference. (11, p. 284)

logical

90. Other inferences are empirical. When we need to have some specialized experience to arrive at the correct inference, the inference is _____ . (11, p. 284)

empirical

91. As children mature, they improve dramatically in their abilities to draw _____ . (11, p. 285)

inferences

92. An important part of the process is activating relevant prior knowledge. Scripts and semantic networks are ways of describing this relevant _____ _____ . (11, p. 285)

prior knowledge

93. A script is a very general event sequence known to most members of a culture. Going to the doctor, going to school, and going to funerals are all _____ . (11, p. 285)

scripts

94. A semantic network is a set of concepts related to each other. The more experience one has with a particular idea or concept, the richer will be that person's _____ _____ . (11, p. 286)

semantic network

95. The information processing view of intelligence is reflected in the work of Sternberg, who proposed a componential model. He claims we can better understand intelligence if we think in terms of information processing _____ . (12, p. 286)

components

96. Sternberg has identified five such _____ . (12, p. 286)

components

97. The higher-order control processes used for executive planning and decision making, Sternberg calls _____ . (12, p. 286)

metacomponents

98. Sternberg refers to processes to carry out a problem-solving strategy as _____ components. (12, p. 286)

performance

99. Processes used in learning new information, such as rehearsal, are known as _____ components. (12, p. 286)

acquisition (or storage)

100. Sternberg refers to those processes involved in accessing previously stored information as _____ components. (12, p. 286)

retention (or retrieval)

101. Those processes used in generalization, so we don't have to learn each new thing entirely from scratch, are called _____ components. (12, p. 286)

transfer

102. Reading is a critical skill and another aspect of _____ development. (13, p. 288)

language

103. Our alphabetic system of writing evolved from the Egyptian system, which began about 3500 B.C. Our _____ system is one of three in use in the world today. (13, p. 288)

alphabetic

104. One alternative to the alphabetic system is the syllabic system. Japanese Katakana is an example of a _____ writing system. (13, p. 288)

syllabic

105. The third system is logographic. Chinese writing, in which each visual symbol corresponds to a word, is a form of _____ writing. (13, p. 288)

logographic

106. Just as our writing system has evolved through many stages, the method of teaching reading developed by Rozin and Gleitman also moves through several _____ . (13, p. 288)

stages

107. The first stage is the semasiographic, in which children learn that meaning can be represented _____ . (13, p. 289)

visually

108. The second stage is logographic, in which children learn that some pictures stand for certain _____ . (13, p. 289)

words

109. The third stage is phoneticization, in which the children learn that some symbols correspond to certain _____ . (13, p. 289)

sounds

110. In the fourth, or syllabary, stage, children learn _____ that correspond to spoken syllables. (13, p. 289)

symbols

111. The fifth stage of the Rozin and Gleitman method is the alphabet stage, in which children learn that _____ characters correspond roughly to phonemes. (13, p. 289)

alphabetic

112. Apparently, children have very little trouble with the first four _____ . (13, p. 289)

stages

113. However, they are not able to move easily into the _____ stage. The authors conclude that the motivational aspects of the five-stage method may be its strongest feature. (13, p. 289)

fifth

114. Historically, there have been three major methods of teaching _____ : ABC, whole-word, and phonics. (13, p. 290)

reading

115. Although it worked for generations of our ancestors, the ABC method is today in ill repute, and most current methods use components of both the whole-word and _____ approaches. (13, p. 290)

phonics

116. Many people, when they read, say the words to themselves so well they can almost hear them. This phenomenon, called speech coding, is discouraged by some speed reading _____ . (13, p. 291)

experts

117. Nonetheless, _____ _____ may contribute to interpreting the meaning of words being read, and to the short-term memory for recently read words. (13, p. 291)

speech coding

Well done! You might want to review the learning objectives before you try out the self test. Keep up the good work.

Self Test

1. A child who has a rounded, somewhat chubby body build is called a(n) (1, p. 261)
   a. endomorph
   b. mesomorph
   c. ectomorph
   d. eunuchoid

2. Middle and late childhood is characterized by (1, p. 261)
   a. rapid growth
   b. stability in the special senses
   c. slow, consistent growth
   d. deterioration of vision

3. During the stage of concrete operations, children (4, p. 263)
   a. become less egocentric
   b. lose the capacity of reversibility
   c. give up relativism permanently
   d. become able to manipulate abstractions

4. The motivation for the development of Binet's first intelligence test was (6, p. 269)
   a. the availability of a major government grant
   b. the need to identify those children who could best profit from schooling
   c. laws which demanded tests for special education
   d. the goal of identifying mental retardation

5. The Wechsler tests are preferred by many psychologists because they (7, p. 271)
   a. were written by an American
   b. are entirely nonverbal
   c. use factor analysis
   d. are divided into subtests

6. Cattell proposed that intelligence is composed of two factors, (7, p. 272)
   a. young and old
   b. formal and informal
   c. general and specific
   d. fluid and crystallized

7. The best example of a culture-free test available today is the (8, p. 276)
   a. Peabody Picture Vocabulary Test
   b. Raven Progressive Matrices Test
   c. Chitling Test
   d. Dove Counterbalance General Intelligence Test

8. According to Guilford, creativity is reflected in (9, p. 278)
   a. divergent thinking
   b. convergent thinking
   c. fluid intelligence
   d. associative flow

9. A very general event sequence known to most people in a given culture, such as going to a party, is called a (11, p. 285)
   a. script
   b. semantic network
   c. literal inference
   d. specialized experience

10. One of the problems with Piaget's theory of cognitive development is that (5, p. 266)
    a. he identified more stages than there really are
    b. children cannot pass conservation tasks during the concrete operations stage
    c. some cognitive abilities emerge earlier and more slowly than he predicted
    d. his focus on measurement of intelligence prevented him from seeing qualitative changes

Individual Learning Activity

The discovery and measurement of creativity is an exciting and sometimes amusing pursuit. To demonstrate that, I am asking you to develop a test of creativity, based on the suggestions of Guilford.

Perhaps you recall that Guilford defined creativity in terms of divergent thinking, a process that generates a large number of possible responses. He further identified these characteristics of creative thinking: word fluency, ideational fluency, associative fluency, expressional fluency, spontaneous flexibility, adaptive flexibility, redefinition, and originality.

Your task is to prepare at least two or three items, and administer this new test to at least ten of your friends, classmates, and fellow earthlings. Note the differences in their responses! So, at least, you have discovered some ways in which individuals differ. What good is that? Piaget would ask. Well, how would you answer that?

The difficult part of measuring creativity is trying to decide which responses are most creative. Some authors have simply looked at low frequency responses and called them the more creative ones. Others have tried to find some social or physical value in the responses, as a criterion to accepting them as creative. In terms of your test, you as the author will have the pleasure of deciding on what basis to define a response as creative. Be prepared to defend your rationale in terms appropriate to the design of your test. (This is an example of construct validity.)

Incidentally, completing this activity will not make you more creative, but it will probably make you more aware of the limits of our knowledge about creativity and its measurement. Good job! Take a break.

Answers to the Self Test

1. a	6. d
2. c	7. b
3. a	8. a
4. b	9. a
5. d	10. c

10 Social, Emotional, and Personality Development

Preview

During middle and late childhood, peers, teachers, and other adults become more important to the child. Parents continue to be concerned with aggression and discipline and add concerns about chores, allowances, and independence. Parents now use less physical punishment and turn to deprivation of privileges, appeals to self-esteem, guilt-arousing arguments, and encouragement toward responsibility.

The coregulation process provides a transition period in which parents gradually relinquish control while monitoring the child's behavior at a distance, using contacts effectively, and teaching the child to monitor his or her own behavior. Parents and children develop expectations of each other, and label each other in terms of broad categories. Parents with more than one child are likely to engage in social comparison. Marital relationships often change as less time is devoted to child rearing.

A considerable portion of the child's day is spent in peer interaction. Children who give reinforcers, who are good listeners, and who are happy, enthusiastic, concerned about others, and show self-confidence without conceit, are the most popular. Physical attractiveness, higher intelligence, and middle-class background also contribute to popularity. The formation of peer relationships has been studied from the perspective of information processing, revealing that intention-cue detection is important in being accepted. As cognitive development advances, children acquire more social knowledge, and develop scripts involving specific plans and goals.

Friendships involve specific attachments including a sense of security, trust, and pleasure, and they become much more prevalent in the elementary years and adolescence. As children get older, they describe friends more in terms of interpersonal constructs. Intimacy in friendships involves self-disclosure and the sharing of private thoughts, and is most likely to arise during early adolescence. Girls' friendships are characterized by more intimacy than boys' friendships are. Having a close and stable best friend is correlated with self-esteem, but the direction of effect is not clear. Friends are usually similar in terms of race, sex, and age, and have similar attitudes toward school, educational aspirations, and achievement orientations.

In groups, hierarchical structures invariably emerge, and norms develop. Frustration and competition contribute to hostility between groups, but this hostility can often be reduced by establishing a superordinate goal which requires cooperation. Children's groups differ from those of adolescents. Children's groups are usually composed of friends or neighborhood mates, are less formalized, and are less often cross-sexed. Even when children go to integrated schools, groups tend to follow racial and ethnic lines.

Teachers have a major influence on children during the middle childhood years. Teachers who are enthusiastic, can plan, have poise, are adaptable, and are aware of individual differences are more likely to contribute to the child's intellectual development. Erikson says good teachers are trusted and respected, know how to alternate work and play, to recognize special efforts and encourage special abilities, and so they are able to produce a sense of industry rather than inferiority. Personality dimensions (aptitude) and educational technique (treatment) interact in a variety of ways. Students with high achievement orientation do well in flexible classrooms, while students with low achievement orientation do better in a structured classroom. Teachers who work with high-socioeconomic status/high-ability students are usually more successful if they move rapidly and enforce high standards. Teachers who work with low-socioeconomic status/low-ability students are more successful if they are warm and encouraging, and move more slowly through the material.

Highly anxious children do better in structured classrooms, as do highly compulsive children. Children who are low in anxiety or are not compulsive do not seem to be influenced by classroom organization. Teachers in middle-class schools spend more time teaching and evaluate the students' work far more frequently than teachers in lower-class schools.

Social class also influences the aspirations and expectations of children. Although when lower-class parents encourage their sons to advance, the aspirations of the children do rise. Still, teachers and children alike have lower expectations of children from lower-class homes. Teachers with lower-class origins may have different attitudes toward lower-class children than middle-class teachers.

The academic and social development of minority children depends on many factors, including the teacher's expectations, the nature of the curriculum, and the availability of role models. While desegregation itself cannot improve race relations, a multiethnic curriculum, projects focused on racial issues, and mixed work groups can lead to positive changes.

As an important component of self-concept, children develop an understanding of how they are perceived by others. As they grow older, children develop a differentiated view of themselves. They also have a more distinct view of themselves as unique persons, termed an individuated view. Also, the self-concept becomes more stable with age. Compared with adolescents, children evaluate themselves in more concrete terms.

Parents who express affection, are concerned about their child's problems, live harmoniously, participate in friendly joint activities, are available, set and abide by clear and fair rules, and allow the child freedom within defined limits, have children high in self-esteem. In addition, children who do well in school are likely to develop positive self-concepts.

A common technique for measuring self-concept is the Piers-Harris Scale. As in all cases of self-reporting, we must be aware of the possibility that the children may be less than candid. Combining self-reports with peer perceptions and observations of parents and teachers provides a more accurate picture of the child's self-concept. Susan Harter has developed the perceived competence scale for children, consisting of cognitive, social, and physical subscales, as well as one for general self-worth.

In middle childhood, two divergent trends in sex typing emerge: children increase their understanding of cultural sex roles, and the behavior and attitudes of boys become more masculine. Girls do not show an increased femininity during the middle childhood years. Both boys and girls now see that stereotypes are not absolute. However, stereotypes, though inaccurate, can cause personal anguish.

Maccoby and Jacklin, after reviewing over 1600 studies, concluded that females are more verbal, while males are more mathematical and aggressive. Baumrind has suggested that females are socialized to become instrumentally incompetent; which means that their behavior is not seen as socially responsible and purposeful. Social competence, however, characterizes the training and behavior of males, according to Baumrind.

In general, compared to boys, girls seem to have lower expectations for success, lower levels of aspiration, more anxiety about failing, and are more likely to accept failure when it occurs. Girls are likely to attribute failure to internal forces and success to external factors, while boys are more likely to do the converse. Many experts believe that girls are socialized to develop learned helplessness, resulting in both lack of motivation and negative affect. High achievement orientation in girls, which is uncommon, is related to moderate parental permissiveness and attempts to accelerate achievement.

Kohlberg's theory of moral development consists of six stages organized into three levels: preconventional, conventional, and postconventional. Only a minority of individuals reach the postconventional level. Kohlberg's theory is similar to Piaget's in the belief that moral development reflects cognitive development, which results from the interaction of genetic and environmental forces. Both Piaget and Kohlberg believe that peer interaction is a major force, challenging the child to progress to a higher level of moral reasoning.

The distinction between social reasoning and moral reasoning is supported by research with young children, who evaluate moral actions on intrinsic features and social conventional actions in terms of their regulatory status. It also appears that children's understanding of social rules unfolds in a stage-like sequence.

Some children have serious problems, and require professional intervention. Boys are referred to mental health clinics more frequently than girls. Boys and lower-class children in general are referred for undercontrolled, expressive behaviors; while girls and middle-class children in general have problems with overcontrolled, internalized behaviors. Depression shows age-related changes, has both biological and environmental determinants, and occurs less often in childhood than in adulthood. Underachievement may be related to attention, concentration, or learning disorders, or to a passive-aggressive pattern involving hostility expressed indirectly, worry about rivalry and fear of success or failure, and an overall passive-aggressive style of handling stress. School phobia is also common, involving psychogenic physical complaints and school avoidance.

Learning Objectives

1. Describe the adjustments parents make as children progress through the middle childhood years, and characterize the coregulation process. (p. 300)
2. List five factors contributing to popularity. (p. 303)
3. Characterize childhood friendships, and summarize the skills needed and problems encountered in the formation of friendships. (p. 306)
4. List four findings from Sherif's studies of groups of children, and contrast children's groups with adolescent groups. (p. 309)
5. Compare flexible and structured classrooms, and list Erikson's criteria for good teachers. (p. 311)
6. List and describe at least four examples of aptitude X treatment interaction (ATI). (p. 313)
7. Describe three developmental changes in self-concept, and two ways to measure them. (p. 316)
8. Define *self-esteem* and list eight parental attributes associated with high self-esteem in children. (p. 317)
9. Describe childhood changes in sex-typed behavior, and sex differences. (p. 318)
10. Connect Baumrind's arguments about sex differences and instrumental competence to the concept of learned helplessness. (p. 320)
11. Trace Kohlberg's theory of moral development, and identify each of the six stages. (p. 321)
12. List and describe at least three emotional problems which occur in childhood, and describe depression and underachievement. (p. 328)

Key Terms

For each key term, write the definition in the space provided.

coregulation process (1, p. 301) _____

intention-cue detection (2, p. 304) _____

intimacy in friendship (3, p. 306) _____

flexible classrooms (5, p. 311) _____

structured classrooms (5, p. 311) _____

Aptitude-Treatment Interaction (6, p. 313) _____

aptitude (6, p. 313) _____

treatment (6, p. 313) _____

instrumental competence (10, p. 320) _____

learned helplessness (10, p. 321) _____

preconventional level (11, p. 332) _____

conventional level (11, p. 322) _____

postconventional level (11, p. 322) _____

passive-aggressive (13, p. 330) _____

school phobia (13, p. 331) _____

Guided Review

1. Children spend more time with peers, teachers, and other adults during middle and late childhood, so they spend less time with their _____ . (1, p. 300)

   parents

2. At the same time, new issues such as chores, allowances, and self-entertainment become the focus of interaction between parent and _____ . (1, p. 301)

   child

3. During the elementary school years, discipline becomes easier for _____ as children become capable of reasoning. (1, p. 301)

   parents

4. In lieu of physical _____ , parents are more likely to use guilt-arousing appeals or statements encouraging personal responsibility. (1, p. 301)

   punishment

5. Parents help their children learn to control themselves, and begin to relinquish parental _____ . (1, p. 301)

   control

6. The coregulation process allows parents to relinquish _____ in specific areas, while giving the child moment-to-moment autonomy. (1, p. 301)

   control

7. By the middle childhood years, parents have formed expectations of their children, and the children have likewise developed _____ of their parents. (1, p. 302)

   expectations

8. As children grow older, so too do _____ , and marital relationships change, particularly for women. (1, p. 302)

   parents

9. In addition to interacting with their parents, children also encounter age mates, or _____ .
(2, p. 303)

peers

10. Popularity among peers is important to _____ . (2, p. 303)

children

11. Giving reinforcements, listening carefully, and being yourself (happy, enthusiastic, concerned for others) are likely to _____ popularity. (2, p. 303)

increase

12. Being physically attractive and intelligent also contribute to _____ . (2, p. 303)

popularity

13. Peer relationships lead children to think about social events. From the information processing perspective, the steps of decoding social cues, interpretation, response search, selection of an optimal response, and enactment make up the information processing view of _____ relationships. (2, p. 304)

social

14. An important aspect of appropriate social behavior is intention-cue detection. Children may be avoided by others if they misinterpret the motives of others, which they may do if they make errors in _____ detection. (2, p. 304)

intention-cue

15. In addition to regular peer relations, children become particularly close to some peers, and develop specific attachments called _____ . (3, p. 306)

friendships

16. Children develop a sense of trust in, and derive pleasure from being with, their _____ .
(3, p. 306)

friends

17. As children get older they are more likely to describe their _____ in terms of interpersonal constructs. (3, p. 306)

friends

18. Some friendships are characterized by intimacy. Self-disclosure and the sharing of private thoughts are essential components of _____ friendships. (3, p. 306)

intimate

19. The friendships of girls are more likely to be _____ than are the friendships of boys. (3, p. 307)

intimate

20. Having a close and stable, if not intimate, _____ is positively correlated with self-esteem. (3, p. 308)

friend (or friendship)

21. There is usually great similarity in age, sex, and race, and similarity in attitudes toward school and in educational aspirations, among _____ . (3, p. 308)

friends

22. Children sometimes operate as members of groups. Sherif has discovered that hierarchical structures invariably emerge in _____ of children. (4, p. 309)

groups

23. Norms also develop in all _____ . (4, p. 309)

groups

24. Frustration and competition contribute to _____ between groups. (4, p. 309)

hostility

25. This hostility can be reduced by setting up a superordinate goal which requires _____ between the groups. (4, p. 309)

cooperation

26. Children's groups differ from adolescent _____ in several ways. (4, p. 309)

groups

27. Members of _____ groups are often friends or neighborhood playmates, and the groups themselves are less formal. (4, p. 309)

children's

28. Also, groups of _____ are likely to consist of members of one sex or another. (4, p. 309)

children

29. Even in integrated schools, groups tend to follow racial and social class lines. Mixtures are likely to occur only in _____ groups. (4, p. 309)

formal

30. Children spend much of their waking time in activities affiliated with schools. The development of the child is greatly influenced by the small society which constitutes the typical _____ . (5, p. 311)

school

31. Classrooms may be structured or flexible. In _____ classroom settings, children are more likely to interact with the teacher on a one-to-one basis. (5, p. 311)

flexible

32. Teachers who are enthusiastic, able to plan, have poise and adaptability, and are aware of individual differences, have _____ who are likely to show intellectual development. (5, p. 312)

students

33. Erikson points out that good _____ stimulate industry rather than inferiority in their students. (5, p. 312)

teachers

34. Moreover, Erikson says, good teachers are trusted and respected, know how to alternate play and work, and how to recognize special efforts and encourage special abilities in their _____ . (5, p. 312)

students

35. Aptitude and treatment interact. Personality variables and academic potential are referred to as _____ , while educational technique is called treatment. (6, p. 313)

aptitude

36. Students with high achievement orientation do better in a flexible classroom, while children with low achievement orientation do better in a _____ classroom. (6, p. 313)

structured

37. Teachers who work with high-socioeconomic status/high-ability students are most successful if they move quickly and enforce _____ standards. (6, p. 314)

high

38. Teachers who are successful with low-socioeconomic status/low-ability students are warm and encouraging, but move more _____ through the material. (6, p. 314)

slowly

39. Teachers who are impulsive tend to produce students who are _____ . (6, p. 313)

impulsive

40. For children who are neither anxious nor compulsive, the classroom organization is not important. Very _____ students do best in a highly structured classroom. (6, p. 314)

anxious or compulsive (it's the same result!)

41. Social class is an important variable in a child's performance in _____ . (6, p. 314)

school

42. Teachers have lower expectations of children from _____-class homes. (6, p. 315)

lower

43. The books children read in school are geared to _____-class values and experiences, and representations of _____-class families are idealized. (6, p. 314)

middle, middle

44. During middle childhood, the self-concept continues to develop. Children gain in the ability to understand how they are viewed by others, as their _____ develop. (7, p. 316)

self-concepts

45. Three developmental changes characterize the maturing of the _____ . (7, p. 316)

self-concept

46. First, children develop a differentiated view of themselves as they grow. Their self-perceptions are no longer simplistic (all good or all bad, for example) but are now _____ . (7, p. 316)

differentiated

47. Older children also develop a more individuated self-concept. Labeling themselves by their unique qualities or differences reflects an _____ self-concept. (7, p. 317)

individuated

48. The older child's self-concept is also more stable. As children grow older, they can more easily integrate new information about themselves, leading to a self-concept which is more _____ . (7, p. 317)

stable

49. Many researchers use the labels _____ and self-esteem interchangeably. (8, p. 317)

self-concept

50. The value children place on themselves and their behavior defines _____ . (8, p. 317)

self-esteem

51. Feeling proud or evaluating oneself as very capable would be manifestations of _____ _____ . (8, p. 317)

self-esteem

52. Coopersmith has been interested in the parental antecedents of _____ _____ . (8, p. 317)

self-esteem

53. He found that parents who express affection, are concerned about the child, live harmoniously, participate in friendly joint activities, are available when needed, set and abide by clear and fair rules, and allow the child freedom, have children high in _____ _____ . (8, p. 317)

self-esteem

54. The Piers-Harris Scale consists of eighty items designed to measure a child's _____ _____ . (8, p. 317)

self-esteem

55. Susan Harter has recently developed the Perceived Competence Scale, a measure of _____ _____ . (8, p. 318)

self-concept

56. Her scale separately assesses four domains. Cognitive, social, physical, and general self-worth make up the four _____ . (8, p. 318)

domains

57. However, with self-reporting there can be problems. Obtaining peer perceptions, and observations of parents and teachers, provides a better overall picture than _____ alone. (8, p. 318)

self-reporting

58. In middle childhood, two divergent trends in sex typing occur. Children increase their understanding of cultural _____ roles, defined as masculine or feminine. (9, p. 318)

sex

59. Simultaneously, the behavior of boys becomes more closely aligned with the _____ sex role. (9, p. 318)

masculine

60. During middle childhood, _____ do NOT show an increased interest in _____ activities. (9, p. 318)

girls, feminine

61. Thanks to careful examination and appraisal, sex roles are being slowly eliminated. People of both sexes may one day feel completely free of the social _____ _____ . (9, p. 319)

sex roles

62. The _____ _____ are a type of stereotype, and as such are arbitrary, and fluctuate with the culture. (9, p. 319)

sex roles

63. Some people think that sex roles simply reflect real sex differences. But research has discovered very few real _____ _____ . (9, p. 319)

sex differences

64. Maccoby and Jacklin reviewed more than 1600 studies purporting to show _____ _____ . (9, p. 319)

sex differences

65. They found that females are consistently more verbal than _____ . (9, p. 319)

males

66. Males, on the other hand, are more mathematical and aggressive than _____ . (9, p. 319)

females

67. Many people wonder whether these _____ _____ are innate or could result from experience. (9, p. 320)

sex differences

68. Sex differences in aggression appear by age three years, and occur among nonhuman primates and across a variety of human cultures, leading to the belief that it is an _____ sex difference. (9, p. 320)

innate

69. Differences in the verbal abilities of boys and _____ do not show up consistently until age eleven, and differences in mathematical ability are not clear until adolescence. (9, p. 319)

girls

70. Thus, differences in verbal and mathematical ability may be influenced by _____ . (9, p. 319)

experience

71. Baumrind has suggested that males are socialized toward instrumental competence. Behavior which is socially responsible and purposeful constitutes _____ _____ . (10, p. 320)

instrumental competence

72. Females, according to Baumrind, are socialized to engage in socially irresponsible and purposeless behavior, or toward _____ _____ . (10, p. 320)

instrumental incompetence

73. Women who as adults are career and achievement oriented usually show signs of this in childhood. Similarly, women who prefer traditionally _____ activities also were attracted to such activities in late childhood and adolescence. (10, p. 321)

feminine

74. In longitudinal studies, achievement behavior is consistent over time. One aspect of _____ is expectancy for success. (10, p. 321)

achievement

75. In general, girls have lower _____ for _____ , lower levels of aspiration, and more anxiety about failing, than boys. (10, p. 321)

expectancy, success

76. Perhaps because they are more anxious about _____ , girls are more likely to avoid risking failure, and are more likely to accept failure, than are boys. (10, p. 321)

failure

77. Girls are more likely to attribute _____ to internal factors, like their own inability. (10, p. 321)

failure

78. Boys, on the other hand, blame failure on _____ factors. (10, p. 321)

external

79. Girls are more likely to attribute success to _____ factors, such as good luck. (10, p. 321)

external

80. Boys are more likely to attribute success to _____ factors, such as superior knowledge. (10, p. 321)

internal

81. Because they attribute success to _____ factors, over which they have little control, girls may develop learned helplessness. (10, p. 321)

external

82. Both lack of motivation and a negative affect make up the paradigm we call _____ _____ . (10, p. 321)

learned helplessness

83. Someone who has learned to feel _____ sees the world as a hopeless place, and is not motivated to do very much. (10, p. 321)

helpless

84. A person who repeatedly experiences failure is likely to develop _____ _____ . (10, p. 321)

learned helplessness

85. If girls are indeed socialized toward instrumental _____ , in which their behaviors are not socially valued as useful, it is easy to see how they could develop learned helplessness. (10, p. 321)

incompetence

86. Achievement orientation in girls is associated with uncommon parenting. To encourage achievement in their daughters, _____ must be moderately permissive. (10, p. 321)

parents

87. Most parents are not very _____ with daughters, even if they are with their sons. (10, p. 321)

permissive

88. The different ways _____ treat their children may be related to sex differences in the way society assigns moral responsibility. (10, p. 321)

parents

89. Lawrence Kohlberg has developed a prominent theory of _____ development. (11, p. 321)

moral

90. Kohlberg proposes that _____ _____ occurs in six stages. (11, p. 322)

moral development

91. Kohlberg claims that most children less than nine years old are at the premoral level. Stages 1 and 2 make up the _____ level. (11, p. 322)

conventional

92. Adolescents who behave in delinquent ways are also often found to be reasoning at the _____ level. (11, p. 322)

preconventional

93. From the late elementary years on, most children reason at the conventional level. Stages 3 and 4 make up the _____ level. (11, p. 322)

conventional

94. Conformity to an upholding of the laws and conventions of society simply to maintain the status quo, characterizes moral reasoning at the _____ level. (11, p. 322)

conventional

95. Only a small minority of persons ever reach the postconventional level. Stages 5 and 6 of Kohlberg's theory relate to the _____ level. (11, p. 323)

postconventional

96. For the person who reasons at the _____ level, social laws and codes must conform with his or her own moral principles, or the person will follow the internal principles rather than the laws. (11, p. 322)

postconventional

97. Note that in _____ theory, the focus is on moral reasoning, not moral behavior. (11, p. 321)

Kohlberg's

98. There have been several criticisms of Kohlberg's theory of _____ _____ . (11, p. 323)

moral development

99. Some experts contend that _____ development is much more culture-specific than Kohlberg believes. (11, p. 323)

moral

100. Others argue that moral reasons can always act as a shelter for _____ behavior. (11, p. 324)

immoral

101. Still other experts disagree with _____ research strategy, suggesting that children and adolescents may not identify with the characters portrayed in the stories. (11, p. 324)

Kohlberg's

102. Carol Gilligan asserts that _____ stages place too much emphasis on a justice perspective and too little emphasis on a care perspective. (11, p. 324)

Kohlberg's

103. According to Gilligan, the emphasis on the _____ perspective may make Kohlberg's theory more appropriate to the moral development of males than to that of females. (11, p. 324)

justice

104. Recently, some experts have distinguished between _____ reasoning and social conventional reasoning. (11, p. 325)

moral

105. Conventional rules are thought to be arbitrary and lack prescription, while _____ rules are seen as not being arbitrary and do involve prescription. (11, p. 325)

moral

106. Research has indicated that even very young children can readily distinguish between moral reasoning and _____ conventional reasoning. (11, p. 326)

social

107. Researchers have also shown that the child's understanding of _____ rules develops in a stage-like fashion. (11, p. 327)

social

108. Some children are burdened by behavioral problems and emotional disturbances, and require referral to mental health clinics. Boys are _____ far more frequently than girls. (12, p. 328)

referred

109. Social class and sex are important as predictors of the nature of problems or _____ . (12, p. 328)

disturbances

110. Lower-class children and boys tend to have undercontrolled, externalized behaviors, while middle-class children and girls tend to have overcontrolled and _____ behaviors. (12, p. 328)

internalized

111. Childhood depression is a very serious disorder. Most people are surprised to learn that, since we rarely think of children as being _____ . (12, p. 330)

depressed

112. Both biological and environmental determinants seem to contribute causally to _____ . (12, p. 330)

depression

113. There are also clear, age-related changes in the nature and expression of childhood _____ . (12, p. 330)

depression

114. One of the most common reasons children are referred to guidance clinics is underachievement. Sociocultural factors may contribute to school _____ . (12, p. 330)

underachievement

115. However, disturbed family patterns may also lead to a pattern called passive-aggressive _____ . (12, p. 330)

underachievement

116. Excessive, unexpressed hostility, usually toward parents, is frequently found in cases of _____ underachievement. (12, p. 330)

passive-aggressive

117. Children who demonstrate _____ patterns also worry excessively about rivalry with siblings and parents, and thus learn to fear both failure and success. (12, p. 330)

passive-aggressive

118. Some children develop an intense fear of going to school, often with painful somatic symptoms. They try to avoid going to school at all, but are not ill. They simply have a school _____ . (12, p. 331)

phobia

119. Children with school _____ often have overprotective parents who foster their dependence. (12, p. 331)

phobia

It is clear, since you worked this far, that you are not an underachiever! Great! So, go do something nice for yourself. You earned it. Then, take another glance at the learning objectives, and do your best on the self test.

Self Test

1. During middle and late childhood, parents and children develop a coregulation process, in which parents (1, p. 301)
   a. give up all control over the child's behavior
   b. monitor the child without the child's awareness
   c. encourage children to be personally responsible
   d. retain control over only immediate decisions

2. Popularity is likely to result from (2, p. 303)
   a. being born in the right neighborhood
   b. good listening skills
   c. careful grooming
   d. affiliating with popular children

3. Sherif's naturalistic experiments have taught us that (4, p. 309)
   a. aggression is an important component of all groups
   b. tightly-knit groups do not need norms for the regulation of behavior
   c. frustration is the best way to bind the group together
   d. top and bottom status positions are filled first

4. Friendship groups in middle and late childhood are formed along the basis of (3, p. 308)
   a. shared school activities
   b. social and ethnic lines
   c. academic ability
   d. popularity

5. Girls more often than boys, attribute _____ to _____ factors. (10, p. 321)
   a. success; internal
   b. failure; internal
   c. failure; external
   d. failure; chance

6. Parents who want to have children high in self-esteem should (8, p. 317)
   a. hide their concern about the child's problems
   b. encourage the child to join groups
   c. be relatively permissive
   d. express affection

7. During middle childhood, (9, p. 318)
   a. children ignore sex roles
   b. boys become more masculine
   c. girls become more feminine
   d. boys become more feminine

8. Maccoby and Jacklin concluded that (9, p. 319)
   a. boys are more verbal than girls
   b. no sex differences are innate
   c. boys are more mathematical than girls
   d. girls are more social than boys

9. According to Kohlberg, most people make moral decisions based on the rules of parents or the broader society, and thus reason at the _____ level. (11, p. 323)
   a. preconventional
   b. premoral
   c. conventional
   d. postconventional

10. Boys are more likely than girls to be referred to mental health clinics for problems relating to (12, p. 328)
   a. undercontrolled behavior
   b. overcontrolled behavior
   c. attentional deficits
   d. depression

Individual Learning Activity

In this chapter you learned about several examples of aptitude X treatment interaction. You also read about the effects of several demographic variables, such as sex and social class, on educational outcomes. In this exercise, you will have the opportunity to personally explore still another aspect of this complex situation.

Before explaining just what we are getting involved in, please take a few minutes to imagine that you are an elementary teacher, perhaps in third or fourth grade. Pay no attention to the subject matter of these grades, or to the level of difficulty; you need not worry about these things. Think about the type of classroom situation you would like to have. In the space below, sketch the floor plan for your room, which will house about thirty children at full capacity.

From your floor plan you can probably get a fairly good idea of the type of interaction you will have with students. What will it be like? Will students initiate it? Will there be very much one-to-one communication?

Another important variable is classroom discipline or orderliness. Each teacher decides how best to define expectations for those children in that room. Take a few minutes to think about what types of expectations you have about how students should behave in your classroom. Now, list at least ten rules of the classroom which you would employ. Many teachers post such a list somewhere in the room. Make your list with the idea that you would post it for students and visitors to see. Write your list here:

1. _____
2. _____
3. _____
4. _____
5. _____
6. _____
7. _____
8. _____
9. _____
10. _____

What can these rules tell you about yourself as a teacher? Let's look at them. First, determine if each one is prescriptive or proscriptive. That is, does the rule say what to do or what not to do? It may surprise you to know that children violate proscriptive rules far more frequently than prescriptive rules. Some psychologists have shown that young children cannot activate proscriptive rules behaviorally until several years after they can remember and repeat them, with thresholds at about age five and one-half for girls, and six to six and one-half for boys. However, even in adulthood, proscriptive rules tend to be broken far more frequently than prescriptive rules.

According to Baumrind's taxonomy, authoritarian teachers generate more proscriptive rules, and more specific rules, while authoritative teachers are more likely to use prescriptive and more general rules. How would you categorize your rules? Can you think of yourself as primarily authoritarian or authoritative? What would be the consequences of each pattern on your students?

It is also important, of course, to ask how you would enforce these rules you have set down. Would you use praise for compliance, punishment for infractions, or a combination of the two? This is another aspect of authoritarian versus authoritative teaching, and we all know what we prefer in our teachers, and what seems to work best empirically.

Now, as a last step, go back to your list and rewrite the proscriptive rules into prescriptive rules. For example, a rule which says, "NO shouting in the classroom," can be easily reworded to say, "Please speak softly in the classroom." See how much better that sounds?

As a fringe benefit, I should tell you that these types of distinctions apply to situations other than teaching and parenting; they apply to all human relationships. Thanks for completing this exercise.

Answers to the Self Test

1. c	6. d
2. b	7. b
3. d	8. c
4. b	9. c
5. b	10. a

11 **Physical and Cognitive Development**

Preview

G. Stanley Hall is widely regarded as the father of the scientific study of adolescence. Hall, responding to Darwin's views, believed that all development is controlled by genetically determined physiological factors. Hall saw adolescence as a period of *sturm und drang* (storm and stress), full of contradictions and wide swings in mood and emotion.

Modern psychologists do not share Hall's views of adolescence. Yet, many negative stereotypes of adolescents have developed. Adelson points out that this is a generalization gap; the stereotypes result from the tendency to study the abnormal and deviant behaviors of adolescence, rather than the normal ones.

We now see adolescence as that transition from childhood to adulthood, beginning in biology and ending in culture. Early adolescence corresponds roughly to the junior high school years, with late adolescence relating to the senior high school years.

The age of menarche has been declining an average of four months per decade for the past century, probably as a result of improved nutrition and health. Frisch and Revelle have documented that menarche occurs at certain body weight and fat ratios, as does the growth spurt.

The development of primary and secondary sexual characteristics is a major component of adolescence. Just as exocrine glands secrete substances such as saliva, sweat, and milk, so ductless or endocrine glands secrete hormones into the bloodstream, to control organs from a distance. Androgens and estrogens, and only in females progesterone, secreted by gonads in response to signals from the pituitary gland, control the emergence of primary and secondary sexual characteristics. For a time, skeletal growth may be independent of other aspects of growth. The adolescent growth spurt for girls precedes that for boys by about two years. By the end of the junior high years, most boys have caught up to the girls in height and weight.

In males, the increase in size of penis and testes is followed by the appearance of pubic hair, minor voice changes, the first ejaculation, rapid growth, axillary hair, more voice changes, and finally facial hair. In females, breast enlargement and pubic hair emergence are followed by a widening of the hips and rounding of the body contours, followed by menarche, the first menstruation.

Exploratory and experimental sex play becomes purposeful sexual behavior. Many adolescents restrict themselves to petting. Masturbation, more common among boys than girls, is the most common sexual outlet. Male sexual fantasies involve specific sexual activity, while female sexual fantasies focus more on future roles of bride, lover, etc. It is only toward the end of adolescence that males see sex as part of human communication, and females become aware of their sensual potential.

Homosexual contacts occur more frequently before the age of fifteen and involve boys more often than girls. Acceptance of homosexuality is widespread, although less than fifteen percent of boys and ten percent of girls report having had a homosexual contact during adolescence.

Attitudes of adolescents about sexual behavior have changed to the point of greater acceptance of sexual involvement, particularly within a loving and affectionate relationship. Attitudinal acceptance far outstrips participation, but the majority of adolescents report having sexual intercourse by the age of eighteen. It is rare for sexually active adolescents to use any form of birth control, and many are misinformed about the female's times of fertility, so it is not surprising that the birthrate for teenagers continues to rise.

Early maturation appears to have positive social and psychological effects, particularly for boys. For girls the effects of early maturation are mixed, and include some social pressures for which the girl may be unprepared.

Cognitive development heralds the arrival of the stage of formal operations, which Piaget characterized as the most advanced stage of thinking. Abstract thinking is the hallmark of this stage, and makes possible deductive-hypothesis testing, contrary-to-fact reasoning, idealism, and the understanding of metaphor. There are considerable individual differences in the development of the characteristics of formal operations.

Adolescents engage in a number of cognitive monitorings, and develop a form of egocentrism in which they often believe that others share their thoughts and perspectives, and sometimes play to this "imaginary audience." As adolescents get older, this egocentrism diminishes. Being in the stage of formal operations also enables the adolescent to develop an implicit personality theory.

The organization of school, particularly junior high and middle schools, is theoretically based on the cognitive and social needs of adolescents. Many critics charge that our junior high schools are just watered-down versions of high schools, and foster passivity rather than autonomy. When a transition to a new school is combined with the onset of puberty, the adjustment is difficult. Therefore, middle schools may be better suited to girls and junior high schools better matched to the developmental timing of boys.

Stephanie Feeney listed characteristics of teachers who are effective with adolescents, citing traits such as security in their identities, comfort with their sexuality, and ability to exercise natural authority.

A job helps the adolescent develop a positive attitude toward work, to learn from other adults, to learn how the business world works, and to learn how to manage money. As long as the number of hours worked is limited, no negative effect on grades is likely, although working adolescents often feel less involved in school. Working adolescents also spend less time with their families. Working, however, brings independence and freedom, and demonstrates the limitations of life.

Learning Objectives

1. Contrast Hall's view of adolescence with the view held by modern psychology, and comment on the validity of stereotypes. (p. 339)
2. Describe changes in the age of menarche and factors associated with that trend. (p. 341)
3. Describe the roles of pituitary and gonadal hormones, and trace the development of sexual characteristics. (p. 342)
4. Trace the changes in height and weight typical during adolescence. (p. 343)
5. Describe the typical pattern of sexual maturation, and comment on the range of individual variation. (p. 344)
6. Describe adolescent changes in sexual attitudes and behavior, including sexual fantasies, self-stimulation, homosexuality, and heterosexual contact. (p. 344)
7. Summarize the psychological aspects of puberty, and the effects of early and late maturation. (p. 348)
8. Define formal operational thought and its intellectual manifestations: abstract reasoning, deductive hypothesis testing, contrary-to-fact reasoning, idealism, and an understanding of metaphor. (p. 351)
9. Describe social cognition, including cognitive monitoring, egocentrism, and the development of an implicit personality theory. (p. 354)
10. Differentiate the benefits of junior high schools versus middle school for early and late developers. (p. 359)
11. List at least four characteristics of teachers who are effective with adolescents. (p. 360)
12. List the advantages and disadvantages of working during adolescence. (p. 360)

Key Terms

For each key term, write the definition in the space provided.

adolescence (1, p. 341) _____

early adolescence (1, p. 341) _____

late adolescence (1, p. 341) _____

menarche (2, p. 341) _____

amenorrhea (2, p. 341) _____

puberty (2, p. 342) _____

hormones (3, p. 342) _____

androgens (2, p. 342) _____

estrogens (2, p. 342) _____

progesterone (2, p. 342) _____

deductive hypothesis testing (8, p. 352) _____

contrary-to-fact reasoning (8, p. 353) _____

metaphor (8, p. 353) _____

implicit personality theory (9, p. 357) _____

Guided Review

1. The concept of adolescence is relatively new. G. Stanley Hall is generally regarded as the father of the scientific study of _____ . (1, p. 329)

   adolescence

2. Charles Darwin had a great impact on _____'s thinking. (1, p. 339)

   Hall

3. Thus, _____ believed that all development is controlled by genetically determined physiological factors. (1, p. 000)

   Hall

4. Hall saw the period of _____ as one of storm and stress. (1, p. 339)

   adolescence

5. The German phrase *sturm und drang* means _____ and _____ . (1, p. 339)

   storm, stress

6. According to _____ , adolescence is marked by contradictions and wide swings in mood and emotion. (1, p. 340)

   Hall

7. Many people see adolescents as rebelling against their _____ . (1, p. 340)

   parents

8. Yet research shows very few or no differences in attitudes between _____ and their _____ . (1, p. 340)

   adolescents, parents

9. Adelson points out that many of our stereotypes of adolescents are incorrect, and that we suffer from a generalization gap, not a _____ _____ . (1, p. 340)

   generation gap

10. Menarche, the first menstruation, is a major event during a girl's _____ . (2, p. 341)

    adolescence

11. The age of _____ has been declining at about the rate of four months per decade for the past century. (2, p. 341)

menarche

12. The most likely reason for this trend in the age of _____ is improved nutrition and health. (2, p. 341)

menarche

13. Frisch and Revelle have shown that menarche is also associated with _____ and the percentage of body mass attributable to fat. (2, p. 341)

weight

14. Teenage anorexics and athletes are likely to experience _____ , or lack of menstruation. (2, p. 341)

amenorrhea

15. The menstrual cycle is under the control of hormones secreted by ductless or _____ glands. (3, p. 345)

endocrine

16. Other glands, called _____ glands, secrete their products directly through ducts. (3, p. 342)

exocrine

17. The pituitary gland, at the base of the brain, is also called the _____ _____ , because it controls the actions of other endocrine glands. (3, p. 342)

master gland

18. In response to gonadotropins, which are hormones secreted by the pituitary gland, the gonads secrete gonadal _____ . (3, p. 342)

hormones

19. Gonadal _____ come in two distinct types: androgens and estrogens. (3, p. 342)

hormones

20. The testicles primarily produce testosterone, an _____ , while the ovaries primarily produce estrodial and progesterone, which are _____ . (3, p. 342)

androgen, estrogens

21. However, thanks to the adrenal glands, males and females have both _____ and _____ . (3, p. 342)

estrogens, androgens (either order)

143

22. In females, _____ dominate, while in males, _____ are found in greater concentrations. (3, p. 342)

estrogens, androgens

23. Puberty involves a rapid growth spurt, which typically begins for _____ two years earlier than for members of the other sex. (4, p. 343)

females

24. Although females start earlier, by the end of junior high years, most _____ have caught up. (4, p. 343)

males

25. Marked weight gain also coincides with the onset of _____ . (4, p. 343)

puberty

26. During early adolescence, _____ tend to outweigh _____ ; but by age fourteen, most of the latter have caught up. (4, p. 343)

females, males

27. Another important feature of _____ is the development of sexual characteristics. (5, p. 344)

adolescence

28. For males, the most noticeable aspects of sexual maturation include penis elongation, growth of the testes, and the emergence of _____ hair. (5, p. 344)

pubic

29. For females, two marked aspects of sexual maturation are the growth of pubic hair and the enlargement of the _____ . (5, p. 344)

breasts

30. Some adolescents mature earlier than average, and some mature _____ . (5, p. 344)

later

31. During adolescence, exploratory sex play turns into purposeful _____ behavior. (6, p. 344)

sexual

32. However, many adolescents choose not to engage in _____ _____ . (6, p. 344)

sexual intercourse

33. The most common sexual outlet in adolescence is _____ . (6, p. 344)

masturbation

34. As a rule, adolescent _____ begin to masturbate earlier and masturbate more frequently than adolescents of the other sex. (6, p. 346)

males

35. Sexual fantasies of adolescent _____ focus specifically on sexual activity, while the fantasies of _____ often focus on future roles. (6, p. 345)

males, females

36. Haeberle claims that it is only near the end of adolescence that _____ learn to view sex as a part of human communication, and _____ learn to appreciate the robust sensuality of their bodies. (6, p. 345)

males, females

37. There are three major findings regarding homosexuality during _____ . (6, p. 346)

adolescence

38. First, _____ contacts occur more often before the age of fifteen, and involve males more often than females. (6, p. 346)

homosexual

39. Second, the acceptance of _____ is widespread, although males have some trouble with male homosexuality. (6, p. 346)

homosexuality

40. Third, in spite of liberal attitudes, very few adolescents report having had _____ experiences. (6, p. 346)

homosexual

41. Attitudes toward heterosexual relationships have also become more _____ in recent decades. (6, p. 347)

liberal

42. A typical adolescent _____ may be to accept sexual involvement within the context of a loving and affectionate relationship. (6, p. 347)

attitude

43. In late adolescence, satisfaction with petting declines, and the incidence of _____ _____ increases. (6, p. 347)

sexual intercourse

44. During periods when they are having sexual intercourse regularly, the frequency of masturbation typically increases for _____ and decreases for _____ . (6, p. 346)

females, males

45. By the age of eighteen, the majority of adolescents have engaged in _____ _____ , at least once. (6, p. 347)

sexual intercourse

46. Most adolescents who do engage in _____ _____ use no contraceptives, resulting in a fairly high rate of _____ . (6, p. 348)

sexual intercourse, pregnancy

47. Not all adolescents mature at the same ages; there is great variation in the age of sexual _____ . (7, p. 348)

maturation

48. Early maturation seems to have consistent, positive effects for _____ . (7, p. 348)

males

49. The benefits of early _____ are not as clear for females, where body image and school performance are likely to suffer. (7, p. 348)

maturation

50. Major changes in cognitive functions also occur during _____ . (8, p. 350)

adolescence

51. According to Piaget, the stage of formal operations begins during _____ . (8, p. 353)

adolescence

52. The stage of _____ _____ is the most advanced stage of thinking, according to Piaget. (8, p. 353)

formal operations

53. The stage of _____ _____ involves thinking that is for the first time primarily abstract, rather than concrete. (8, p. 351)

formal operations

54. One of the first signs of this abstract thinking is the adolescent's ability to use a new style of problem solving called _____ _____ . (8, p. 352)

deductive-hypothesis testing.

55. The person can more readily confirm or reject abstract hypotheses on the basis of _____ _____ . (8, p. 352)

deductive-hypothesis testing

56. Another aspect of formal operations is the ability to consider hypotheses which conflict with reality. This is called _____ reasoning. (8, p. 353)

contrary-to-fact

57. In addition, formal operations involves an enthusiastic _____ , often displayed in fantasies about the future. (8, p. 353)

idealism

58. The stage of _____ _____ also includes the appreciation of metaphor. (8, p. 353)

formal operations

59. A figure of speech in which an expression with one literal meaning is used to describe another event, is called a _____ . (8, p. 353)

metaphor

60. Many studies show, however, that there are wide individual differences in the time at which adolescents develop _____ _____ . (8, p. 353)

formal operations

61. John Flavell has defined social cognition. Thinking about social or psychological processes involving the self and/or others is called _____ _____ . (9, p. 354)

social cognition

62. Many studies of _____ _____ focused on monitoring social thoughts. (9, p. 354)

social cognition

63. Adolescent egocentrism and the development of an implicit personality theory are also aspects of _____ _____ . (9, p. 354)

social cognition

64. Elkind believes that _____ involves a unique sort of egocentrism. (9, p. 356)

adolescence

65. The _____ acts as if others are as preoccupied with his feelings and thoughts as he is. (9, p. 356)

adolescent

66. According to _____ , this form of _____ accounts for the boorishness and preoccupation with body parts that young adolescents often display. (9, p. 356)

Elkind, egocentrism

67. As thoughts about oneself and others are weighed and organized, an implicit _____ theory emerges. (9, p. 357)

personality

68. This _____ _____ has three elements not present during childhood. (9, p. 357)

personality theory

69. First, unlike the younger child, the adolescent considers new information in light of previous information, and does not rely on _____ observations. (9, p. 357)

concrete

70. Second, the _____ appreciates that human behavior is variable in different circumstances. (9, p. 357)

adolescent

71. Third, the adolescent looks for deeper, more complex causes of _____ . (9, p. 357)

personality (or behavior)

72. Information about the physical and cognitive development of adolescents has been used to design school environments. But many experts assert that the junior high school is just a watered down version of _____ school. (10, p. 359)

high

73. These same critics argue that schools should provide unique curricular and extracurricular offerings designed specifically for the special needs of _____ . (10, p. 359)

adolescents

74. The type of school organization (junior high versus middle school) may influence the adjustment of the individual _____ . (10, p. 359)

adolescent

75. It is well known that a transition to a new school coupled with the onset of _____ makes the adjustment to both more difficult. (10, p. 359)

puberty

76. Since females mature earlier than males, the structure of the _____ school should better serve their needs. (10, p. 359)

middle

77. Being less mature at the same age, males should fare better staying in elementary school for another year, and then going to the _____ _____ school. (10, p. 359)

junior high

78. Feeney has listed some characteristics of _____ who are effective in working with adolescents. (11, p. 360)

teachers

79. She suggests that good teachers can recall their own vulnerability, are secure in their adult identities, and comfortable with their _____ . (11, p. 360)

sexuality

80. Moreover, she says teachers should be comfortable using natural (versus arbitrary) _____ . (11, p. 360)

authority

81. Ultimately, Feeney says, good teachers must know themselves and understand _____ to be able to help teenagers. (11, p. 360)

adolescence

82. Many adolescents hold part-time jobs. Research has shown that having a job creates a positive attitude toward _____ . (12, p. 360)

work

83. By having a _____ , the adolescent learns how the business world works, how to manage money, and how to budget time. (12, p. 361)

job

84. Working adolescents spend less time on schoolwork, and less time with their _____ , but just as much time with their _____ , as nonworking adolescents. (12, p. 361)

families, peers

85. Like growing up, _____ introduces teenagers to the limitations of their own lives. (12, p. 361)

working

Good job! You have now completed this review of chapter 11. After you take a short break, be sure to look over the learning objectives and then do your best on the self test.

Self Test

1. Hall conceptualized adolescence as a period of (1, p. 339)
    a. passivity and conformity
    b. storm and stress
    c. political radicalism
    d. economic unrest

2. Recent studies have shown that the age of the young female at the time of menarche (2, p. 341)
    a. is partly controlled by weight and body fat
    b. has stopped the trend toward earlier ages
    c. is entirely genetically controlled
    d. is unrelated to fertility or sexual interests

3. During the growth spurt (4, p. 343)
    a. girls grow faster than boys
    b. boys catch up by age twelve
    c. girls begin earlier than boys
    d. three or four years pass

4. The actual production of estrogens or androgens is (3, p. 342)
    a. carried out by the pituitary
    b. controlled by the thalamus
    c. dependent on body mass and fat distribution
    d. monitored and controlled by the pituitary

5. The individual variation in sexual maturation is (5, p. 344)
    a. determined by nutritional intake
    b. greater now than in the past decades
    c. greater than the typical length of the growth spurt
    d. determined by exercise and physical acitivity

6. For the majority of adolescents, the major sexual outlet is (6, p. 344)
    a. sexual fantasies
    b. sexual intercourse with loving and affectionate partners
    c. masturbation
    d. homosexual encounters

7. The sexual fantasies of an adolescent male are typically focused on (6, p. 345)
    a. explicit sexual activity
    b. hopeful future opportunities
    c. romantic and loving relationships
    d. masturbation or petting

8. Masturbation (6, p. 346)
    a. reduces fertility
    b. causes insanity
    c. decreases during months when the person engages in sexual intercourse
    d. is more common among males than females

9. Formal operations (8, p. 352)
    a. promotes deductive-hypothesis testing
    b. involves three stages
    c. begins consistently at puberty
    d. replaces the childish implicit personality theory

10. The belief that others are thinking the same things you are is called (9, p. 356)
    a. personal fable
    b. transparent self
    c. egocentrism
    d. social monitoring

Individual Learning Activity

Gathering information about the sexual behavior, even sexual fantasies, of adolescents is difficult. The design of any research in this area must take into account the sensitivity of sexual issues, particularly for adolescents, and the concomitant likelihood that some subjects will provide false data. Sometimes, fabrication of answers is motivated by guilt or shame, and the person will deny sexual experiences which would be embarassing to acknowledge. Sometimes, the opposite is true, and the person will claim sexual experiences they have not had, simply to comply with what they believe to be the norm, or to gain acceptance among peers. So, knowing very much about the sexual activites of adolescents is difficult.

Your assignment here is to design a study which will provide further information about the sexual activities of adolescents. Several areas invite research. A considerable amount of sexual behavior which is not sexual intercourse, does occur among adolescents, and it would be helpful to know how they react to these noncoital experiences. What constitutes readiness for any type of sexual encounter? How do sexual activities influence the person's self concept? How do these same activities influence the relationship within which they occur? Before we can answer any of these questions, we must first decide how to gather the information we need. Most studies of adolescent sexuality involve questionnaires which the subjects fill out anonymously. Let's try to design one.

First, what do you want to know? A good way to start is to simply ask the questions directly. Have you ever engaged in sexual intercourse? Have you masturbated to orgasm? Have you engaged in petting? Do you see any problem with these questions?

Yes. The most obvious problem is that yes and no answers are not entirely helpful. Not only are these closed questions, but their format makes them ripe for less than honest responses. Moreover, the information you would get would be minimal. Now, try these: Have you ever had the measles, and if so, how many? Now we're getting somewhere. How old were you when you first had sexual intercourse? How frequently do you masturbate, in times per week or month?

OK, let's write down at least three or four questions we think will provide information. Write them here:

_____

_____

_____

_____

As you look over your questions, please consider this. Many young adolescents are not familiar with technical words. In fact, I was once surprised to find that the majority of a class of seventh grade boys did not know the word *penis*! Perhaps you should include some parenthetical slang terms in your questions? A good way to find out if your questions are understandable is to conduct a pilot test of your questionnaire on a dozen or so subjects. Then, you can revise the questions they have difficulty with.

After you have revised your questions so they meet the dual requirements of being easily understood and producing the type of information you want, what else must you do before you begin gathering data? How about informed consent? Are you asking minor children sensitive questions? Do you need their parents' consent to do this? Where will you gather your data? Perhaps in a school? Will the school cooperate? Isn't research fun?

Aside from designing the questions and gathering the data, what benefits will your study provide? How will your data fit with published studies to increase our knowledge? How will that knowledge help us and others?

This exercise was designed to introduce you to the design and conduct of survey research, focusing on sexual issues in adolescence. Congratulations on completing it. You will find these skills helpful throughout your academic, professional, and personal life.

12 Social, Emotional, and Personality Development

Preview

Adolescents push strongly for independence from their parents' authority, and at the same time come more heavily under the pressure of their peers. Parents who adopt authoritarian strategies have adolescents who show little autonomy. Democratic, and to a lesser extent permissive, parenting produces more competent and better adjusted adolescents. Democratic parenting is best for the development of overall competence. Early in adolescence, there is an increase in parent-adolescent conflict, due to biological changes, and the fact that most parents, between thirty and forty-five years old, are encountering more difficult life experiences themselves. The conflict between adolescents and parents peaks during early adolescence, is stable through the high school years, and then lessens, particularly if the adolescent goes away to college. Some conflict is good, since it is related to identity development.

Adolescents whose parents divorce experience the event as a painful one, and survive best if they distance themselves and remain relatively uninvolved in the conflict. Later, they are likely to recall the divorce as a hindrance to growing up, show concern about their own marriages, and hope that their children will have intact homes.

It is in the area of sexual behavior that the adolescent daughters of divorced and widowed mothers most differ. Daughters of widows are more inhibited, rigid, and restrained around men, while daughters of divorcees are more likely to seek the attention of males, show early heterosexual behavior, and are more open and uninhibited.

Parental and peer influences undergo many transformations. For children in the third grade, they are directly contradictory. By the time the child is in sixth grade, when peer influence has increased significantly, the two are not in direct opposition and each operates in different situations. For children in the ninth grade, when parent-child conflict peaks, the two are again opposed, and the adolescent's attempts to achieve independence meet with increasing parental restrictions.

Children's groups differ from those of adolescents, in that children's groups are usually composed of friends or neighborhood mates, are less formalized, and are less often cross-sexed. Crowds, cliques, and friendships characterize adolescent groups. Crowds are likely to be dominated by athletes and popular girls. Group identity often overrides personal identity, which may depend heavily on money, cars, and clothes.

Dating is a relatively new phenomenon, emerging in the 1920s. Today, dating serves four purposes: recreation, status and achievement, socialization, and mate selection. In dating relationships, females are more likely than males to reveal sensitive, intimate feelings, and to pursue personality exploration.

Adolescents develop formal theories about the self. At first, the theory is somewhat tenuous, hinging on idealized self images. As a result of experience, the older adolescent modifies the theory of the self to be more realistic.

Erikson's theory describes identity development, which reaches crisis proportions in adolescence. During the psychological moratorium world views become important, and the adolescent experiments with various roles, emerging with a sense of identity that is both refreshing and acceptable. The adolescent who does not succeed experiences identity confusion, and is often withdrawn, or replaces personal identity with that of a crowd. By late adolescence, occupational choices are paramount, augmented with choices relating to sexuality, politics, religion, and moral values.

Marcia identified four modes of resolution of the identity crisis. Those adolescents experiencing identity diffusion have experienced no crisis and made no commitments. Those in moratorium have experienced the crisis and are sorting out roles. Those in foreclosure have experienced no conflict, but made a commitment or had one forced on them by authoritarian parents. Those adolescents who have experienced the crisis and made a commitment have achieved identity. There is some evidence that college experiences increase the likelihood of entering a moratorium and eventually achieving personal identity.

Marijuana is used by many adolescents, as are alcohol and cigarettes. Parental use of drugs, and associating with friends who smoke it are related to personal use of marijuana.

A juvenile delinquent is an adolescent who breaks the law or engages in illegal behavior. Minority delinquents are probably overrepresented in the total numbers due to their inability to influence the judicial system. Most delinquents come from families with poor marital relationships, and are not close to their parents. For the most part, intervention programs have not been very successful, and the problem of delinquency has been seen more as mental illness than as criminality. Achievement Place, with its token economy, is an exception in that it works to reduce recidivism among delinquents.

The incidence of adolescent suicide continues to rise sharply, ranking third in causes of death among adolescents. Suicidal adolescents say that their parents nag and criticize them, and withhold affection from them. Any major loss or stressful event may precipitate a suicide attempt, and discussions of suicide must be taken seriously. Crisis intervention centers can sometimes be helpful in helping a suicidal person not make a rash decision.

Anorexia nervosa is a serious eating disorder involving severe malnutrition, emaciation, amenorrhea, an obsession with activity, and a preoccupation with body size coupled with a distorted perception of the body.

Learning Objectives

1. Describe changes in parenting during adolescence, including the nature of parent-adolescent conflicts. (p. 367)
2. Recount the effects of divorce on adolescents, and list prominent characteristics of the sexual behavior of daughters of divorced and widowed mothers. (p. 372)
3. Summarize the role of peers during adolescence, including adolescent groups, crowds, and cliques. (p. 374)
4. List the functions of dating, and identify sex differences in dating practices. (p. 377)
5. Trace the development of the adolescent's theory of the self, and the role of experience. (p. 379)
6. Present the key elements of Erikson's theory of identity formation, and Marcia's elaboration of four modes of resolution. (p. 379)
7. Describe the extent of use of marijuana and alcohol, and known correlates of the use of these drugs. (p. 382)
8. Define *juvenile delinquency,* and characterize efforts to rehabilitate delinquents. (p. 385)
9. Summarize what is known about adolescent suicide and its prevention. (p. 389)
10. List four characteristics of a person suffering from anorexia nervosa. (p. 390)

Key Terms

For each key term, write the definition in the space provided.

crowd (3, p. 375) _____

clique (3, p. 375) _____

identity diffused (6, p. 382) _____

identity confused (6, p. 382) _____

foreclosure (6, p. 382) _____

moratorium (6, p. 382) _____

identity achieved (6, p. 382) _____

juvenile delinquent (8, p. 385) _____

token economy (8, p. 388) _____

anorexia nervosa (10, p. 390) _____

Guided Review

1. It seems to be the very nature of _____ that they push for autonomy and independence from their parents. (1, p. 367)

   adolescents

2. At the same time that adolescents are striving for independence from their parents, they rapidly come under increasingly intense pressure from their _____ . (1, p. 367)

peers

3. We know that authoritarian parenting restricts the adolescent's development of _____ . (1, p. 368)

independence

4. Yet both permissive and democratic _____ seem to increase autonomy or independence. (1, p. 368)

parenting

5. When we look at the overall competence and adjustment of the adolescent, we see that the best adjustment is associated with _____ parenting. (1, p. 368)

democratic

6. Early in adolescence, the level of _____ between parents and the child increases. (1, p. 368)

conflict

7. Certain biological changes, including sexuality, contribute to the rise in the level of _____ . (1, p. 368)

conflict

8. Another source of conflict has to do with the _____ , who are typically between thirty and forty-five years old, and entering middle age. (1, p. 368)

parents

9. Conflict appears to escalate during early _____ , then level off, and actually decline after the high school years. (p. 369)

adolescence

10. Parents should know that some _____ is a good thing, since it is associated with identity exploration. (1, p. 369)

conflict

11. Sometimes adolescents are called upon to survive the divorce of their _____ , a very painful experience. (2, p. 372)

parents

12. Those adolescents who fare best are typically those who distance themselves and remain uninvolved in the _____ surrounding the divorce. (2, p. 372)

conflict

13. Looking back on the _____ from the vantage point of adulthood, these children regret that they did not grow up in an intact family. (2, p. 372)

divorce

14. Hetherington has shown that _____ has a marked impact on adolescent daughters, far different from the effects of the death of the father. (2, p. 372)

divorce

15. It is in the area of _____ behavior that differences between daughters of divorced and widowed mothers appear. (2, p. 372)

sexual

16. Daughters of _____ mothers tend to seek the attention of men, engage in early sexual behavior, and are more open and uninhibited. (2, p. 372)

divorced

17. The daughters of _____ mothers are more likely to be inhibited, rigid, and restrained around men. (2, p. 372)

widowed

18. According to Hetherington, _____ women are more anxious, unhappy, and hostile toward men, and more negative toward marriage than are widowed women. (2, p. 372)

divorced

19. Daughters of _____ women tend to marry younger, and to select mates with drug problems and poor work records. (2, p. 373)

divorced

20. Daughters of _____ women tend to marry men with puritanical characters. (2, p. 373)

widowed

21. As adolescents become independent of parents, they are more influenced by peers. In decisions involving basic values and vocation, they are more likely to listen to their _____ . (3, p. 374)

parents

22. In areas of friendships, they are more likely to listen to their _____ . (3, p. 374)

peers (or friends)

23. Although at the time of sixth grade, the influences of parents and peers were aligned, by the ninth grade they are in _____ . (3, p. 374)

conflict

24. The adolescent's attempt to be independent meets with the strongest parental objections at the time of the _____ grade. (3, p. 375)

ninth

25. In the later high school years, there is greater agreement between _____ and _____ . (3, p. 375)

parents, peers (either order)

26. Children's groups differ from adolescent _____ in several ways. (3, p. 375)

groups

27. Members of _____'s groups are often friends or neighborhood playmates, and the groups themselves are less formal. (3, p. 375)

children

28. Also, groups of _____ are likely to consist of members of one sex or another. (3, p. 375)

children

29. Adolescents socialize in crowds, cliques, and friendships. The largest and least personal is the _____ . (3, p. 375)

crowd

30. Smaller size, more intimacy, and more group cohesion characterize _____ . (3, p. 375)

cliques

31. Leading _____ are often dominated by athletes and popular girls. (3, p. 376)

crowds

32. The identity as part of a group may override _____ identity. (3, p. 376)

personal (or a similar word)

33. While group activities often provide an initial opportunity to get to know members of the other sex, more serious contacts occur through the practice of _____ . (4, p. 377)

dating

34. Dating today serves four major functions. Recreation, status and achievement, socialization, and _____ selection are all valid functions of dating. (4, p. 377)

mate

35. On dates, _____ are more likely to disclose intimate feelings and seek personality exploration. (4, p. 378)

females

36. In _____ , individuals develop formal theories of the self. (5, p. 379)

adolescence

37. Although the theory of the self begins as a very tenuous and idealistic one, in later adolescence, as a result of _____ , the theory becomes more realistic. (5, p. 379)

experience

38. According to Erikson, the major developmental task of adolescence is the development of _____ . (6, p. 379)

identity

39. The gap between the security of childhood and the autonomy of adulthood, Erikson calls the psychological _____ . (6, p. 379)

moratorium

40. Adolescents can experiment with various roles during the _____ _____ . (6, p. 379)

psychological moratorium

41. Trying out different _____ , selecting those you like, and making them part of you constitutes the creation of your identity. (6, p. 379)

roles

42. Failure to resolve the identity crisis results in what Erikson calls _____ _____ . (6, p. 379)

identity confusion

43. Adolescents who drop out of school, run away from home, or stay out all night, may be experiencing _____ _____ . (6, p. 379)

identity confusion

44. According to Erikson, at the heart of the development of identity are choices about _____ . (6, p. 380)

occupation (or career, or vocation)

45. Marcia has identified four modes of resolution of the _____ crisis. (6, p. 382)

identity

46. According to Marcia, these four modes are identity diffused or confused, foreclosure, moratorium, and _____ achieved. (6, p. 382)

identity

47. Adolescents who have experienced no crisis and made no commitments are said to be _____ _____ . (6, p. 382)

identity diffused (or confused)

48. Those who have made commitments without crisis, or who have had commitments forced upon them, are said to be in _____ . (6, p. 382)

foreclosure

49. Foreclosure is most likely in families where the parents are _____ . (6, p. 382)

authoritarian

50. Those adolescents in midst of crisis who have not yet made commitments are in the _____ . (6, p. 382)

moratorium

51. Those who have experienced the crisis and selected and committed to roles, are referred to as _____ _____ . (6, p. 382)

identity achieved

52. Many experts believe that going to college increases the likelihood of entering the _____ . (6, p. 382)

moratorium

53. The chances of successful development of identity commitment _____ with each additional year of college experience. (6, p. 382)

increase

54. Marijuana is an illicit _____ commonly used by many adolescents. (7, p. 382)

drug,

55. Alcohol and cigarettes are also widely used by adolescents, but these _____ are licit. (7, p. 384)

drugs

56. There is a strong positive correlation between parental use of _____ and adolescent use of _____ . (7, p. 384)

drugs, drugs

57. Associating with friends who smoke marijuana is ＿＿＿＿＿＿＿＿＿＿＿ likely to influence an adolescent than parental drug use. (7, p. 385)

more

58. Adolescents are ＿＿＿＿＿＿＿＿＿＿ likely to drink alcohol than to smoke marijuana. (7, p. 383)

more

59. The most frequently abused drug in the country is ＿＿＿＿＿＿＿＿＿＿ . (7, p. 384)

alcohol

60. An adolescent who commits a crime or engages in criminal behavior, whether caught or not, is termed a ＿＿＿＿＿＿＿＿＿＿ ＿＿＿＿＿＿＿＿＿＿ . (8, p. 385)

juvenile delinquent

61. Blacks and other minority groups may well be overrepresented in the total number of ＿＿＿＿＿＿＿＿＿＿ because they are less able to influence the court system. (8, p. 385)

delinquents

62. Many delinquents come from homes where the ＿＿＿＿＿＿＿＿＿＿ are inconsistent, or rejecting, or overly punitive. (8, p. 387)

parenting

63. Many intervention efforts have been made, but only Achievement Place has been routinely successful in reducing the pattern of ＿＿＿＿＿＿＿＿＿＿ . (8, p. 387)

delinquency

64. At ＿＿＿＿＿＿＿＿＿＿ ＿＿＿＿＿＿＿＿＿＿ , adolescents earn points in a token economy for a wide range of academic and prosocial behaviors. (8, p. 388)

Achievement Place

65. Since 1950 the rate of adolescent ＿＿＿＿＿＿＿＿＿＿ has tripled. (9, p. 389)

suicide

66. In fact, after accidents and murder, suicide is the third leading cause of ＿＿＿＿＿＿＿＿＿＿ among adolescents. (9, p. 389)

death

67. Any person who talks about committing ＿＿＿＿＿＿＿＿＿＿ should be taken seriously. (9, p. 390)

suicide

68. Adolescents who attempted _____ but lived, said that their parents nagged and criticized them, and withheld affection from them, more than did the parents of a nonsuicidal control group. (9, p. 389)

suicide

69. Severe family problems, or any major loss in a person's life may precipitate a _____ attempt. (9, p. 390)

suicide

70. Crisis centers, using specially trained volunteers and professionals, can often help deter a person from committing _____ . (9, p. 390)

suicide

71. Severe malnutrition, emaciation, and amenorrhea characterize the adolescent female suffering from _____ _____ . (10, p. 390)

anorexia nervosa

72. The person who has anorexia nervosa literally tries to starve to death, and does not feel in control of her _____ . (10, p. 390)

life

73. She is likely to be overly preoccupied with body size, and obsessed with _____ , which she believes will help her reduce her weight. (10, p. 390)

activity

Speaking of activity (but not of compulsion), can you believe that's the end of this review? That wasn't so bad, was it? After you reward yourself appropriately for completing this exercise, please take a few minutes to look over the learning objectives, then give the self test your best effort.

Self Test

1. Adolescent girls who are overly active, flirtatious, and sexually aggressive typically have fathers who (2, p. 372)
   a. divorced their wives
   b. died
   c. are loving and kind
   d. are authoritarian

2. Daughters who marry puritanical men have mothers who were (2, p. 373)
   a. divorced
   b. widowed
   c. unmarried
   d. unhappy

3. Father absence is correlated with daughters who (2, p. 373)
   a. are promiscuous
   b. refuse to have children
   c. avoid their mothers
   d. have fewer orgasms

4. Overall competence and adjustment of the adolescent is most likely when the parenting style is (1, p. 368)
   a. permissive
   b. authoritarian
   c. democratic
   d. laissez-faire

5. The adolescent who argues frequently with his parents, tries out several jobs in the first two years of high school, and ultimately goes on to college, should be considered (6, p. 369)
   a. arrested in moratorium
   b. likely to become a delinquent
   c. developing appropriately
   d. foreclosed

6. The peak of conflict between parental views and the views of peers usually occurs during the _____ grade. (3, p. 374)
   a. third
   b. sixth
   c. ninth
   d. eleventh

7. Great intimacy, group cohesion, and small size define the adolescent (3, p. 375)
   a. friendship
   b. clique
   c. group
   d. gang

8. The adolescent who selects a lifetime career goal without considering alternatives is in a condition termed (6, p. 382)
   a. crazy
   b. foreclosure
   c. identity confusion
   d. moratorium

9. Those suffering from anorexia nervosa typically (10, p. 390)
   a. focus intently on body shape
   b. avoid structured exercises
   c. have overprotective parents
   d. die within six months of diagnosis

10. The juvenile delinquent who is sent to Achievement Place is likely to be surprised by the (8, p. 388)
    a. need to earn points to obtain privileges
    b. high frequency of physical punishment
    c. hospital-like atmosphere
    d. incredible social isolation

Individual Learning Activity

There are two major issues here which have both professional and personal import for each of us. In lieu of the typical activities we have been doing thus far, in this chapter I would like to suggest we consider some real discovery learning, by selecting either one of these two options.

1. Explore the issue of the abuse of marijuana and alcohol by consulting community resources. In every community, not necessarily on or associated with your campus, you will find several professional resources. You might check the yellow pages of the phone book, ask your professor for suggestions, or just check it out with friends, to find clinics and other agencies who deal with the issues of drug and alcohol abuse. (In many communities, they are still treated separately out of tradition, or due to respect for the archaic notion that alcohol is not a drug, or out of social deference to groups like AA—Alcoholics Anonymous.)

After you have located some of these resources, arrange to visit them and gather information. What is the rate of clinic referral in your community? How does the agency propose to help people with problems? What do they do in the name of education? Prevention? How do they know when they are being successful? Listen carefully to determine what assumptions they make about the nature of the "problem" they are treating.

2. The issue of adolescent suicide touches every life. It is a very rare person indeed who does not know someone who has attempted suicide, perhaps successfully (?). As your author suggests, crisis centers can often be helpful. I think it is ludicrous to say that they are not terribly effective because many people who actually commit suicide did not call them. What about the many people who do call them and then do not commit suicide? Is this not a more rational measure of success?

After locating a crisis center in your community, arrange to visit it. Discover how they recruit and train volunteers for the work, and what a typical shift of work at the crisis center is like. How many calls do they receive each day, and what is the range of calls in terms of their nature? How many volunteers work there? I believe you'll be pleased at what you learn. Crisis centers across the country provide some excellent training in interpersonal skills, empathic listening, and general helping skills, which we can all use in our daily lives, whether we aspire to a helping profession or not. Please consider giving some of your time and talents to such a worthy effort.

Answers to the Self Test

1. a	6. c
2. b	7. b
3. d	8. b
4. c	9. a
5. c	10. a

Section VI Early Adulthood

13 Physical and Cognitive Development

Preview

The stage of youth is an extended period of training and education, and involves those who have not yet settled questions of their relationship to society, vocations, social roles, and life style. Decision-making ability does not seem to be fully formed in youth. Economic independence and autonomous decision making signal the end of youth and the beginning of adulthood. The most widely recognized social marker of adulthood is the first "permanent" full-time job. Stability characterizes the period of youth; with individual differences in self-esteem and achievement orientation being the most stable.

Physical growth, stamina, and prowess reach their zenith between ages eighteen and thirty, and young adults are at the healthiest stage of the life span as well. However, at this age there is an increase in cigarette smoking and other bad health habits which will take their toll later. Young adults rebound from stress and exertion easily, and may learn to abuse their bodies. It is important to begin preventive health care at this time, including proper nutrition, rest, and exercise. Physical health at age thirty appears to be a good indicator of life satisfaction at age seventy, more so for men than women.

While only minute changes occur in the brain of the young adult, the lens of the eye begins to lose elasticity. Muscle tone and strength begin their slow decline about the age of thirty. At the same time, the basal metabolism rate (BMR) gradually drops, as does caloric burn-off; and there is an increase in body fat beginning in the late twenties. Although men are also concerned with these changes, weight consciousness and fears of obesity are particularly troublesome for women.

Biological cycles may influence a person's psychological orientation. For example, most women feel anxious or depressed during the last few days of their menstrual cycle, and more optimistic at the time of ovulation. These mood changes may result from the fluctuating hormone levels of the menstrual phases.

Sexuality is an important aspect of personality. In recent years, an attitude of acceptance toward premarital sexual intercourse has developed, reflecting a high incidence of coital experience in unmarried twenty-five-year-olds. In marriage, sexual satisfaction is highly linked to overall happiness. The frequency of sexual intercourse declines slowly with years of marriage. Younger cohorts of women report more willingness to participate in sexual experimentation, more involvement in oral-genital contact, more frequent orgasms, and greater physical satisfaction.

While wide individual differences in frequency of sexual intercourse and satisfaction exist, the most common reason for sexual abstinence is marital conflict. Males report more sexual interest, while women report more sexual frustration. Extramarital sexual intercourse is not broadly condoned, and fewer than 2 percent of married adults engage in mate swapping or swinging. Exclusive homosexuality characterizes about 4 percent of the males and 3 percent of the females in America. Despite numerous hypotheses and extensive research, the etiology of homosexual preference remains obscure.

Piaget proposed that formal operational thought, achieved in adolescence, characterizes adult thinking. Some cognitive structuralists believe that for many people, formal operational thought is not consolidated until adulthood. Labouvie-Vief points out that formal thinking may be a faulty choice for adults, since the idealism may impede realistic and pragmatic orientation to the world. Improvement in logical thinking is seen during the college years. Labouvie-Vief's work suggests the possibility of a fifth stage, beyond formal operations, which would involve relativistic, pragmatic, contextual thinking.

Haan agrees with the contextual perspective; and stresses that adaptation is never final, and that additional formal cognitive structures are involved in adult adaptation. Haan also believes that young adults overaccommodate. Besides formal logic, Haan postulates that the use of structures such as morality, social understanding, and affective attitudes characterize adult thought. Schaie also emphasizes the importance of social matters and contextual considerations. He has proposed four stages of cognitive development: acquisitive, achieving, responsible, and reintegrative.

Fischer believes there are ten cognitive structural stages, including three which emerge in adulthood. Level 7 marks the first abstract thinking, permitting the person to construct a simple abstract set. Level 8 is called abstract mapping, which permits identity comparisons. Level 9 is called abstract system, and level 10 is the system of abstract systems, and permits the integration of identities throughout the life cycle. All the Piagetian revisionists assert that formal operations is not the dominant characteristic of adult thinking, and that social involvement is important in adult cognition.

Studying the total productivity of creative people in the arts, sciences, and humanities, Dennis found that peaks of productivity vary from discipline to discipline, with the twenties being the least productive decade.

There are three major theories of vocational choice. Eli Ginsberg's theory includes a fantasy stage (to age eleven), a tentative stage (eleven to seventeen), and the realistic stage (seventeen to twenty-five). While Ginsberg's theory has been criticized on the basis of limited norms and failure to account for individual differences, his general focus on increasing realism during adolescence is probably correct. Donald Super's theory of vocational choice emphasizes self-concept. According to Super, beginning at about age fourteen to eighteen, individuals go through stages of crystallization, specification, implementation, stabilization, and consolidation. John Holland's theory is based on matching careers to the basic personality types, of which he delineates six: realistic, intellectual, social, conventional, enterprising, and artistic. Most individuals entering occupations go through phases of exploration, planning, and decision making. The choice of an occupation is narrowed by sociocultural factors; with channels for upward mobility being largely educational. Research shows that the adult occupational cycle includes four stages: selection and entry, adjustment, maintenance, and retirement.

Divorce has been increasing in incidence, perhaps as both the cause and the effect of economic independence for women. Although most college women anticipate both a career and family, the combination often causes role overload; and women with children find they have fewer options. Women who return to higher education or careers after marriage and children show high levels of commitment; and women who are employed often are more satisfied and have higher self-esteem than full-time homemakers.

Since work plays a central role in our modern social organization, workers at all levels experience stress from unemployment. While managers are more sensitive to economic downturns and have more to lose, their reactions to losing their jobs are less severe than those of less skilled workers. Lack of trust is common among unemployed workers, as are alcohol and drug abuse and depression.

Learning Objectives

1. Describe the period of youth and trace the course of development of autonomy and economic independence. (p. 400)
2. Identify young adulthood as the peak of physical performance and health, pointing out changes in the sensory and muscular systems, the BMR, and weight consciousness. (p. 401)
3. Identify the nature and incidence of changes in mood associated with the menstrual cycle. (p. 406)
4. Describe premarital and marital sexual activity, attitudes and values, and homosexuality in early adulthood. (p. 406)
5. Describe the contextual perspective on adult thinking, including the work of Labouvie-Vief, Haan, Schaie, and Fischer. (p. 410)
6. Comment on consistency and change in creativity and productivity over the course of adult life. (p. 413)
7. Recount and compare the theories of vocational choice proposed by Ginsberg, Super, and Holland; and describe the succinct stages in entering an occupation. (p. 414)
8. Describe the role of sociocultural factors in occupational choice, and list the major aspects of the role of women in higher education and career positions. (p. 417)
9. Trace the contour of work in adulthood, and describe those aspects appropriate to early adulthood. (p. 418)
10. Describe the effects of unemployment on workers, and contrast the responses of managers and line workers to losing their jobs. (p. 419)

Key Terms

For each key term, write the definition in the space provided.

youth (1, p. 400) _____

basal metabolism rate (BMR) (2, p. 403) _____

obesity (2, p. 403) _____

circadian rhythms (3, p. 406) _____

adult contextual model (5, p. 410) _____

acquisitive stage (5, p. 411) _____

achieving stage (5, p. 412) _____

responsible stage (5, p. 412) _____

reintegrative stage (5, p. 412) _____

abstract mapping (5, p. 412) _____

abstract system (5, p. 412) _____

system of abstract systems (5, p. 412) _____

fantasy stage (7, p. 414) _____

tentative stage (7, p. 415) _____

realistic stage (7, p. 415) _____

Guided Review

1. Many postteenagers spend an extended period of time in education or other preparation for work; this period of time is referred to as _____ . (1, p. 400)

    youth

2. Questions such as relationship to society, vocations, and social roles are not yet answered by those in the period of _____ . (1, p. 400)

    youth

3. Economic independence and autonomous decision making signal the end of youth and the beginning of early _____ . (1, p. 400)

adulthood

4. Perhaps the most important social signal of early adulthood is the first relatively permanent full-time _____ . (1, p. 400)

job

5. The dominant picture one gets of an individual during the period of _____ is one of stability, with very little change. (1, p. 401)

youth

6. Characteristics such as achievement orientation and self-esteem were relatively _____ during the transition from youth to early adulthood. (1, p. 401)

stable

7. The physical status and health of the individual attain their peak during _____ _____ . (2, p. 401)

early adulthood

8. However, some poor _____ habits, such as smoking, will take their toll later. (2, p. 402)

health

9. Young adults also should be careful not to excessively stress their bodies; while they may bounce back easily now, they could develop habits which would be problematic _____ . (2, p. 403)

later

10. Only very slight changes can be noted in the brain and sensory organs during _____ _____ . (2, p. 403)

early adulthood

11. However, the _____ of the eye loses some of its elasticity, leading to problems focusing on near objects. (2, p. 403)

lens

12. Around age thirty, _____ tone and strength begin to decline. (2, p. 403)

muscle

13. In the mid to late twenties there is an increase in body _____ . (2, p. 403)

fat

14. Obesity may become a problem at this time, since the individual is experiencing a slow _____ in the basal metabolism rate (BMR). (2, p. 403)

decline

15. Weight consciousness is particularly troublesome for _____ , who may devote major efforts to weight control, trying to remain lithe and younger-looking. (2, p. 404)

women (or females)

16. From early adolescence until some point in middle adulthood, a woman experiences cycles of hormone secretion which bring about the _____ cycle. (3, p. 406)

menstrual

17. Bardwick reports increased incidence of depression and anxiety near the end of the _____ _____ . (3, p. 406)

menstrual cycle

18. Higher levels of self-esteem and confidence are found in women at the time of _____ . (3, p. 406)

ovulation

19. About _____ percent of all women experience mood shifts related to phases of the _____ _____ . (3, p. 406)

75, menstrual cycle

20. Traditionally, it was believed that premarital _____ was more acceptable for males than for females. (4, p. 406)

sex

21. Recently, an attitude of acceptance of _____ _____ has emerged. (4, p. 406)

premarital sex

22. By age twenty-five, 97 percent of males and 81 percent of females have engaged in _____ sexual intercourse. (4, p. 406)

premarital

23. Compared with women of cohorts past, it would appear that young women in the 1970s and 1980s are less _____ about enjoying sexual activity. (4, p. 407)

inhibited

24. In married women, the frequency of _____ is correlated with overall happiness. (4, p. 408)

orgasm

25. The majority of individuals in our society do not condone _____ sex. (4, p. 408)

extramarital

26. Fewer than 2 percent of married couples engage in _____ _____ , sometimes called "swinging." (4, p. 408)

mate swapping

27. In the past two decades, we have heard much about homosexuality. Approximately 4 percent of all American males and 3 percent of females are exclusively _____ . (4, p. 408)

homosexual

28. Despite active research efforts and numerous theories, the cause of _____ eludes scientists. (4, p. 409)

homosexuality

29. During early adulthood, sexual development is accompanied by cognitive _____ . (5, p. 410)

development

30. According to Piaget, during adolescence the stage of _____ _____ is attained. (5, p. 410)

formal operations

31. Adult thought simply continues this stage of formal operations, according to _____ . (5, p. 410)

Piaget

32. Some cognitive-structuralists assert that it is not until early _____ that many individuals actually consolidate their formal operational thinking. (5, p. 410)

adulthood

33. Individuals in early adulthood do in fact engage in more _____ _____ thought than adolescents do. (5, p. 410)

formal operational

34. Gisela Labouvie-Vief argues that Piaget's model is insufficient for the analysis or interpretation of _____ thought. (5, p. 410)

adult

35. Accordingly, Labouvie-Vief has proposed the _____ contextual model of cognitive development. (5, p. 410)

adult

36. According to _____ , formal thinking may be inappropriate for adults, because the abstract idealism prevents the person from having a pragmatic orientation to the real world. (5, p. 410)

Labouvie-Vief

37. As students move successively through their college years, the absolute nature of logic _____ . (5, p. 410)

declines

38. According to _____ , this permits a new integration of the practical aspects of adulthood into logical thinking. (5, p. 410)

Labouvie-Vief

39. Thus, the ideas of _____ suggest the possibility of a fifth stage of cognitive development, which emerges in adulthood. (5, p. 411)

Labouvie-Vief

40. Norma Haan agrees with _____ that a contextual perspective is necessary to an understanding of adult cognitive function. (5, p. 411)

Labouvie-Vief

41. Haan also believes that young adults adapt not just by accommodating but by _____ . (5, p. 411)

overaccommodating

42. According to _____ , other mental structures such as morality, social understanding, and affective attitudes join with logical thinking to characterize adult thought. (5, p. 411)

Haan

43. K. Warner Schaie has proposed a four-stage model of _____ cognitive development. (5, p. 411)

adult

44. According to _____ , the acquisitive stage occurs during childhood and adolescence. (5, p. 411)

Schaie

45. In early adulthood, according to _____ , the individual turns from acquiring new knowledge to a focus on achieving potential, the so-called achievement stage. (5, p. 411)

Schaie

46. Middle _____ corresponds to the responsible stage, according to Schaie, and later adulthood is the reintegrative stage. (5, p. 412)

adulthood

47. Schaie believes that in late adulthood, motivational aspects become more important in _____ activity than at any other time in life. (5, p. 412)

cognitive

48. Kurt Fischer believes that there are ten (count 'em!) stages in human _____ development, with the last three occurring in adulthood. (5, p. 412)

cognitive

49. According to Fischer, a simple abstract set becomes possible in stage _____ . (5, p. 412)

seven (7)

50. The next stage, which Fischer calls abstract mapping, involves a person's ability to relate his or her _____ identity to that of another. (5, p. 412)

abstract

51. Level 9 is called an abstract system, and entails the coordination of one's own identities with those of significant _____ and with societal expectations. (5, p. 412)

others

52. Fischer's most advanced stage is called the system of _____ systems, and involves the coordination of identities across the life span. (5, p. 412)

abstract

53. All of these revisionists' theories share one element: all assume that Piaget's notion of formal operational thought does not describe _____ cognition. (5, p. 412)

adult

54. On a related subject, Wayne Dennis measured the productivity of creative people, and found that the twenties was the least _____ decade. (6, p. 413)

productive

55. Also, the peak ages of _____ varied with the discipline or specialty of the creative person. (6, p. 414)

productivity

56. There are several contemporary theories of vocational choice. Ginsberg's _____ emphasizes fantasies children have. (7, p. 414)

theory

57. According to Ginsberg, until age eleven children are in the _____ stage. (7, p. 414)

fantasy

58. From age eleven to seventeen, boys and girls are in what _____ calls the tentative stage. (7, p. 415)

Ginsberg

59. According to Ginsberg, adolescents assess their interests, capacities, and values during this _____ stage. (7, p. 415)

tentative

60. At age seventeen or eighteen, the individual enters the realistic _____ , which extends through the twenties. (7, p. 415)

stage

61. Exploration and eventually crystallization comprise the _____ stage, according to Ginsberg. (7, p. 415)

realistic

62. Donald Super's _____ of vocational choice is based on the importance of the individual's self concept. (7, p. 415)

theory

63. According to Super, there are five phases of _____ development. (7, p. 415)

vocational

64. From age fourteen to eighteen, crystallization occurs. Adolescents develop ideas about work which mesh with their global self _____ during _____ . (7, p. 415)

concept, crystallization

65. Specification extends from age eighteen to twenty, and involves narrowing the vocational _____ . (7, p. 415)

choices

66. Implementation stretches from age twenty-one to twenty-four. Young adults complete their education or training and enter the work world during _____ . (7, p. 415)

implementation

67. According to _____ , stabilization is the next stage. (7, p. 415)

Super

68. From age twenty-five to thirty-five, the decision on a specific career is made. This is called _____.
(7, p. 415)

stabilization

69. After thirty-five, consolidation occurs. According to Super, adults seek higher status positions within their careers during _____. (7, p. 415)

consolidation

70. John Holland claims that people choose careers which match their personalities. According to Holland, there are six major _____ types. (7, p. 416)

personality

71. The realistic _____ shows masculine traits, and is best at farming, truck driving, or construction. (7, p. 416)

personality

72. The intellectual _____ type is best suited for careers in math and science. (7, p. 416)

personality

73. The social _____ type shows feminine _____ , and is suited for teaching, social work, or counselling. (7, p. 416)

personality, traits

74. The conventional _____ _____ is well suited for work as a bank teller, secretary, or file clerk. (7, p. 416)

personality type

75. According to _____ , the enterprising type enjoys leading others and dominating them. These people make good salesmen and politicians. (7, p. 416)

Holland

76. The artistic _____ type naturally does well in _____ and writing. (7, p. 416)

personality, art

77. Even _____ admits that his categories of _____ types may be too simplistic. (7, p. 416)

Holland, personality

78. By whatever means they choose, by the end of adolescence most people enter some type of _____.
(7, p. 416)

occupation

79. In entering an _____ , people should take time to explore alternative career paths, then plan and make decisions. (7, p. 416)

occupation

80. Decisions about which _____ to enter are influenced by sociocultural factors. (8, p. 417)

occupation (or career)

81. The divorce rate has been _____ in recent years, and is a reason many women seek work. (8, p. 417)

rising (or increasing)

82. The increasing rate of _____ may also be in part due to the increased economic independence of _____ . (8, p. 417)

divorce, women

83. Although most college women anticipate both marriage with children and a _____ , many later find this combination produces role overload. (8, p. 418)

career (not husband—that's redundant)

84. Those women who return to a career or to _____ after marriage and children, are highly committed. (8, p. 418)

college

85. In general, women who are employed have _____ levels of self-esteem and life satisfaction than do full-time homemakers. (8, p. 418)

higher

86. There are four major stages in the occupational cycle. The four _____ are: selection and entry, adjustment, maintenance, and retirement. (9, p. 418)

stages

87. Daniel Levinson calls the second stage, _____ , the "Age 30 Transition." (9, p. 418)

adjustment

88. Just as career choices are often difficult, so too is unemployment. Professional, skilled, and semi-skilled workers are all affected by _____ . (10, p. 419)

unemployment

89. In the areas of income and self-image, _____ have more to lose from unemployment, and are, therefore, more sensitive to economic downturns than are line workers. (10, p. 419)

managers

90. Comparing steelworkers and managers one year after layoff, the Buss-Redburn study showed that the
_____ were more distrustful and aggressive one year after layoff. (10, p. 419)

steelworkers

91. However, one year after layoff, the _____ were using more over-the-counter drugs and were reporting more family problems. (10, p. 419)

managers

92. Overall, the _____ seemed to handle the stresses of unemployment better. (10, p. 419)

managers

Self Test

1. The transition from youth to early adulthood is often socially recognized by the announcement of (1, p. 400)
   a. marriage
   b. graduation from college
   c. the first pregnancy
   d. a full-time job

2. Adults are healthiest during (2, p. 402)
   a. early adulthood
   b. middle adulthood
   c. later adulthood
   d. the decade of the forties

3. A woman is likely to show the highest self-esteem and confidence when she is (3, p. 406)
   a. newly divorced
   b. ovulating
   c. menstruating
   d. postmenopausal

4. For women, satisfaction in marriage is related to (4, p. 408)
   a. trying different partners
   b. reading sex manuals
   c. discovering what she likes and telling her partner
   d. engaging in more frequent intercourse with orgasm

5. According to Piaget, (5, p. 410)
   a. there is a fifth stage of cognitive development
   b. adults use formal operations
   c. adults have the capacity to analyze formal operational thought itself
   d. formal operational capacity is lost in later adulthood

6. It would appear that across many disciplines, the least productive decade for creative adults is the decade of the (6, p. 413)
   a. twenties
   b. forties
   c. fifties
   d. sixties

7. It is fairly well agreed upon among researchers that the real cause of homosexuality is (4, p. 409)
   a. a weak or distant father and strong mother
   b. being raised by parents who are sexually unhappy
   c. being seduced by a homosexual as a child
   d. unknown

8. An essential feature of the adult contextual model is that it (5, p. 410)
   a. disproves Piaget's theory
   b. suggests that adult cognition becomes realistic
   c. invokes a fifth stage of rational development
   d. equates moral thinking with rational thinking

9. According to Donald Super, vocational choice is related to a person's (7, p. 415)
   a. fantasy
   b. personality
   c. self-concept
   d. cognitive attributes

10. For those women who seek both a career and a family, life satisfaction is (8, p. 418)
    a. highest if she meets both sets of demands alone
    b. less than that of the full-time homemaker
    c. limited to career satisfaction
    d. in jeopardy if she fails to deal with role overload

Individual Learning Activity

This activity is very likely to have personal benefits for you, particularly if you are not yet certain about your own occupational choice. Although there is much disagreement about the nature of vocational choice, as reflected in the three theories you read about in this chapter, there is no disagreement with the statement by Donald Super that exploration of alternatives is the most important aspect of career development.

In response to this type of thinking, over the past ten years, virtually every high school, college, and university has instituted some form of program to assist students to discover their most suitable occupation. To begin, locate the office on your campus which is responsible for this function. It may be called counselling, or student services, or perhaps career planning. Check it out. Go there (you may benefit by making an appointment), and find out what they have to offer. Perhaps they have several tests of aptitude and/or interest which you can take to see with which career paths your interests align. Perhaps, as at the college where I teach, they have an interactive computer program which asks you questions, and, based on your answers, provides you with a list of likely career opportunities, and a profile of your aptitudes and interests which the counselor will then discuss with you.

If you can do so, try out the tests. After you have done this, and have seen the results, ask yourself these questions: Which of the three theories seems to describe the assumptions underlying the tests I took? Which theory best describes the attitudes and assumptions of the counselor or student services worker with whom I spoke? How would that person have responded differently to me if she or he had been influenced by either of the other theories? How would my test results have been interpreted by the authors of each of these theories?

The key here is twofold: first, to realize whatever personal benefit you can from the exploration of alternatives for yourself; second, to appreciate that the tests and help of the professionals you encountered were predicated on or at least influenced by the assumptions underlying one or more of these theories.

Answers to the Self Test

1. d	6. a
2. a	7. d
3. b	8. b
4. d	9. c
5. b	10. d

14 Social, Emotional, and Personality Development

Preview

During the past fifty years, personal fulfillment has been as important as the goal of a stable marriage. Most adults marry at least once, and have fewer children than older cohorts. The combination of higher life expectancy and lower childbearing rates means more years of marriage without children at home. At the same time, divorce rates are rising.

Marital roles are often renegotiated several times. Mate selection typically begins with physical attraction, proceeding to the discovery of similar values and attitudes. Although some sociologists contend that mates are selected to complement self-perceived weaknesses in personality, a combination of similarity and complementarity is involved in most courtships.

Early marriage involves exploration and the evaluation of expectations. Role assignments may be influenced by financial conditions, while birth control permits the delay of parenthood. Communication is a very important aspect of early marriage, as is passion and sexual intimacy. Loyalty and sensitivity to feelings are considered more important to middle-aged and older adults. Good marriages emerge from mutually rewarding relationships in which each partner assumes responsibility, and negotiation occurs.

The greatest degree of dissatisfaction surrounds the early childrearing years, when role conflict or overload is likely. There is less sharing of household tasks as well as less companionship between husbands and wives.

Compared with adults in 1940, today's women are more egalitarian in their attitudes toward marriage, but men today still believe that they should be dominant. Contemporary adults of both sexes are more in favor of financial independence than were adults of 1940. Contemporary women express more regret over marriage than their 1940 counterparts, while for men there are no differences. These changes are in line with the trend toward greater sex role equality in society at large.

Marital satisfaction and conflict may be viewed from the perspective of behavior exchange theory, emphasizing hedonism and competence in marital relationships. Distressed couples use aversive controls to try to precipitate changes in the partner, while competent couples use support and understanding. Notions of reciprocal determinism and cognitive determinants should also be considered in any effective model of marital satisfaction. Over the life span, there is some coherence and continuity in relationships, internalization of earlier relationships, carrying forward of relationships to influence new ones, and cohort differences in relationship expectations and demands.

The parental role, planned or accidental, requires interpersonal skills and emotional stamina for which there is little or no education or training. The current trend is toward fewer children, with planning of timing and number of children. Therefore, women have more freedom to pursue careers, men invest more time in fathering, and home care is supplemented by institutional child care, as infants spend less total time with their mothers. Parenthood brings many changes in the marital relationship too. Lack of maternal skill at feeding the infant is related to tension and conflict, while the quality of the marriage predicts maternal affection for the infant.

At any given time, slightly more than one third of adults are unmarried. More women than men are unmarried, due to their greater numbers and the reduction in the number of men at wartimes. Moreover, many women are emotionally more mature and better adjusted than men, as a result of the feminist movement, and of making use of personal growth opportunities. Many single adults cite personal freedom as an advantage.

Adults who were married and experienced divorce, desertion, or widowhood, work through the grief process. Marriage at an early age, low income levels, low educational levels, and premarital pregnancy all increase the risk of divorce. Divorced couples often continue to have a relationship, particularly when they have children. Divorce is often more traumatic for women than men, producing many displaced homemakers. Both men and women suffer lowered self-esteem following divorce, and find that the establishment of a new, satisfying, intimate heterosexual relationship is often the most important factor in their later perception of themselves.

Erikson recommends that identity be firmly established before intimacy arrives. He defines intimacy in both sexual and friendship terms. Five styles of interaction, including intimate, preintimate, stereotyped, pseudointimate, and isolated, have been identified. Research confirms that individuals with a firm sense of identity are more likely to attain intimacy.

Weiss believes that emotional isolation and social isolation are distinct types of loneliness, and that both close emotional attachments and outside social ties are needed. Rubin adds that for people in high-pressure jobs, aloneness can heal, while loneliness hurts. Loneliness is more prevalent among unmarried, divorced, and widowed individuals.

An important aspect of the development of intimate relationships is commitment. At the same time that young adults are trying to establish an identity, they must cope with achieving independence from parents, developing an intimate relationship, and increasing friendship commitments. There is a delicate balance between intimacy/commitment and independence/freedom in an individual's personality and in relationships with others, which may vary according to the sociohistorical context of each person.

Childhood personality measures are not generally good predictors of adult personality characteristics. The California Longitudinal Study, using the Q-sort technique, found some evidence for personality consistency, particularly in dimensions more directly concerned with the self, such as cognitive investment and emotional control. In the Fels Longitudinal Study, it was found that sex-typed characteristics tended to show stability from the elementary school years to early adulthood. The New York Longitudinal Study of temperament showed consistency only in person-environment interaction. Therefore, Freud's ideas that personality is fixed during the first five years of life have been rejected, but personality at any age builds on previous experiences.

Learning Objectives

1. Trace recent trends in life goals and expectations, and relate them to rates of marriage, childbearing, and divorce. (p. 427)
2. Describe the sequence of courtship, early marriage, and the childbearing years, focusing on appropriate roles. (p. 428)
3. List and describe at least three cohort effects in attitude and role expectations involved in marriage relationships. (p. 430)
4. Summarize the findings on marital satisfaction and conflict, from both behavior exchange and relationship construction views. (p. 431)
5. Describe the nature of the parental role, changes in parenting behaviors, and the relationship of parenthood to marital relationships. (p. 433)
6. Explain the particular situations of adults who never married, or who are divorced or widowed, including sex differences in their reactions. (p. 438)
7. Trace the development of intimacy and its variations, and loneliness and isolation, as well as the relationship between intimacy/commitment and independence/freedom. (p. 439)
8. Review the findings of the three major longitudinal studies, and summarize the ability to predict adult personality from earlier measures. (p. 445)

Key Terms

For each key term, write the definition in the space provided.

behavior exchange theory (4, p. 431) _____

displaced homemaker (6, p. 439) _____

intimacy (7, p. 439) _____

intimate style (7, p. 441) _____

preintimate style (7, p. 441) _____

stereotyped style (7, p. 441) _____

pseudointimate style (7, p. 441) _____

isolated style (7, p. 441) _____

emotional isolation (7, p. 442) _____

social isolation (7, p. 442) _____

Q-sort technique (8, p. 446) _____

Guided Review

1. Most adults expect to find a mate and get _____ . (1, p. 427)

   married

2. Indeed, until about 1930, the goal of a stable _____ was seen as a major endpoint of early adulthood. (1, p. 427)

   marriage

3. In the past fifty years, however, personal fulfillment has become as important a goal for adults as a stable _____ . (1, p. 427)

   marriage

4. Most Americans, however, still _____ , at least once. (1, p. 427)

   marry

5. Another trend is that toward having fewer _____ per married couple. (1, p. 427)

   children

6. Thus, while over 90 percent of married couples have _____ , the average number of children per couple is declining. (1, p. 427)

   children

7. At the same time, the average person is living longer. This increase in life expectancy, coupled with lower reproduction rates, means that the typical couple will spend more time without _____ at home. (1, p. 428)

   children

8. The rate of divorce is increasing. If the current rate trend continues, soon a married couple will have a better than 50 percent likelihood of experiencing _____ . (1, p. 428)

   divorce

9. The marital relationship develops in stages. During the course of the _____ , roles are renegotiated several times. (2, p. 428)

   relationship

10. Courtship is the name given to the first _____ of the emerging marital relationship. (2, p. 428)

    stage

11. In selecting a mate, most of us are initially drawn to someone by _____ appearance. (2, p. 428)

    physical

12. The relationship is maintained if we find we have _____ interests and attitudes. (2, p. 428)

similar

13. The more things we have in _____ , the greater the likelihood we will spend more time together, and eventually discuss _____ . (2, p. 428)

common, marriage

14. Some sociologists believe that mate selection involves not similarities but _____ needs. (2, p. 428)

complementary

15. Complementary needs are defined as those opposite qualities in another person which _____ for perceived inadequacies we might have. (2, p. 428)

compensate

16. Most of us choose a mate based on both _____ of interests and values, and _____ needs. (2, p. 428)

similarities, complementary

17. The early years of _____ involve exploration and evaluations of our expectations in terms of the reality we discover. (2, p. 428)

marriage

18. Communication in marriage is more characteristic in _____ adulthood than in middle or later adulthood. (2, p. 429)

early

19. Passion and sexual intimacy are more important to _____ adults. (2, p. 429)

young

20. Loyalty and sensitivity to feelings are more valued by _____ adults. (2, p. 429)

older

21. Courtship and early marriage are often focused on the resolution of the extent to which the relationship leads to intimacy. Intimacy is enhanced by behavior which is _____ rewarding. (2, p. 429)

mutually

22. The birth of the first _____ brings new concerns, as well as new roles. (2, p. 430)

child (or baby)

23. Many adults report the greatest amount of marital _____ when they have infants and young children to care for. (2, p. 430)

dissatisfaction (!)

24. With both family and occupational demands peaking, role conflict and role overload contribute to marital _____ in early adulthood. (2, p. 430)

dissatisfaction

25. Just as there are cohort differences in expectations about marriage, so are there _____ effects in terms of specific role expectations within marriage. (3, p. 430)

cohort

26. Comparing contemporary women with women in Terman's 1940 study, it is clear that contemporary women have a _____ egalitarian view of marriage. (3, p. 430)

more

27. While contemporary women do not widely believe that the man should be dominant in the relationship, most contemporary men, like their 1940 counterparts, believe that the man should be _____ in marriage. (3, p. 430)

dominant

28. Compared to the 1940 sample, contemporary men and women agree that married individuals should be more financially _____ . (3, p. 430)

independent

29. Contemporary men believed they should take an _____ role in parenting, while their 1940 counterparts were less inclined to do so. (3, p. 430)

active

30. Compared to the 1940 women, contemporary women were more likely to express _____ and dissatisfaction in their marriages. (3, p. 431)

regret

31. Although there were no such cohort differences for men, contemporary women were far more likely to seriously consider _____ or separation than the 1940 women were. (3, p. 431)

divorce

32. There are two major views of marital satisfaction and conflict. The behavior exchange theory emphasizes the hedonism and competence involved in _____ . (4, p. 431)

marriage

33. The hedonism component involves the assumption that each partner's _____ is determined by the reinforcement value of the other partner. (4, p. 431)

satisfaction

34. The other element of the behavior exchange theory, _____ , is reflected in the mastery of specific relationship skills. (4, p. 431)

competence

35. All marriage partners want to change their mates at some time. Distressed (unhappy) couples are likely to try to _____ their mates by using aversive controls. (4, p. 432)

change

36. More satisfied couples are likely to behave competently, trying to effect _____ through the use of understanding and support. (4, p. 432)

change

37. The other major view of marital satisfaction is the relationship construction view, which begins by focusing on the early _____ with parents. (4, p. 432)

relationships

38. It is commonly observed that there is some continuity and coherence in the many _____ a person has throughout life, and that some aspects of these early relationships are internalized. (4, p. 433)

relationships

39. In addition, people tend to carry forward old relationships which then influence new _____ . (4, p. 433)

relationships

40. Thus, the construction of a _____ relationship involves many factors from the individual partners' backgrounds. (4, p. 433)

marital

41. Some people become parents by carefully planning, but most become parents by _____ . (5, p. 433)

accident

42. There are many myths about parenting. The notion that the birth of a child will save a failing marriage is one of those _____ . (5, p. 434)

myths

43. Currently, the trend is to have fewer _____ per marriage, a trend facilitated by adequate birth control. (5, p. 434)

children

44. With fewer children, and the reduced demands of child care, a _____ has more opportunity for other things. (5, p. 434)

woman (or mother)

45. There are a number of connections between parenting roles and the _____ relationship. (5, p. 435)

marital

46. For example, in one study it was found that tension and conflict between the _____ partners was related to the mother's difficulties in feeding the infant. (5, p. 435)

marital

47. Also, the mother's ability to enjoy and be affectionate with the infant may be linked to the quality of her relationship with her _____ . (5, p. 435)

husband

48. The arrival of the first _____ produces significant role strain for the parents. (5, p. 435)

child

49. Thus with the arrival of children and parenthood, the couple must again renegotiate their respective _____ . (5, p. 435)

roles

50. Although most adults get married at least once, at any given time more than one-third of all adults are _____ . (6, p. 437)

single (or unmarried)

51. Many _____ have remained single due to the "marriage squeeze." (6, p. 437)

women

52. The shortage of _____ in the 1970s, due to the baby boom in the 1940s and 1950s after the war and women's custom of marrying older men, defines the _____ _____ . (6, p. 437)

males, marriage squeeze

53. People who are _____ often complain that the society is marriage-oriented. (6, p. 437)

single (or unmarried)

54. Many _____ adults cite personal freedom as a benefit of being _____ .
    (6, p. 438)

single, single

55. Some persons were previously married, and experienced _____ . (6, p. 438)

divorce

56. Youthful marriage, premarital pregnancy, low educational level, or low income all increase the likelihood of
    _____ . (6, p. 438)

divorce

57. Whether the individual initiates the divorce, or is divorced by the partner, the grief process is the same, as the
    person mourns the death of the _____ . (6, p. 438)

relationship

58. The process of separation and _____ is usually emotionally charged and complex, with
    prior social scripts that are difficult to break. (6, p. 438)

divorce

59. While the time prior to the decision may be the most difficult for both partners, the actual divorce is often more
    traumatic for _____ . (6, p. 439)

women

60. The term, displaced _____ , describes the situation many divorced women find themselves
    in. (6, p. 439)

homemaker

61. It is critical for divorced adults to create a positive _____ identity in order to deal with the
    issues of loneliness and financial hardship. (6, p. 439)

single

62. One of the most marked changes in _____ parents during the first year following divorce is
    the decline in their feelings of competence. (6, p. 440)

divorced

63. Erikson claims that we should not attempt intimacy until we have established a firm sense of _____ .
    (7, p. 439)

identity

64. Erikson defines _____ in terms of both sexual relationships and friendship. (7, p. 439)

intimacy

65. One classification of _____ involves five styles of interaction. (7, p. 441)

intimacy

66. These five _____ are: intimate, preintimate, stereotyped, pseudointimate, and isolated. (7, p. 441)

styles

67. The _____ _____ individual forms and maintains one or more deep and long-lasting love relationships. (7, p. 441)

intimate style

68. The _____ _____ individual has mixed emotions about commitment, and offers love without obligations. (7, p. 441)

preintimate style

69. Superficial relationships, particularly same-sex friendships, are preferred by the _____ _____ individual. (7, p. 441)

stereotyped style

70. The _____ person pretends to have a long-term heterosexual relationship, but in fact the relationship has no real depth or closeness. (7, p. 441)

pseudointimate

71. The _____ _____ individual withdraws from social encounters, and has no intimate attachment to anyone. (7, p. 441)

isolated style

72. Research has confirmed Erikson's view that those with a stable sense of _____ are most likely to achieve intimacy. (7, p. 442)

identity

73. Robert Weiss has pointed out two types of loneliness: emotional isolation and social _____. (7, p. 442)

isolation

74. The loss of an emotional attachment, such as occurs in a divorce, is likely to result in _____ isolation. (7, p. 442)

emotional

75. Weiss asserts that people need both emotional ties and strong _____ friendships in order to avoid loneliness. (7, p. 442)

social

76. It is important to distinguish between aloneness and _____ . (7, p. 442)

loneliness

77. According to Rubin, people in high pressure jobs can be healed by _____ , but all of us are hurt by loneliness. (7, p. 442)

aloneness

78. Unmarried, divorced, and widowed individuals are more at risk for _____ . (7, p. 442)

loneliness

79. In early adulthood, individuals are called upon to work at more than one task simultaneously. At the same time that they are developing an identity, they are also working at achieving _____ from parents. (7, p. 443)

independence

80. Also, while they are striving for _____ , they are also increasing their friendship commitments. (7, p. 443)

intimacy

81. The interrelationship between intimacy/commitment and independence/freedom may vary according to the sociohistorical context, but in any case the _____ is delicate. (7, p. 444)

balance

82. One aspect of developmental psychology which has long intrigued students is the question of whether adult personality could be predicted on the basis of childhood _____ measures. (8, p. 446)

personality

83. Freud asserted that the individual's _____ was fixed by age five years, as a result of interaction with parents and other adults. (8, p. 446)

personality

84. Fortunately, we no longer believe _____ notions, but subject such assumptions to research. (8, p. 446)

Freud's

85. Three longitudinal studies have given us some perspective on the issue of the stability or predictability of adult _____ . (8, p. 446)

personality

86. The California _____ Study used the Q-sort technique to obtain trait ratings, and found some consistency in all categories. (8, p. 446)

Longitudinal

87. Those dimensions most closely concerned with the self, such as cognitive investment and emotional control, showed the greatest _____ over time. (8, p. 446)

stability

88. In fact, emotional _____ appears to influence the overall course of life, predicting health status, early death, problem drinking, and even IQ. (8, p. 446)

control

89. In the Fels _____ Study it was discovered that sex-typed characteristics show some stability from the elementary years to early adulthood. (8, p. 447)

Longitudinal

90. This study, completed in the late 1950s, may not reflect our culture's changing _____ standards. (8, p. 447)

sex-role

91. The New York Longitudinal Study, spearheaded by Thomas, Chess, and Birch, examined the _____ of temperament from birth into adulthood. (8, p. 447)

stability

92. The New York study found that the only predictable aspect of the period from infancy through adolescence is that the _____ will experience person-environment interaction. (8, p. 448)

individual

93. According to Thomas, Chess, and Birch, major changes in development are produced by changes in either the _____ or the environment. (8, p. 448)

person

Well, you have finally arrived at the end of this review. Please look over the learning objectives, and then do your best on the self test.

Self Test

1. Marriages in early adulthood are characterized by (2, p. 429)
   a. communication
   b. loneliness
   c. companionship
   d. sensitivity to feelings

2. The greatest degree of marital dissatisfaction typically occurs when (4, p. 430)
   a. the last child has left the nest
   b. the first child reaches adolescence
   c. the children are very young
   d. there are no children

3. Marital satisfaction (5, p. 435)
   a. is higher in childless marriages
   b. declines consistently over time
   c. influences the mother's interaction with the infant
   d. is higher during pregnancy

4. A recent trend indicates that in contemporary America, (1, p. 427)
   a. more people than ever are seeking marriage partners
   b. personal satisfaction is sought primarily outside of marriage
   c. people are waiting longer to get married
   d. married couples are having fewer children

5. Compared to their counterparts of 1940, contemporary (3, p. 430)
   a. women seek more egalitarian marriages
   b. men are more satisfied with their marriages
   c. women are less likely to regret marriage
   d. men want to be less dominant in the marriage

6. The likelihood of divorce is increased by (6, p. 438)
   a. higher income
   b. advanced education
   c. premarital pregnancy
   d. remaining childless

7. Divorce is often thought to be more difficult for women, because they (6, p. 439)
   a. are almost always surprised by it
   b. have a harder time "letting go" of the mate
   c. are less well prepared to live independently
   d. are usually blamed by their friends for the divorce

8. Compared to older adults, young adults have marriages which are more focused on (2, p. 429)
   a. passion and sexual intimacy
   b. appreciation and respect
   c. love and trust
   d. realistic expectations of success

9. The hedonism stressed by the behavior exchange view of marital satisfaction can be expressed in terms of (4, p. 431)
   a. listening skills
   b. negotiating strategies
   c. residual relationships from the past
   d. shared pleasures

10. Those aspects of adult personality which are most stable, and thus less likely to be subject to change by a marital partner, are those which are also (8, p. 446)
    a. common to members of both sexes
    b. linked to temperament
    c. revealed in the New York Longitudinal Study
    d. related to emotional control

Individual Learning Activity

As you learned in this chapter, relationships involving courtship, marriage, love, and intimacy, follow certain paths in their emergence. It is possible to develop models of the development of such relationships, which will then permit the assessment of relationships against some standards. Some of the research reported in this chapter may help form the basis for such a model, but our task here is the design of research to accomplish this.

If you ask a wide-ranged group of adults to describe what they consider is important in marriage, or in an intimate relationship, or both, their responses will give you some idea where they are within the contours of the variables you are measuring. For example, we could ask people these types of questions:

1. What are the three most important elements in your marriage?
2. How can you tell whether you really have an intimate relationship with someone?
3. What are two common reasons why marriages fail?
4. How has your marriage changed in the past five years?
5. How do you expect your marriage will change in the next five years?
6. What characteristics do you most treasure in your mate?

These questions will allow us to gauge the relative position in the course of marriage, of a number of subjects in our sample.

Now, suppose we wanted to measure their position on some other variable? Let us say we wanted to determine their level of intimacy? Obviously, all we would have to do is add items to the list, or better yet, scramble items into the list, which would reliably measure these other variables. (We are not going to worry about determining reliability at this point; that is beyond the scope of this activity.)

To get a clear image of this task, please decide on a variable to measure, and write at least three questions which would provide you with some information about how the person is doing on that variable.

1. _____

2. _____

3. _____

4. _____

Let's suppose that you have collected your data, and have arrayed the responses to reflect what you consider to be a logical progression. Now, you have responses from each subject which reflect that person's level of attainment on two different variables. This is the essence of a correlational study, as you probably remember. You could compute a correlation coefficient to express the degree of relationship statistically. More important from a theoretical perspective, however, you could try to connect the concepts logically. Let's try that.

The easiest way to do that is to print each level of each variable (type of relationship) on a small index card, and arrange the cards in what you believe to be the proper sequence. Now, examine the data to see if the responses of your subjects support your arrangement. If not, rearrange your cards until they match the sequence your subjects reported.

This brief exercise demonstrates the basic elements in the derivation of theories and models, and in the extraction and testing of hypotheses. In all aspects of theories and models, data that are not quite in alignment with the hypothesis derived from the theory, cause us to adjust that aspect of the theory, however slightly. As we obtain more data on adult development, it should be possible to construct far more detailed models and theories, and tie together the many strands of adult development into a comprehensive fabric.

Answers to the Self-Test

1. a	6. c
2. c	7. c
3. c	8. a
4. d	9. d
5. a	10. d

15 Physical and Cognitive Development

Preview

Many physical changes characterize middle adulthood. These physical changes are clear indicators of middle age. Accommodation of the eye declines sharply, making it difficult to see near objects clearly without corrective lenses. At the same time, the retina becomes less sensitive to low levels of illumination. Hearing also declines, particularly for the higher pitches and especially for men. Bodies get shorter as muscles weaken and intervertebral disks deteriorate. A general decline in physical fitness is accompanied by a focus of concern on health status, particularly heart disease, cancer, and weight. Women show a much greater concern about weight than men, and other aspects of aging, such as facial wrinkles and gray hair, are interpreted as being more favorable for men than for women.

Those who are healthiest at mid-life tend to have calm, self-controlled, and responsible personalities. As coronary arteries narrow and cholesterol levels increase, blood pressure rises. Life style is a major factor in cardiovascular disease, with Type A persons being at highest risk. The link between psychological factors and cancer is less well marked than that for heart disease, but people who are diagnosed as having cancer have frequently had recent major losses, and the suppression of the immune system is the suspect intermediary, based on knowledge of psychoneuroimmunology.

Menopause marks the end of menstruation and the cessation of childbearing capacity. Menopause often includes hot flashes and vaginal atrophy, both resulting from decreased estrogen levels. While some women become depressed at the time of menopause, no causal link is known. Estrogen replacement therapy is controversial, and associated with increased risk of uterine cancer.

The male climacteric arrives later than menopause in the female, and progresses much more slowly. The climacteric occurs over a much longer time period, and refers to the loss of the ability to reproduce. Erection is slowed, but maintained for longer times. Sexual desire does not necessarily decline, but potency does. In middle adulthood, sexual frequency declines, partly displaced by career interests, family matters, and lower energy levels. Men continue to report greater sexual interest and activity levels than women. For women, sexual activity depends on the availability of a partner.

Cattell and Horn have distinguished between crystallized intelligence, which increases across the life span, and fluid intelligence, which rises through adolescence, levels off during early adulthood, and declines in middle and later adulthood. Schaie, Baltes, and Labouvie-Vief, who represent the contextualist perspective, argue that cross-sectional designs may have misled Horn and Cattell, and that longitudinal designs show much later peaks of intellectual functions. Moreover, Baltes and Willis showed that practice on fluid abilities improves test performance among old people.

From an information processing perspective, tasks which rely on short-term memory show little or no decline with age, while tasks requiring long-term memory show substantial age-related differences. Organization, semantic elaboration, and mental imagery, all helpful in encoding into long-term memory, are less efficient in middle adulthood than earlier, although appropriate techniques can overcome the deficiency. While recall performance falls off with age, recognition ability does not. Increasing recall time allows middle-aged adults to perform as well as younger adults.

Personal characteristics, such as attitudes, interests, health-related factors, and previously acquired knowledge and skills, also determine the level of intellectual performance. Most individuals maintain their ability to use well-learned knowledge and skills into old age. Some apparent age differences may be due to the types of materials used. Memory for unfamiliar nonverbal information is especially susceptible to age-related deficits in middle age and beyond. In addition, recall tasks may suffer because they demand difficult search strategies; while recognition tasks require only direct access mechanisms.

In middle adulthood, the status and income of most men peak, as they do for women who have long employment histories. Mid-life is often seen as a major turning point in careers, with adjustment of hopes to realistic possibilities. Levinson observes that for many men there is sadness over unfulfilled dreams. Feelings of constraint by bosses, wives, and children can lead to rebellion in the form of extramarital affairs, divorce, alcoholism, suicide, or career change.

Leisure refers to the pleasant time after work when people are free to pursue activities and interests of their own choosing. In recent years, television viewing has dominated leisure activities, although both television viewing and newspaper reading have decreased slightly since 1975. Sports are also important in leisure activities. Gould suggests that the middle-age years are a time to reassign priorities for leisure time, as money and freedom permit personal exploration.

Learning Objectives

1. Describe physical changes in middle adulthood, including changes in vision, hearing, and stature. (p. 457)
2. Characterize health status and concerns in middle adulthood, and the connections between psychological variables and cardiovascular disease and cancer. (p. 458)
3. Contrast menopause and the climacteric, and related sexual changes in women and men. (p. 462)
4. Distinguish between fluid and crystallized intelligence, and trace each through the adult years. (p. 466)
5. From the information processing perspective, describe memory functions and their limits in middle adulthood. (p. 467)
6. List and describe three control processes which provide strategies for the enhancement of memory function. (p. 469)
7. Define characteristics of the learner, learning materials, and the task itself which contribute to age differences in memory performance. (p. 471)
8. Trace the course of work through the middle-adult years, identifying the peaks of satisfaction and income, and the changes made at this important turning point. (p. 474)
9. Describe the preferred leisure activities at mid-life, and the strategies for adapting leisure preferences to changing status and life-styles. (p. 475)

Key Terms

For each key term, write the definition in the space provided.

Type A person (2, p. 460) _____

Type B person (2, p. 460) _____

psychoneuroimmunology (2, p. 461) _____

menopause (3, p. 462) _____

male climacteric (3, p. 463) _____

free recall (5, p. 469) _____

semantic or categorical elaboration (6, p. 470) _____

leisure (9, p. 475) _____

Guided Review

1. Many physical changes characterize middle _____ . (1, p. 457)

   adulthood

2. Between forty and fifty-nine years of age, the eye loses much of its ability to _____ , and most adults require eyeglasses for near vision. (1, p. 457)

   accommodate

3. There is also some evidence that the retina becomes less sensitive to low levels of _____ , which may well account for increased night blindness by middle-aged drivers. (1, p. 457)

   illumination (or light)

4. By age forty, hearing also begins to decline, with loss of _____ pitched sounds first. (1, p. 457)

high

5. Hearing loss occurs for men more than women, perhaps because _____ are more often exposed to noise in their occupations. (1, p. 457)

men

6. Muscular strength also _____ during middle adulthood. (1, p. 457)

declines

7. As the back muscles weaken, the individual becomes a bit _____ , a process which is also aided by the slow deterioration of the intervertebral disks of the spine. (1, p. 457)

shorter

8. In middle adulthood, these changes do not go unnoticed; the individual is likely to begin to show some concern about her or his general _____ . (2, p. 458)

health

9. The focus of health concerns is typically on three areas: cardiovascular disease, _____ , and weight. (2, p. 458)

cancer

10. The number one cause of death in the United States is _____ disease, followed by cancer. (2, p. 458)

heart

11. Smoking-related _____ is often first diagnosed in middle adulthood. (2, p. 458)

cancer

12. Partly because of the continued slowing of the basal metabolism rate (BMR) and the increase in sedentary activities, obesity is a critical health problem in _____ adulthood. (2, p. 459)

middle

13. The concern about weight is a much more serious matter to _____ than to members of the other sex. (2, p. 459)

women

14. In our culture, some signs of aging, such as facial wrinkles or gray hair, are thought to be more attractive for _____ than for members of the other sex. (2, p. 459)

men

15. Psychological factors may be associated with good health. In fact, the strongest association with good health at middle age was a calm, self-controlled and responsible personality, a pattern usually established by _____ . (2, p. 460)

adolescence

16. Let's look now at the cardiovascular system. The capacity of the heart to pump blood diminishes during _____ adulthood. (2, p. 460)

middle

17. Also, the coronary arteries become more narrow, and blood pressure _____ . (2, p. 460)

increases (or rises)

18. As cholesterol levels rise, the accumulations add to the thickness of the walls of the arteries, making a stroke or _____ _____ more likely. (2, p. 460)

heart attack

19. Life style appears to be associated with the incidence of _____ disease in middle adulthood. (2, p. 460)

cardiovascular (or heart)

20. Individuals categorized as Type A have a higher than average risk of _____ _____ . (2, p. 460)

heart disease

21. Excessive competition, an accelerated pace of activities, impatience with normal timing of activities, the struggle to do more than one thing at a time, and hostility all characterize the _____ person. (2, p. 460)

Type A

22. The absence of these behavioral tendencies characterizes the _____ person. (2, p. 460)

Type B

23. The articulation of the Type A and Type B persons has led to the measurement of the individual reactivity to actual stress rather than at rest alone, permitting physicians to more accurately predict _____ problems. (2, p. 461)

coronary (or heart)

24. While the link between psychological factors and heart disease is quite clear, the link between psychological factors and _____ is less clear. (2, p. 461)

cancer

25. There appears to be some link between life stress and _____ , with many people having had serious losses shortly before their positive diagnosis. (2, p. 461)

cancer

26. It is suspected that the impact of emotional losses reduces the efficiency of the immune system. It is known that stress and the absence of, or inability to engage in, some form of coping ability seem to increase susceptibility to diseases mediated by the _____ system. (2, p. 461)

immune

27. Psychoneuroimmunology is the study of the way in which psychological factors influence the vigor and viability of the _____ system. (2, p. 461)

immune

28. Middle adulthood is also characterized by a number of sexual changes. The end of menstruation and of fertility is _____ . (3, p. 462)

menopause

29. The two troublesome symptoms produced in response to lowered estrogen levels brought on by menopause are _____ _____ and atrophy of the lining of the vagina. (3, p. 462)

hot flashes

30. Some women become depressed at about the time of menopause, but menopause does NOT cause _____ . (3, p. 462)

depression

31. Most women experience menopause with very mild symptoms, and cope well without medical intervention. However, some women elect to undergo estrogen replacement therapy, abbreviated as _____ . (3, p. 462)

ERT

32. However, women who take exogenous estrogen appear to have an increased risk of uterine _____ . (3, p. 462)

cancer

33. Menopause is exclusively for women, but during his sixties and seventies, a man experiences the _____ . (3, p. 463)

climacteric

34. The man's climacteric is later and more gradual than the woman's _____ . (3, p. 463)

menopause

192

35. The climacteric is accompanied by several gradual changes in sexual functioning. As a man gets older, it takes him longer to have an _____ . (3, p. 463)

erection

36. However, he becomes capable of maintaining the _____ for a longer time. (3, p. 463)

erection

37. As adults age, the frequency of sexual activity _____ . (3, p. 463)

declines

38. Because desire does not decrease as sharply as activity levels, many adults remain _____ active into very old age. (3, p. 464)

sexually

39. Even in middle adulthood, there continue to be sex differences in sexuality. Commonly, _____ report higher levels of sexual interest and more frequent sexual activity than their partners of the other sex. (3, p. 464)

men

40. One factor very important in predicting the frequency of sexual activity for women is the availability of suitable _____ . (3, p. 464)

partners

41. Although there are gradual declines in potency and terminal points in fertility, it is good to remember that we are all _____ beings until we die. (3, p. 464)

sexual

42. In the meantime, let's turn our attention to cognitive development. Raymond Cattell and John Horn have defined fluid and crystallized _____ . (4, p. 466)

intelligence

43. Cattell and Horn believe that crystallized intelligence, which is based on cumulative learning experiences, _____ throughout the life-span. (4, p. 466)

increases

44. Cattell and Horn also believe that _____ intelligence increases through adolescence, levels off in early adulthood, then declines. (4, p. 466)

fluid

45. Prior to the work by Horn and Cattell, psychometric measures of _____ had indicated that verbal abilities tended to increase in adulthood, whereas perceptual-motor abilities tended to decrease. (4, p. 466)

intelligence

46. Schaie, Baltes, and Labouvie-Vief argue that Horn's cross-sectional designs mislead him, and point out that in their own longitudinal design, the peaks of intellectual functions occurred much _____ . (4, p. 467)

later

47. These same critics, who represent the contextualist perspective, argue that it may be possible to reverse some of the observed _____ by exercising the appropriate functions. (4, p. 467)

decline

48. The information processing perspective allows us to look at the question of decline in _____ in much more detail. (5, p. 467)

intelligence

49. Experimental psychologists have routinely observed _____ in intelligence test scores at some point in adulthood. Some researchers argue that the decline begins early, at about age thirty. (5, p. 467)

decline

50. Baltes and Schaie disagree, arguing that declines except those due to health or emotional problems, occur only in _____ adulthood. (5, p. 467)

later

51. A more careful analysis of the evidence shows that whether one observes a _____ in performance may be a function of the type of task involved. (5, p. 467)

decline

52. Tasks that use short-term memory show little or no _____ over the course of early and middle adulthood. (5, p. 469)

decline

53. However, tests which require the use of _____ memory do show major age-related declines in performance. (5, p. 469)

long-term

54. Information is encoded into _____ memory using three processes: organization, semantic elaboration, and mental imagery. (6, p. 469)

long-term

55. Encouraging subjects to use techniques which invoke these processes improves the cognitive performance of those individuals in _____ adulthood. (6, p. 470)

middle

56. It is also important to examine the characteristics of the learner in cognitive experiments. Attitudes, interests, health-related factors, and previously acquired knowledge and skills are important in predicting _____ performance. (7, p. 471)

cognitive (or intellectual)

57. The nature of the materials used in research is also important to consider. Unfamiliar materials, particularly nonverbal ones, are more problematic for _____ subjects to learn and remember. (7, p. 471)

older

58. We must also consider the nature of the memory task itself. Tests of memory may be of two varieties: recall and _____ . (7, p. 472)

recognition

59. While performance on recall tasks declines with age, there is no noticeable decline on tasks of _____ . (7, p. 472)

recognition

60. One argument regarding recall versus recognition tasks points out that _____ requires more difficult search procedures, while recognition tasks permit direct-access memory functions. (7, p. 472)

recall

61. Most workers reach the peak of status and income levels during _____ adulthood. (8, p. 474)

middle

62. Many authors describe the mid-life career experience as a major turning point. The individual at _____ must adjust idealistic hopes to fit well with realistic possibilities. (8, p. 474)

mid-life

63. Many men feel trapped or constrained at _____ , and may rebel. (8, p. 475)

mid-life

64. This _____ may appear in the form of extramarital affairs, divorce, alcoholism, suicide or a change in career. (8, p. 475)

rebellion

65. Also at mid-life we turn our attention more to how we will use our nonwork or _____ time. (9, p. 475)

leisure

66. Since the mid-1970s there has been a leveling off or slight decline in _____ viewing, a popular leisure activity, and a decline as well in newspaper reading. (9, p. 475)

television

67. College educated persons are likely to watch less television and are more likely to read a _____ daily. (9, p. 475)

newspaper

68. Sports activities, whether for participation or viewing as a spectator, are also important _____ choices for many adults. (9, p. 475)

leisure

69. As more money is available, and more freedom of vacation opportunities is enjoyed, _____ continues to be an important component of middle adulthood. (9, p. 477)

leisure

Well done! You have completed this guided review. Please take the time to review the learning objectives, then do your best on the self-test.

Self Test

1. In middle adulthood, the individual (1, p. 457)
   a. loses the capacity to see distant objects
   b. demonstrates a decrease in blood pressure
   c. has increased cardiac output
   d. loses the capacity to hear high pitched sounds

2. The menopause and the climacteric signal the end of (3, p. 462)
   a. potency
   b. attractiveness
   c. sexuality
   d. fertility

3. Cancer related to cigarette smoking is usually first detected (2, p. 458)
   a. soon after a major loss
   b. only in Type B persons
   c. by the end of early adulthood
   d. in people who are easy-going and noncompetitive

4. The risk of stroke and heart attack increase in middle adulthood due to (2, p. 460)
   a. major losses in relationships and hopes for the future
   b. elevated blood pressure and cholesterol levels
   c. menopause and the climacteric
   d. changes in career plans

5. Horn and Cattell assert that in later life there is a decline in (4, p. 466)
   a. crystallized intelligence
   b. fluid intelligence
   c. skills learned at school
   d. cognitive flexibility

6. Schaie, Baltes, and Labouvie-Vief contend that Horn is in error, due to his use of (4, p. 466)
   a. cross-sectional designs
   b. longitudinal designs
   c. mixed cross-sectional and longitudinal designs
   d. subjects with cardiovascular disease

7. Information processing studies conclude that the decline in function in later adulthood is particularly noticed in areas of (5, p. 469)
   a. recognition
   b. long recall times
   c. short-term memory
   d. long-term memory

8. The performance of middle-age adults will match that of younger adults when (7, p. 470)
   a. short-term memory is involved
   b. attention is divided
   c. organizational techniques are suggested
   d. no cardiovascular disease is evident

9. An important reason why middle-aged adults may have problems with memory tasks is that (7, p. 472)
   a. recall tasks require strenuous search efforts
   b. recognition is more difficult than other types of retrieval strategies
   c. they are used to dealing with more complex tasks than most researchers provide
   d. they are distracted by their own efforts to avoid life transitions

10. The mid-life career experience is often described as a turning point because at this time (8, p. 475)
    a. most women leave the work force and retire
    b. men are likely to rebel against felt constraints
    c. promotions are rare
    d. leisure becomes much more important than work

Individual Learning Activity

In this chapter we examined in brief, some of the physical changes which occur during middle adulthood. In the past two decades, we have seen adults become much more concerned about their health and their physical status. One manifestation of this is the plethora of diet and fitness books on sale everywhere (even in most college bookstores!). Another sign is the rapid growth of expensive spas and health fitness facilities. Yet another is the change in focus of most college and university physical education departments, as fitness and wellness replace exercise and activities courses.

These changes reflect concern on the part of adults, about their health and the risk of disease. We have become sensitized to hypertension and other cardiovascular ailments, and almost every American now knows that heart disease is the major cause of death. Yet, do we not fear other (less frequent and less preventable) causes as much or more than heart disease?

Let's design a simple instrument to discover what the major concerns and fears about health and disease are. We might ask people a few very simple questions. We might ask them what the most likely causes of death for people their age or slightly older are. We might also ask them whether they believe they are at risk for any health problems. Begin by writing at least five sample questions here:

1. _____

2. _____

3. _____

4. _____

5. _____

You might also want to ask your prospective research subjects what they think they could do, and what they actually do, to minimize their risks and prolong their health. You may be surprised to find that many people do not actively do anything to deal with those outcomes they most fear. Why is this?

If you actually ask these types of questions to adults of varying ages, do you expect to get responses which vary as a function of age? Why or why not? Would you expect the person's sex to be important in determining how they might answer? Would men fear heart disease more, and women cancer more? Why might this be? Are the diseases somehow psychologically important in a sex-linked way?

Now, let's suppose that you wanted to somehow influence these adults to modify their behavior in some way to prolong their health. Would their responses on these types of questions help you design a project to enhance health? How could you appeal to their fears, and strengthen their resolve to take action? Would education be an important aspect of your effort? What do the responses to your sample questions suggest that these subject need to learn? Do they understand the relationship of life style and other psychological variables to their health status?

What we have done here is shown how a fairly simple idea, or observation, can be developed into a research project, which can yield very useful information, particularly for those interested in influencing people, educating them, or helping them to achieve their goals.

Answers to the Self Test

1. d	6. a
2. d	7. c
3. a	8. c
4. b	9. a
5. b	10. b

16 Social, Emotional, and Personality Development

Preview

Love is important throughout life. Berscheid and Walster have distinguished between passionate love, which is intense, romantic, and involves a search for fulfillment, and companionate love, which involves the affection we feel for those with whom we have a long-term relationship. For most people, intimacy deepens over time, and passion is transformed into tenderness. According to Levinger, mutuality supports love relationships over time. There are age differences in love relationships, with passion and sexual intimacy more important in early adulthood, and tender feelings of affection and loyalty more important in later life. At all ages, people rate emotional security as the most important factor in love, followed by respect, communication, help and play behaviors, sexual intimacy, and loyalty. Women prize emotional security more than men do; men value loyalty more. There are no sex differences in the extent to which communication and sexual intimacy are important.

Launching of children from the family of origin to an independent adulthood is an important event. As more adults are living to older ages, there are more postchildrearing years. Those who speak of the empty nest syndrome assume that parents derive great satisfaction in childrearing and now sense a feeling of emptiness when the children leave home. But the majority of families appear to support the upswing thesis, an improvement in marital satisfaction when children leave home. The magnitude of this upswing may be enhanced by the high divorce rate of unhappy couples earlier in adulthood, and by increased satisfaction for women from their careers.

During the past two centuries dramatic population changes have serious implications for intergenerational relationships. Today we are likely to see more three- and four-generation families, often involving divorced and blended families. Social and historical forces serve to moderate intergenerational relationships. Intergenerational transmission is enhanced when these forces encourage consistency in values or behavior, and is reduced when social forces are at odds between generations. There is considerable and frequent contact between the generations, with almost all families having contact at least on a monthly basis.

Within families, both similarity and discontinuity exist. Parent-child similarity is highest in religious and political areas, lowest in sex roles, life styles, and work orientation. Yet parents and children remain closely bonded. Friends or peers moderate family influences in areas such as sexual behavior or drug use, while parental influences are strongest in achievement, work, and education. In most cases, parental and peer influences are complementary. Daughters retain more involved relationships with their parents, particularly their mothers, than do sons. The mother's relationship with her own mother is a powerful force in her relationship with the infant, and the infant's perception of the mother.

According to Erikson, middle-aged parents are involved in generativity, helping a new generation enter adulthood. At the same time, their own aging parents become more dependent on them. Interdependencies are renegotiated, and physical departures are rehearsed as young adults assume roles outside the family of origin. When middle-aged parents become grandparents, they reflect on the beginnings and endings of the life cycle. Young adults carry forward their parental influences to impact their work, marital, and own parental behaviors. The middle generation assumes the role of a bridge between younger and older generations.

Several personality theories characterize adult development. Erikson focuses on generativity, the need to assist the younger generation in developing and leading useful lives. Gould describes seven stages or transformations, emphasizing the turbulence of striving to handle crises in adulthood. Gould's theory is based on clinical observations and questionnaire returns, with no reliability checks or statistical analysis. Levinson collected biographies from forty middle-aged men, and developed a theory emphasizing developmental tasks. Peck expanded Erikson's notion of generativity to include four challenges: valuing wisdom versus valuing physical powers; socializing versus sexualizing in human relationships; cathectic flexibility versus cathectic impoverishment; and mental flexibility versus mental rigidity. Vaillant has also expanded Erikson's intimacy and generativity stages, adding two stages called career consolidation and keeping the meaning versus rigidity. All these approaches are similar in their overall outline of adult development from identity to final integration. Yet, these theories are based on minimal kinds of observations, are crisis-oriented, and neglect individual variations.

The focus on crisis has been popular. Levinson sees the middle-aged adult suspended between the past and the future. Vaillant sees the forties as the time for reassessing and recording the truth about adolescence and early adulthood, and believes that only a minority of adults experience a mid-life crisis. Those who ascribe to the life-events framework emphasize that attention should be paid to how various events influence the individual.

Neugarten believes that the central theme in adulthood is developing a sense of timing of major events in the life cycle. She believes that those few who do experience crises do so because of an interruption in the rhythm of adult development. Middle adulthood is a time of transition. Expectations of physical decline may influence perceptions of events. This is also a time when people must relinquish some power and status to younger adults.

In earlier versions of the life-events framework, the assumption was that life events forced personality changes. More recent, modified versions focus on the sociohistorical circumstances in which life events occur. In addition, it is important to note the age or life-stage of the individual, the probability of the event's occurrence, and the stressfulness of the event. Predictable events are typically less stressful. Both internal and external factors mediate the effects of life events on the individual. The life-events framework may be criticized as placing too much emphasis on change, and the lack of significance of the personal importance of the event. Lazarus has found that the frequency of major life events declines with age, but that life-events lists may exclude many events significant to older people.

Two theoretical approaches to personality development exist, one focused on similarities, the other on individual differences. According to Sarason, an individual's response to stress is influenced by at least five factors: the nature of the task or stress; the skills available; personality characteristics; social supports available; and the individual's history of stress-arousing experiences.

Longitudinal studies provide evidence for both stability and change in adulthood. Neugarten found stability in adaptive characteristics, and consistent age differences in intrapsychic dimensions. She sees adulthood as moving from active to passive mastery, accompanied in older adults by interiority. Costa and McCrae found stability in their three major dimensions: neuroticism, extraversion, and openness to experience. The California Longitudinal Study has yielded reports suggesting both stability in early adulthood and change in mid-life. Recent reports indicate that life satisfaction at age seventy can be predicted from some variables measured in the decade of the thirties.

Learning Objectives

1. Distinguish between passionate and companionate love, and trace the course of attachment and love relationships through adulthood. (p. 483)
2. Contrast the empty nest syndrome with the upswing thesis to characterize parental reactions to launching their offspring into adulthood. (p. 486)
3. Describe intergenerational relationships and the population trends which impact them. (p. 487)
4. Characterize intergenerational transmission in infancy, adolescence, and early adulthood, identifying the changing roles of the middle generation. (p. 489)
5. Identify parent-peer orientations and sex differences in intergenerational transmission. (p. 492)
6. Compare the personality theories and contributions of Erikson, Gould, Levinson, Peck, and Vaillant. (p. 494)
7. Criticize the crisis model of middle adulthood, and focus on issues of timing and time perspective. (p. 497)
8. Contrast the life-events framework and the issue of individual differences in middle adulthood. (p. 499)
9. Summarize the findings on stability and inconsistency in adult development of major longitudinal studies. (p. 504)

Key Terms

For each key term, write the definition in the space provided.

passionate love (1, p. 483) _____

companionate love (1, p. 483) _____

empty nest syndrome (2, p. 486) _____

upswing thesis (2, p. 486) _____

transformation (6, p. 494) _____

seasons of a man's life (6, p. 495) _____

valuing wisdom versus valuing physical powers (6, p. 496) _____

socializing versus sexualizing in human relationships (6, p. 496) _____

cathectic flexibility versus cathectic impoverishment (6, p. 496) _____

mental flexibility versus mental rigidity (6, p. 496) _____

career consolidation (6, p. 496) _____

keeping the meaning versus rigidity (6, p. 496) _____

mid-life crisis (7, p. 498) _____

life-events framework (8, p. 499) _____

active to passive mastery (9, p. 504) _____

interiority (9, p. 504) _____

Guided Review

1. Attachment and love are important throughout life. Berscheid and Walster have distinguished two types of _____ relationships. (1, p. 483)

love

2. Passionate _____ is intense, and involves a search for complete fulfillment. (1, p. 483)

love

3. By contrast, companionate love is much less _____ , and involves the feelings of affection we share with good friends. (1, p. 483)

intense

4. According to Levinger, relationships develop over time, moving from a surface type of relationship to a more intense, mutual style of _____ . (1, p. 483)

relationship

5. Over time, the passionate fires of youth are transformed into the the deeper, more tender _____ of old age. (1, p. 484)

love

6. Accordingly, researchers have found age differences in the nature of satisfying love relationships. Passion and sexual intimacy are more important to _____ adults. (1, p. 484)

young

7. By contrast, loyalty and sensitivity to feelings are more valued by _____ adults. (1, p. 484)

older

8. Aside from the age differences, there are many similarities in the nature of satisfying love relationships. At all ages, emotional security was ranked as the most important ingredient in a _____ relationship. (1, p. 484)

love

9. In this same study, by Reedy, Birren, and Schaie, there appears to be a shift toward increased valuing of security, fidelity, trust, and commitment in love _____ . (1, p. 485)

relationships

10. Eventually, children grow up and leave home, an event commonly referred to as _____ , which may remind you of the christening of a new ship. (2, p. 486)

launching

11. Because of the increasing life expectancy, and the trend to fewer children per family, the number of years a couple has to themselves after the children are launched is _____ . (2, p. 486)

increasing

12. A traditional view of this postchildrearing period suggested that parents lost their major life roles, and languished in the _____ nest. (2, p. 486)

empty

13. More recently, we have noted an increase in marital satisfaction in the postparental years, supportive of the upswing _____ . (2, p. 486)

thesis

14. One reason for this _____ thesis is that divorce is still increasing, and previously unhappy couples are no longer represented as couples in the postparental group. (2, p. 487)

upswing

15. Still another reason for the upswing may be that marital _____ for women is higher because they derive more satisfaction from career opportunities. (2, p. 487)

satisfaction

16. Besides parent-child and peer relationships, there are some interaction patterns which span generations. Intergenerational _____ can involve many different age segments. (3, p. 487)

relationships

17. Recent demographic changes in our population have had dramatic impact on _____ relationships. (3, p. 487)

intergenerational

18. Today, for example, the typical person lives longer and has fewer children. We see many families encompassing three or four _____ . (3, p. 487)

generations

19. Social and historical forces, which research depicts as cohort or period effects, serve to moderate _____ relationships. (3, p. 487)

intergenerational

20. Intergenerational transmission is enhanced to the extent that there is similarity between the _____ in terms of values and attitudes. (3, p. 487)

generations

21. Evidence suggests that there is considerable and frequent contact among family members of different _____ . (3, p. 488)

generations

22. Contact permits us to assess similarities. Parents and children are typically very _____ in their responses to issues of religion and politics. (3, p. 489)

similar

23. Intergenerational transmission begins even in infancy. The nature of a mother's relationship with her own mother is related to the mother's feelings toward the _____ , and by age four years, to the infant's perception of the mother. (4, p. 489)

infant

24. According to Erikson, middle-aged parents are involved in the crisis of _____ . (4, p. 489)

generativity

25. Generativity means the parents are helping a new group of children become _____ . (4, p. 489)

adults

26. At the same time, these _____ are experiencing the aging of their own parents, who need comfort and support from their middle-aged offspring. (4, p. 490)

parents

27. As children move from adolescence to adulthood, their interdependencies with their own _____ are renegotiated. (4, p. 490)

parents

28. Many of the young adult's social roles influence the relationship with the _____ of origin, and vice versa. (4, p. 490)

family

29. Thus, as the young adult marries and assumes an occupational role, ties with the _____ are carried forward to impact achievement motivation, marital relationships, and childrearing philosophies. (4, p. 491)

parents

30. In intergenerational _____ , the middle generation serves as a bridge between younger and older generations. (4, p. 492)

relationships

31. In areas such as sexual behavior and the use of illicit drugs, peer influences moderate intergenerational _____ , which is in turn more influential in achievement, work, and educational issues. (5, p. 492)

transmission

32. There are also sex differences. On entering adulthood, daughters continue to have more involved _____ with their parents, particularly their mothers, than do sons. (5, p. 492)

relationships

33. Now let's turn our attention to the individual, and the developing personality. There are several
_____ theories competing for our allegiance. (6, p. 494)

personality

34. According to Erikson, the crisis of middle adulthood is generativity. Individuals at this time need to assist the
_____ generation in developing and leading useful lives. (6, p. 494)

younger

35. Those without _____ of their own need to find substitutes, by volunteer efforts, foster parenthood, or through friends. (6, p. 494)

children

36. Another perspective is that of Gould, who suggests that _____ adulthood is as turbulent as adolescence, but that resolution of the crisis now leads to healthier, happier living. (6, p. 494)

middle

37. A major limitation of _____ theory is that it is based entirely on clinical observations and questionnaire data. (6, p. 494)

Gould's

38. Daniel Levinson also has suggested a theory of adult _____ development, based on his analysis of biographical material about forty middle-aged men. (6, p. 495)

personality

39. Levinson suggests that certain developmental tasks need to be mastered at each stage of development. One of those stages involves what Levinson calls becoming one's own man, abbreviated _____ . (6, p. 495)

BOOM

40. According to Levinson, middle adulthood involves four conflicts: being young versus being old, being constructive versus being destructive, being masculine versus being feminine, and being attached to others or _____ from them. (6, p. 494)

separated

41. Peck has suggested an expansion of Erikson's stages of adult development, and like Levinson suggests that we face four challenges in the middle _____ years. (6, p. 496)

adult

42. One of these challenges involves valuing wisdom versus valuing physical powers. Another is socializing versus _____ in relationships. (6, p. 496)

sexualizing

43. Peck also points to the challenges of cathectic flexibility versus cathectic impoverishment and mental flexibility versus mental _____ . (6, p. 496)

rigidity

44. Even Peck is not alone! George Vaillant has also suggested adding stages to Erikson's theory. Specifically, Vaillant wants to add two stages: career consolidation and what he calls keeping the meaning versus _____ . (6, p. 496)

rigidity

45. Please note that both Peck and Vaillant warn us of the dangers of developing _____ in middle adulthood. (6, p. 496)

rigidity

46. All these theories also share other common features. For example, they all suggest that adulthood begins in the transition from identity to _____ and ends in some final integration of the two. (6, p. 496)

intimacy

47. Most of these theories also suggest that some experience of crisis is normal during middle _____ . (7, p. 497)

adulthood

48. However, they may disagree about how common the crisis is. Levinson, for example, sees almost all mid-life adults experiencing a _____ , while Vaillant claims that crises are a rare experience. (7, p. 498)

crisis

49. One resolution to the argument over whether mid-life crisis is a common experience is provided by the life-events _____ , which focuses more on how events are likely to be interpreted by adults. (7, p. 498)

framework

50. Another view comes from Bernice Neugarten, who claims that the main theme of _____ life is developing a sense of timing of events. (7, p. 498)

adult

51. Neugarten believes that too much emphasis has been put on crisis and not enough on a psychology of _____ in adulthood. (7, p. 498)

timing

52. Thus, the real image of _____ adulthood should probably be one of transition, not crisis. But the expectations may produce the experience. (7, p. 499)

middle

53. For example, people entering _____ adulthood may well expect some physical decline, and thereby interpret events accordingly. (7, p. 499)

middle

54. All these perspectives focus on the individual, almost ignoring the environment. The life-events framework suggests that the _____ in a person's life heavily influence the development of the personality. (8, p. 499)

events

55. While earlier versions were oriented to stress as a component of life, more recent descriptions of the _____ framework have focused on the sociohistorical circumstances in which the events occur. (8, p. 500)

life-events

56. For example, events which are more predictable and for which the person is better prepared are likely to be experienced as less _____ than a sudden, unexpected event. (8, p. 500)

stressful

57. Like other approaches described above, the life-events framework also has some limitations. For example, there is great emphasis on change, and the typical lists of life _____ are certainly not exhaustive, particularly for older adults. (8, p. 500)

events

58. There are two major approaches to personality development; one focused on similarities, the other focused on _____ . (8, p. 501)

differences

59. Sarason, working primarily with the issue of anxiety, has pointed out the importance of considering individual _____ . (8, p. 502)

differences

60. Accordingly, we need an interactionist approach to adult _____ development; one which points out similarities but can account for individual variations. (8, p. 502)

personality

61. Still another issue (or another way of looking at things) addresses the question of stability and change in adult _____ development. (9, p. 504)

personality

62. One of the most famous of all longitudinal studies is that conducted by Neugarten and her research team. They identified a change in adulthood which she characterized as moving from active to _____ mastery. (9, p. 504)

passive

63. She also described another change: an increasing focus on the internal (mental) life, a trend she calls _____ . (9, p. 504)

● **interiority**

64. By contrast, Costa and McCrae identified three relatively consistent indices of adult personality: neuroticism, extraversion, and openness to experience, which they found to be fairly stable throughout _____ . (9, p. 505)

adulthood

65. The California Longitudinal Study is still yielding data, but it appears there is considerable _____ in the adult personality as that study is measuring it. (9, p. 505)

change (or variation)

66. As an example, the researchers attempted to find predictors in early adulthood for life satisfaction in later adulthood. They were able to find only a few significant _____ , and far more for men than for women. (9, p. 506)

predictors

67. All together, then, the evidence suggests we still have much to learn about the development of personality in _____ adulthood. (9, p. 505)

● **middle**

Right! Congratulations on completing another review. This has been a fairly lengthy one, so perhaps you would like to take a short break. Later, you can look over the learning objectives, then use the self test to measure your retention. Good luck!

Self Test

1. The definitive nature of companionate love is that it (1, p. 483)
   a. develops slowly
   b. is less intense than passionate love
   c. is momentary and lacks commitment
   d. is intense and seeks fulfillment

2. According to George Levinger, the "key" to lasting love relationships is (1, p. 484)
   a. sacrifice
   b. fidelity
   c. passion
   d. mutuality

3. It may surprise many people to learn that in a large study by Reedy, Birren, and Schaie, more men than women claimed their relationships were characterized by (1, p. 486)
   a. loyalty
   b. friendship
   c. respect
   d. communication

●

4. The "upswing thesis" is refuting the empty nest syndrome, supported by all of the following EXCEPT: (2, p. 486)
   a. a higher divorce rate
   b. more career opportunities for women
   c. fewer children per family
   d. an earlier age at marriage

5. In our observations of our friends and acquaintances, we should not be surprised to find that the people who visit their parents LEAST are (3, p. 488)
   a. Tom and Cathy, who are recently married
   b. Jack and Jill, who have two young children
   c. Karen and Richard, whose children are both teenagers
   d. Joan and Kurt, who live only three blocks away

6. Parents get blamed for many things, even after their children have grown into early adulthood. Many times, this is inappropriate, but NOT in the case of the young adult child who (5, p. 491)
   a. uses illicit drugs
   b. engages in deviant sexual practices
   c. works hard and gets a promotion
   d. volunteers for the "other" political party

7. Particularly at holiday times, parents of married adults are confused and sometimes even hurt at the behavior of their children. The operative description for these parents is (5, p. 492)
   a. You don't lose a son, you gain a daughter.
   b. We are, after all, a mother-centered society.
   c. Sons are always closer to home than daughters.
   d. Celebrate with his, grieve with hers.

8. Erikson's notions about generativity suggest that (6, p. 494)
   a. you must be a parent to be happy as an adult
   b. parents are happier than non-parents
   c. happiness derives from making a contribution to the younger generation's development
   d. if you don't have children, you should buy some from a Gypsy

9. According to Levinson, the transition to middle adulthood lasts about five years, and involves the conflict of (6, p. 495)
   a. being destructive versus being constructive
   b. socializing versus sexualizing in relationships
   c. keeping the meaning versus rigidity
   d. valuing wisdom versus valuing physical powers

10. The life-events framework, as a way of looking at adult personality development, (8, p. 500)
    a. supports those theories indicating crisis as the norm
    b. assumes that all changes are stressful
    c. is developing a social and historical perspective
    d. indicates increasing stress for the aging adult

Individual Learning Activity

As you can see from reading this chapter, much of the theorizing about the middle adult's personality is based on clinical and anecdotal data. This bothers the scientific community, including most academic psychologists, but it does not stop the proliferation of theoretical perspectives or the widespread publication of these tentative (and tenuous) models. Let's look for a minute at what is involved.

The derivation of most of these "theories" occurred in response to the reaction of one person (the author of each theory) to a series of interviews or questionnaires. Consider the nature of interviews. Even if tightly structured, with a list of questions carefully prepared in advance, each interview is slightly unique. Some interactions go well, some do not. Over the course of an hour or two, any person being interviewed is bound to say something that causes a response by the interviewer which the subject (or client) can interpret as disagreement or surprise. This necessarily influences the interview from that point on, and indeed influences the interviewer's interpretation of the dialogue.

On the other hand, biographical and interview materials are so rich a source of cognitive and affective experience that to ignore them would be absolutely inexcusable. In fact, many people enjoy reading biographies of less than famous people, simply for the rich texture of another life thus portrayed.

I want to encourage you to have the experience of conducting several interviews. Typically, a good clinical interview should last two hours or more, but for purposes of this experience much less time will suffice. It is important to structure the interview carefully in order to elicit the type of information you are going to use. Interview questions, however, must be open-ended. That is, the questions themselves must be worded in such a way that the person cannot answer simply "yes" or "no," but must provide some detail and some self-disclosure to support the response. Also, it is a good idea if the questions permit easy follow-up prompting, such as "Could you please give me an example of that?" or "I'm not too sure I understand that fully; could you tell me a little more about it?" Writing such questions is difficult, so here are a few examples to think about.

1. As you look back over your life, what milestones or major events seem to stand out?
2. How does each of these major events serve to organize your memories of other events and people in your life?
3. What two or three major goals have you already achieved, and what one or two goals are you now working on?
4. What have you found to be the typical course of relationships in your own experience?
5. What do you look forward to in the next five or ten years?

Now that you have seen these samples, please try to write a few of your own:

1. _____

2. _____

3. _____

4. _____

5. _____

Thank you! Now comes the fun part. Simply locate at least three middle-aged adults, and ask each of them at least three questions. (Of course, use the same questions for each person.) Having done that, you are ready to derive your own personal stage theory of middle adulthood. Simply look for common themes, give each a nice name, and array them in what seems an appropriate order. Of course, if you like, you may go on to do a Q-sort to improve the representational ability of your theory, but that would be beyond the scope of this project.

You should, however, ask a few people to look at your theory and comment on it. Don't be too flattered if they claim that you are clearly a visionary mystic to have divined such an accurate perception of adult development. Remember we all seek order in a chaotic world, and sometimes the temptation is to grab hold of whatever order we can. Perhaps that's why so many people bought *Passages*.

Answers to the Self Test

1. b	6. c
2. d	7. b
3. a	8. c
4. d	9. a
5. a	10. c

17 Physical and Cognitive Development

Preview

A greater percentage of the population is growing older. Since 1900, an individual's life expectancy has increased significantly, although the maximum life span has not.

Evidence suggests that heredity, health, education, personality characteristics, and life style are important ingredients in longevity. Researchers have found that continuity and rhythmic regularity of life, moderate diet, realistic life goals, a positive role for the elderly, and a positive self-image have contributed greatly to the long life span of the Abkhasians. In the Duke Longitudinal Study of Aging, the strongest predictors of longevity were physical function, nonsmoking, work satisfaction, and happiness.

Sex differences in longevity have been attributed to social patterns, which include health habits, lifestyles, and occupational choices. Even though sexual equality has become the norm, however, sex differences in longevity have increased. Therefore, we should suspect biological factors as the cause. In practically all animal species, females outlive males. Among humans, women have greater resistance to infectious and degenerative diseases.

Several biological theories attempt to understand the aging process, each with a slightly different perspective on the role of the genes. Hayflick asserts that cells are limited in their capacity to replicate themselves, thus limiting ultimate life span. Genetic error theories argue that aging is caused by a breakdown or error which develops in the DNA-RNA cellular system. Still another biological theory suggests that aging results from the decline in efficiency of the immune system, together with a rise in autoimmunity. Hormonal theory points to aging pacemakers in the brain which cause a sequence of hormonal changes which cause us to age. An alternative hormonal view suggests that blocking hormones begin to be produced soon after puberty, reducing absorption of thyroxine, producing in turn an excess of free radicals, mutations, cross-linkages, a build up of intracellular toxins, and autoimmunity. Macrobiological theories include homeostatic imbalance theory, which suggests that as organ reserve is diminished, so is the ability to withstand stress and restore homeostasis, until even the slightest perturbation results in death. Indeed, after the age of thirty, an individual's mortality rate doubles every eight years. Scientists now agree that there is a biological clock in the body which can be programmed.

In later adulthood, we find numerous physical changes. There is less elastin and more collagen. The maximum heart rate is more limited, and the arteries are narrower and more tortuous. Resting heart rate and blood pressure are both elevated, and less oxygen is transported to brain and lungs. Most researchers have reported changes in the brain including cell loss, inferred from a reduction of total mass, but there is currently some confusion about the extent of cellular losses. Visual changes include night blindness and delayed dark adaptation. Less light reaches the retina, which may also suffer degenerative changes. Visual acuity becomes less efficient with age. For most people, vision can be corrected by lenses until about age seventy, when correction becomes more difficult. Hearing loss in late adulthood typically results from degenerative changes in the cochlea. Wearing two hearing aids, balanced to permit correct orientation to sound sources, is often very helpful. Sensitivity to sweet and salty tastes diminishes before sensitivity to bitter and sour tastes. Sensitivity to pain also diminishes in late adulthood, which may provided a mixed blessing; it can be harmful if it masks injuries or illnesses requiring treatment.

Many of the chronic diseases lead to long-term illness and impairment. The most prevalent chronic diseases are arthritis, hearing impairment, vision impairment, and heart conditions. Women are more likely than men to have arthritis, hypertension, and visual problems, and less likely to have hearing problems. Low income is significantly related to health problems in late adulthood.

The need for intense exercise decreases in later adulthood, although its risks are greatly exaggerated. For most older people, regular exercise and physical activity slow down the deteriorative effects of aging.

Aging produces changes in sexual performance, particularly for the male. Frequency of orgasm drops to once in three coital episodes, and erection results only from more direct stimulation. However, there are no known limits to sexual activity, and sex education among the elderly often leads to improved interest and performance. White has concluded that males are more active sexually than females, that declines in the female's interest or activity reflect changes in the male partner, and that males do show a gradual decline in sexual activity with advancing age. It is important to note that physiological changes in the genitals do not account for the reduction or cessation of sexual activity in either sex, and that most research on sexuality and aging suffers from sample bias and methodological problems.

While there are no apparent age-related declines in selective attention tasks, age differences are clearly seen in divided attention tasks, particularly when many mental operations are required. These limitations involved in divided attention tasks may reflect reduced amounts of processing capacity, another example of reduced reserve capacity.

Memory-span performance is roughly constant from the twenties through the fifties, but declines in the sixties and seventies, perhaps due to a slowing in processing speed. In long-term memory, five control processes suggest specific changes and strategies for improvement. Rehearsal instructions improve recall among elderly subjects. Good organizational activities can reduce otherwise large age effects, as can semantic elaboration training. Imagery instructions also produce improvement, but older adults require more time to make effective use of imagery. There is no convincing evidence for age differences in retrieval processes.

While recall performance is usually better among younger subjects, using recognition tests sometimes attenuates age effects. Young adults do better on recall of "young-familiar" words, while old adults do better on recall of "old-familiar" words. There is no apparent decline in the amount of memory knowledge available for use. Age differences in performance typically involve tasks that remove previously learned relationships or strategies. Furthermore, it appears that there may not be declines in metamemory in aging.

The psychometric approach continues to be characterized by the argument between Horn and Schaie, Baltes, and Labouvie-Vief, over whether there is a drop in fluid intelligence in old age. Schaie, Baltes, and Labouvie-Vief argue that there is a great deal of plasticity in the cognitive functioning of elderly persons, but that our standardized tests were designed to measure stability, in much younger subjects. Nancy Denney points out that it is important to distinguish between unexercised and optimally exercised mental abilities.

Riegel and Riegel have found a developmental drop in IQ which occurs in the five years preceding death, and may be due to physiological or psychological processes. Intellectual decline is more likely in persons who have a chronic illness.

Complex skills, such as fluid intelligence, can be trained and modified in elderly persons, and do transfer to other tasks. Older adults can learn an efficient strategy for solving reasonably simple identification problems.

Productivity remains high in old-age, and enjoyable work may prolong life expectancy. Older workers are absent less often and have fewer accidents than younger workers. Atchley has described adjustment to retirement in seven phases: remote, near, honeymoon, disenchantment, reorientation, stability, and termination. Retirement brings a more leisurely pace and often financial restrictions, as well as a sense of not being part of a work-oriented culture. Some alternatives to sudden and/or forced retirement are phased retirement, slower work pace, and alterations of work roles.

Learning Objectives

1. Trace the changes in life expectancy since 1900, and distinguish between life expectancy and life span. (p. 515)
2. Describe major social patterns associated with long lives, and comment on sex differences in life expectancy, and their sources. (p. 517)
3. List and describe four biological theories of aging, including error theory, immune and hormonal theories, and homeostatic imbalance theory. (p. 520)
4. Describe physical changes associated with old age, including the cardiovascular, nervous, and sensory systems. (p. 522)
5. Summarize the desirability and effectiveness of exercise for very old individuals. (p. 525)
6. Describe sexual functioning among elderly persons, including the effects of sex education. (p. 528)
7. Trace age-related changes in selective and divided attention, processing capacity and speed, the utility of training in control processes in elderly adults, and the importance of task and subject variables in memory functions. (p. 530)
8. Characterize intellectual plasticity in old age, developmental drop, and the distinction between unexercised and optimally exercised abilities, and the relationship between physical health and cognition. (p. 534)
9. Describe the productivity of older workers, trace the course of retirement through Atchley's seven phases, and list alternatives to sudden or forced retirement. (p. 538)

Key Terms

For each key term, write the definition in the space provided.

life expectancy (1, p. 515) _____

genetic error theories (3, p. 521) _____

microbiological theory (3, p. 521) _____

macrobiological perspective (3, p. 521) _____

selective attention (7, p. 530) _____

divided attention (7, p. 530) _____

processing capacity (7, p. 531) _____

processing speed (7, p. 531) _____

rehearsal (7, p. 531) _____

metamemory (7, p. 533) _____

developmental drop (8, p. 535) _____

unexercised ability (8, p. 536) _____

optimally exercised ability (8, p. 536) _____

remote phase (9, p. 539) _____

near phase (9, p. 539) _____

honeymoon phase (9, p. 540) _____

disenchantment phase (9, p. 540) _____

reorientation phase (9, p. 540) _____

stability phase (9, p. 540) _____

termination phase (9, p. 540) _____

Guided Review

1. More and more people are living to an older age. For each of us, this means our life expectancy is _____ .
   (1, p. 515)

   increasing

2. Since 1900, the _____ _____ in this country has increased by
   twenty-two years. (1, p. 515)

   life expectancy

3. Although the _____ _____ has increased dramatically the life span
   has not changed! (1, p. 515)

   life expectancy

4. It is believed that the _____ _____ is limited by biological factors.
   (1, p. 515)

   life span

5. Several investigations have revealed factors which predict longevity. In the Duke Longitudinal Study of Aging, those factors which most strongly predicted _____ were physical function, nonsmoking, work satisfaction, and happiness. (2, p. 517)

longevity

6. While sex differences in longevity may vary somewhat from country to country, in our country, it is well known that _____ live longer. (2, p. 518)

women

7. The _____ differences in life expectancy are linked to health attitudes, habits, lifestyles, and occupational choices. (2, p. 518)

sex

8. Many authors have commented that these sex differences in longevity may result because _____ work in high-stress and hazardous occupations, and have more accidents. (2, p. 518)

males

9. As sex roles change and equality becomes the norm, we might look for these _____ _____ in life expectancy to disappear. (2, p. 518)

sex differences

10. However, the sex differences are widening! Thus, we should reasonably suspect that these differences may be due to biological factors; _____ are more resistant to infection and degenerative diseases than men are. (2, p. 519)

women

11. There are several biological _____ of aging, and each of them attributes an important role to genes. (3, p. 520)

theories

12. Hayflick reports that the cells of the body can only _____ and thus replace themselves a limited number of times. (3, p. 521)

divide

13. Genetic error _____ assert that aging results from some type of breakdown or errors that develop in the DNA-RNA system. (3, p. 521)

theories

14. Yet another biological theory of _____ relates aging to changes in the immune system. (3, p. 521)

aging

15. Each of us has a built in _____ system, which peaks in efficiency in adolescence. (3, p. 521)

immune

16. After adolescence, the efficiency of the _____ system declines. (3, p. 521)

immune

17. We also develop the capacity to attack our own cells, a function called _____ . (3, p. 521)

autoimmunity

18. We may also age because the efficiency of our hormonal system declines, according to _____ theory. (3, p. 521)

hormone (wasn't that easy?)

19. Finch believes that changes in certain brain centers cause neurological and _____ changes which result in aging. (3, p. 521)

hormonal

20. While all these theories of aging have been microbiological, there is also a _____ perspective. (3, p. 521)

macrobiological

21. The most prominent _____ theory is the homeostatic imbalance theory. (3, p. 521)

macrobiological

22. As we age, our organ reserve is reduced, and the loss of _____ _____ reduces our ability to maintain homeostasis. (3, p. 522)

organ reserve

23. If we cannot maintain _____ , or recover from stress, the result is death. (3, p. 522)

homeostasis

24. Proponents of the _____ _____ theory point to the linear decrease in organ reserve and the linear increase in mortality rate to support their views. (3, p. 522)

homeostatic imbalance

25. After age thirty, the individual's _____ rate doubles every eight years. (3, p. 522)

mortality

26. In later adulthood, we find many physical changes. Many of these _____ involve the cardiovascular system. (4, p. 522)

changes

27. There is less elastin and more collagen. The material which gives stretch to the heart and blood vessels is called _____ , and is reduced. (4, p. 522)

elastin

28. At the same time that there is less elastin, there is more _____ , a protein which stiffens vessel walls. (4, p. 522)

collagen

29. The maximum heart rate is reduced. This means that the _____ _____ does not increase as readily in response to stress. (4, p. 522)

heart rate

30. The arteries are more resistant to the flow of _____ , leading to a reduction in blood flow. (4, p. 522)

blood

31. Cardiac output is reduced, increasing the risk of _____ failure in highly stressful conditions. (4, p. 522)

heart

32. And, as a result of the increased resistance to blood flow and the decreased output of blood on each beat, the heart rate and _____ pressure both rise. (4, p. 522)

blood

33. Many of the chronic diseases associated with being _____ lead to long-term illness and impairment. (4, p. 522)

elderly (or old)

34. The four most prevalent _____ conditions are arthritis, hearing impairment, vision impairment, and heart conditions. (4, p. 522)

chronic

35. There are sex differences in health too, with _____ more likely to have arthritis and hypertension, and visual problems. (4, p. 522)

women

36. Low income is also strongly related to _____ problems in late adulthood, with three times as many poor people limited by chronic diseases. (4, p. 522)

health

37. There is some disagreement about changes in the nervous system. Specifically, argument rages over the extent of the loss of _____ associated with aging. (4, p. 523)

neurons

38. Changes also occur in the sensory systems. In vision, dark adaptation slows considerably, making it very difficult for the person to _____ at night. (4, p. 523)

drive

39. Furthermore, there is a reduction in area of the visual _____ , and degenerative changes occur in the retina. (4, p. 523)

field

40. Because of changes within the lens itself, the quality of light reaching the _____ is also reduced, and visual acuity is impaired. (4, p. 524)

retina

41. We can correct most visual problems adequately until about age seventy, after which only one in four adults has good _____ . (4, p. 524)

vision

42. With advancing age, there is also a loss of acuity in hearing, which affects men far more than it does _____ . (4, p. 524)

women

43. Degenerative changes of the cochlea are usually responsible for the loss of _____ . (4, p. 524)

hearing

44. Wearing two hearing aids which are _____ permits the person to orient to sound sources, and helps to reduce confusion. (4, p. 524)

balanced

45. The senses of smell, touch, and taste also become less efficient. Overall, the sensitivity to sweet and salty tastes diminishes faster than does sensitivity to sour and bitter _____ . (4, p. 524)

tastes

46. Also, older people are less sensitive to _____ than younger people are, so they are not as likely to suffer from minor aches and injuries. (4, p. 524)

pain

47. Many older people ask about the advisability of exercise. As people age, the need for _____ is reduced. (5, p. 525)

exercise

48. However, some _____ and physical activity appear to slow down the deterioration of the body. (5, p. 525)

exercise

49. Late adulthood brings some changes in sexual performance, particularly for the _____ . (6, p. 528)

male

50. Orgasm becomes _____ frequent for the male, perhaps occurring only once in two or three coital episodes. (6, p. 528)

less

51. Also, more _____ stimulation is required to produce an erection, but the male can maintain the erection for a longer period of time. (6, p. 528)

direct

52. Although these changes occur, there is no known age _____ to sexual activity. (6, p. 528)

limit

53. Sexual education, involving simply providing information, leads to an increase of sexual interest and _____ . (6, p. 528)

activity (or performance)

54. Except in very old samples where there are no differences, _____ are more sexually active than _____ . (6, p. 528)

males, females

55. When the _____ ceases to be sexually active, it is usually in response to declining interest or ability in the partner. (6, p. 528)

female

56. We now turn our attention to cognitive functions. The _____ _____ view of cognitive functions looks separately at perception, attention, memory, and the characteristics of the material and the learner. (7, p. 530)

information processing

57. There are age differences in attention, but not in all aspects. It is questionable whether there are age differences in selective _____ . (7, p. 530)

attention

58. Difficulties are more likely to be due to age differences in divided _____ tasks. (7, p. 530)

attention

59. Trying to listen to two conversations at once is an example of a _____ _____ task. (7, p. 530)

divided attention

60. Simply ignoring irrelevant noise is easier, a skill called _____ _____ . (7, p. 530)

selective attention

61. One explanation for the difficulty in _____ attention tasks is the concept of limited processing capacity. (7, p. 531)

divided

62. Short-term _____ shows very little decline with age. (7, p. 531)

memory

63. However, there is evidence of some slowing of _____ memory processes. (7, p. 531)

short-term

64. Investigations of long-term memory functions have focused on five control processes. Rehearsal is one such _____ process, and rehearsal instructions improved recall performance. (7, p. 531)

control

65. Older adults do not spontaneously use organization as much as younger adults do, but when instructed to do so, the organization of the material _____ the age effect to some extent. (7, p. 531)

reduced

66. Imagery instructions also improved the long-term memory performance of the _____ , but they required more time to effectively use the imagery than did younger adults. (7, p. 532)

elderly

67. As we might suspect, performance is better on _____ tests than on recall tests. (7, p. 532)

recognition

68. The materials used in these experiments are important. People of all ages do better when we use stimuli with which they are _____ . (7, p. 533)

familiar

69. Can aging adults learn new material? Research shows that they can, but this ability to learn new material is reduced if the _____ material conflicts with previously learned skills or knowledge. (7, p. 533)

new

70. It also appears that the improvements in metamemory commonly seen in children are not necessarily mirrored by _____ in later adulthood. (7, p. 534)

decline

71. The psychometric view is dominated by the debate between Cattell and Horn and Schaie, Baltes, and Labouvie-Vief, over whether _____ intelligence declines with age. (8, p. 534)

fluid

72. Schaie, Baltes, and Labouvie-Vief assert that there is considerable plasticity in cognitive functions among the elderly. The problem, they say, is that our intelligence tests are designed to measure stability, not _____ . (8, p. 534)

plasticity

73. Riegel has found a significant _____ in IQ scores in the five years before death. (8, p. 535)

decline

74. This developmental _____ , as it is called, may be due to physiological or psychological factors. (8, p. 535)

drop

75. Nancy Denney asserts that one should expect to see a decline in those functions and abilities which are not _____ . (8, p. 536)

exercised

76. Denney distinguishes between optimally exercised abilities, which she speculates will _____ less, and unexercised abilities, which should decline more. (8, p. 536)

decline

77. We have talked about health, and about cognition. Many experts wonder if _____ and cognition are related. (8, p. 535)

health

78. People who are ill typically do _____ on intelligence tests. (8, p. 535)

poorly

79. One reason for studying various facets of cognition in old age is the possibility of intervention. Studies have shown that such complex skills as those involved in fluid _____ can be modified and can transfer to new situations. (8, p. 537)

intelligence

80. Until recently, almost everyone had to _____ at age sixty-five, yet many older persons would rather work. (9, p. 538)

retire

81. In fact, productivity in old age is apparently the rule, and not the _____ . (9, p. 538)

exception

82. Older workers have better attendance records and fewer disabling _____ than younger workers. (9, p. 538)

accidents

83. Perhaps because of these facts, the age of mandatory _____ has been raised. (9, p. 538)

retirement

84. Atchley has identified seven phases of _____ : remote, near, honeymoon, disenchantment, reorientation, stability, and termination. (9, p. 539)

retirement

85. People do not prepare for retirement, and act as though it will never come, during the _____ phase. (9, p. 539)

remote

86. Workers usually participate in preretirement programs during the _____ phase. (9, p. 539)

near

87. These _____ programs can be very helpful, although good ones are not available to most people. (9, p. 539)

preretirement

88. Those people who do take advantage of good _____ programs usually have higher income and engage in more activities in retirement. (9, p. 540)

preretirement

89. Just after retirement, many people feel euphoric, a time called the _____ phase. (9, p. 540)

honeymoon

90. Later there is a sense of letdown, perhaps even depression, as the person enters the _____ phase. (9, p. 540)

disenchantment

91. Most disenchanted individuals come to grips with the reality of the situation and decide to make the best of it during the _____ phase. (9, p. 540)

reorientation

92. When the person has established a set of criteria for evaluating choices and carrying through, he or she has entered the phase of _____ . (9, p. 540)

stability

93. As health eventually fails, and the individual becomes dependent on others, retirement enters the _____ phase. (9, p. 540)

termination

94. When a person _____ , his financial resources are reduced. (9, p. 541)

retires

95. In addition, ready or not, he is expected to enjoy a life of _____ instead of work. (9, p. 540)

leisure

96. Some alternatives to sudden _____ include alterations in time spent on the job, alterations in the job itself, and alterations of roles within organizations. (9, p. 541)

retirement

97. Such strategies as phased _____ , taking a slower pace, and lateral transfers could make the shock of retirement much more bearable. (9, p. 541)

retirement

Well, that concludes this review. Feel free to take a break (reward yourself for studying well), before you review the learning objectives. The self test is next.

Self Test

1. Since 1900, the human life span has (1, p. 515)
   a. doubled
   b. increased by 50 percent
   c. not changed significantly
   d. been shortened by new diseases

2. Most of the sex differences in life expectancy are due to (2, p. 519)
   a. occupational differences
   b. the emotional superiority of females
   c. social factors
   d. the female's better resistance to infection

3. Genetic error theory suggests that aging results from (3, p. 521)
   a. errors in taking prescription drugs
   b. having cells destroyed by physical trauma
   c. cell destruction from chemical agents, such as drugs
   d. unrepaired error in the RNA

4. Proponents of homeostatic imbalance theory point to the linear loss of (3, p. 522)
   a. immune system activity
   b. organ reserve
   c. autoimmunity
   d. mortality risk

5. In later adulthood, physical changes include (4, p. 522)
   a. a reduction in elastin
   b. increased elasticity of the aorta
   c. smoother arterial walls
   d. lower heart rate

6. Exercise for an old person (5, p. 525)
   a. is dangerous
   b. is very necessary
   c. slows the effects of aging
   d. prevents heart attacks

7. Men are more likely than women to have (4, p. 522)
   a. arthritis
   b. hypertension
   c. visual impairments
   d. hearing impairments

8. Riegel found a drop in IQ (8, p. 535)
   a. reflecting a regression from formal operations
   b. within the five years before death
   c. associated only with cardiovascular problems
   d. more often among men than women

9. Older individuals (7, p. 530)
   a. are less sensitive to distraction than younger adults
   b. show no declines in short-term memory
   c. perform well on divided attention tasks
   d. have little trouble with selective attention

10. When a recognition test is combined with careful control of encoding strategies or control processes, older adults (7, p. 532)
    a. do almost as well as younger adults
    b. do very poorly
    c. cannot perform on the task at all
    d. find the experience irrelevant and unmotivating

Individual Learning Activity

In this chapter we have learned many things about older individuals, and we have seen that in many cases older people are not treated well, and do not receive their fair share of goods and services. While some of the unfair treatment is due to archaic attitudes, some is due to ignorance. Dispelling ignorance is the obligation of those who have knowledge, so now it is your turn.

This activity is simple in design, but will provide you with a comprehensive review of the chapter, helping you to encode the information into long-term memory in a more meaningful way. Instantly you are a consultant to powerful people everywhere, and your advice will receive the most serious consideration. Got it? Good. Your task is to prepare a list of recommendations, drawn from the literature you reviewed in this chapter, to help teachers, physicians, nurses, therapists of all types, and other professionals who deal with older people. Your list should be divided into four parts:

1. How best to design and control the environment in which older people work with us.
2. How best to present visual information to older people.
3. How best to present verbal information to older people.
4. How best to assess or test older people.

Based on the information in this chapter, you should have no problem drawing up a substantial list. Try to make your suggestions simple but in accord with the evidence on physical and cognitive changes common in older people.

Answers to the Self Test

1. c	6. c
2. d	7. d
3. d	8. b
4. b	9. d
5. a	10. a

18 Social, Emotional, and Personality Development

Preview

Social theories of aging include disengagement theory, activity theory, and social breakdown theory. Disengagement theory argues that successful aging involves the reciprocal disengagement of the individual from society. From research which did not support this theory, Neugarten and her associates developed activity theory, which suggests that activity and involvement are associated with high life satisfaction. These researchers identified four personality styles: integrated, armored-defended, passive-dependent, and unintegrated. Social breakdown theory suggests that aging is promoted through negative functioning involving a poor self-concept and a lack of skills. According to this theory, we can prevent social breakdown by reorganizing our social system to provide respect for the elderly.

Ageism, a form of prejudice against old people, is a particular problem in our culture. While our culture values youth, other cultures revere and respect the elderly for their accumulated wisdom. This is particularly true of cultures where adult responsibilities are reciprocal, such as those of China and Japan.

One of the major concerns of older people is decrease in income, which leads to a high rate of poverty. There may be as many as five million hidden poor among the elderly. Poverty is more likely for women than men, and for nonwhites than for whites. In recent years, a reasonable breadth of social services for the elderly has been developed, and the family continues to play a major role.

Retirement alters life style, particularly in traditional families where both spouses may need to learn more expressive roles. Marital happiness in later life is influenced by each individual's ability to deal with personal conflicts. Individuals, particularly women, who are married are happier than single people, but those older people who have never married have less trouble with loneliness. The Terman subjects indicated increasing numbers of women who said they were less satisfied with their marriages at age seventy than at age thirty, while there were no differences in satisfaction for men. For women, the longitudinal changes matched cohort differences, as did the changes for men, with one exception: the move to more egalitarian views of dominance in marriage appears to be truly developmental, changing from age thirty to age seventy.

Three meanings are attached to the grandparenting role: biological renewal, emotional self-fulfillment, and remoteness or little importance. The three styles of grandparenting are formal, fun-seeking, and distant figure.

Old people place a high value on friendship, which can provide important support at times of divorce or death of a spouse, or when family members are distant, and because families are growing smaller.

Freud believed that in old age we again become narcissistic, and Jung believed that thought in old people is submerged in the unconsciousness, away from reality. More contemporary personality theorists do not agree with these views. Erikson focuses on later life as a crisis of ego integrity versus despair. Reviewing our lives and finding that we have lived well, produces integrity. Looking back and regretting our decisions and life path leads to despair. Peck claims that in old age three issues must be confronted: ego differentiation versus work-role preoccupation, body transcendence versus body preoccupation, and ego transcendence versus ego preoccupation. Butler agrees with Erikson, and suggests that the life review is set in motion by looking forward to death. The life review permits reorganization of past experience and the sharing with family and close friends unknown characteristics of personality. The reciprocal disclosures may permit the emergence of hidden themes of great meaning.

Life satisfaction is determined largely by health and income, and is supported by an active lifestyle. The Terman longitudinal study revealed that coping styles of work persistence and unbroken marriage are major predictors of life satisfaction in old age. Among gifted women, those who worked reported more satisfaction with life.

There is continuing debate over whether sex roles change in late adulthood. The consensus of research findings appears to be that males do show an increase in feminine traits, or a decrease in masculine traits, although females do not show an increase in masculine traits.

A basic underlying theme of stress and coping is that we struggle constantly to make sense of our experiences. This mental and emotional struggle has important implications for health, happiness, success, and interpersonal relationships. Mental health, defined as both the absence of mental illness, difficulties and frustrations, and the capacity to deal effectively with life issues, is a major problem among the elderly. Depression is the most common problem, and is often treated with antidepressant drugs, such as the tricyclics, which also have a sedative effect and help to regulate sleep. Group psychotherapy has also become popular with some success. The most controversial and confounding set of disturbances are grouped together as the dementias, characterized by a deterioration of intelligence and behavior. Alzheimer's disease is the most common of the dementias, accounting for about half of all cases. Although we have some clues to its origins, we have no effective treatment to date. Dementia syndromes may also be caused by drugs, toxins, and physical illness. In at least 10 to 30 percent of all dementia situations, treatment is at least partly successful.

The extent of mental disorders among the elderly is difficult to estimate, since many do not seek treatment and some have more than one problem. Psychologists must be encouraged to work with the elderly, and their care must be made more affordable. Some study of aging should be included in the undergraduate programs in psychology and related areas, to encourage professional interest.

Learning Objectives

1. Compare social theories of aging, including disengagement theory, activity theory, and social breakdown theory. (p. 547)
2. Define *ageism,* and summarize cross-cultural comparisons of treatment of elderly adults. (p. 548)
3. Describe the extent of poverty among the elderly, and provide examples of services available to help them. (p. 549)
4. Trace the pattern of the marriage and family relationships in old age, and the effects of marriage on life satisfaction. (p. 550)
5. List and define the three meanings of grandparenthood, and three styles of grandparenting. (p. 552)
6. Create a brief scenario to demonstrate the importance and sources of friendships in old age. (p. 552)
7. Summarize the positions of Freud and Jung on personality in old age, and compare these with the work of Erikson, Robert Peck, and Robert Butler. (p. 554)

8. Identify the variables important in the determination of life satisfaction, and comment on alleged changes in sex roles. (p. 555)
9. Describe mental health concerns and problems of elderly adults, and the determinants and treatment of the major disorders. (p. 557)

Key Terms

For each key term, please write the definition in the space provided.

disengagement theory (1, p. 547) ⎯⎯⎯⎯⎯⎯⎯⎯⎯⎯⎯⎯⎯⎯⎯⎯⎯⎯⎯⎯⎯⎯⎯

activity theory (1, p. 548) ⎯⎯⎯⎯⎯⎯⎯⎯⎯⎯⎯⎯⎯⎯⎯⎯⎯⎯⎯⎯⎯⎯⎯⎯⎯

social breakdown theory (1, p. 548) ⎯⎯⎯⎯⎯⎯⎯⎯⎯⎯⎯⎯⎯⎯⎯⎯⎯⎯⎯⎯⎯⎯

ageism (2, p. 548) ⎯⎯⎯⎯⎯⎯⎯⎯⎯⎯⎯⎯⎯⎯⎯⎯⎯⎯⎯⎯⎯⎯⎯⎯⎯⎯⎯⎯⎯⎯

life review (7, p. 554) ⎯⎯⎯⎯⎯⎯⎯⎯⎯⎯⎯⎯⎯⎯⎯⎯⎯⎯⎯⎯⎯⎯⎯⎯⎯⎯⎯⎯

life satisfaction (8, p. 555) ⎯⎯⎯⎯⎯⎯⎯⎯⎯⎯⎯⎯⎯⎯⎯⎯⎯⎯⎯⎯⎯⎯⎯⎯⎯

dementia (9, p. 560) ⎯⎯⎯⎯⎯⎯⎯⎯⎯⎯⎯⎯⎯⎯⎯⎯⎯⎯⎯⎯⎯⎯⎯⎯⎯⎯⎯

Alzheimer's disease (9, p. 561) ⎯⎯⎯⎯⎯⎯⎯⎯⎯⎯⎯⎯⎯⎯⎯⎯⎯⎯⎯⎯⎯⎯⎯

Guided Review

1. In addition to biological theories of aging, there are also social ⎯⎯⎯⎯⎯⎯⎯⎯⎯ of aging. (1, p. 547)

   theories

2. Disengagement theory proposes that as the person ages, there should be a mutual ⎯⎯⎯⎯⎯⎯⎯⎯⎯ of the person from society and society from the person. (1, p. 547)

   disengagement

3. Several research studies fail to support hypotheses derived from ⎯⎯⎯⎯⎯⎯⎯⎯⎯ theory. (1, p. 547)

   disengagement

4. Neugarten, Havighurst, and Tobin found that activity and involvement are associated with high levels of life satisfaction, and proposed ⎯⎯⎯⎯⎯⎯⎯⎯⎯ theory. (1, p. 547)

   activity

5. They categorized people in late ⎯⎯⎯⎯⎯⎯⎯⎯⎯ into four personality styles. (1, p. 547)

   adulthood

6. The four ⎯⎯⎯⎯⎯⎯⎯⎯⎯ were: integrated, armored-defended, passive-dependent, and unintegrated. (1, p. 548)

   styles

7. People who were engaged and involved were called ⎯⎯⎯⎯⎯⎯⎯⎯⎯ . (1, p. 548)

   integrated

8. Those who were holding on to middle-aged roles were described as _____ . (1, p. 548)

armored-defended

9. Those individuals who were sometimes apathetic, with low to medium activity levels, were termed _____ . (1, p. 548)

passive-dependent

10. And those who were disorganized, or showed deteriorated cognitive processes or weak emotional control were labeled as _____ . (1, p. 548)

unintegrated

11. Those who were more active and involved, the _____ and _____ types, were found to have the highest life satisfaction. (1, p. 548)

integrated, armored-defended

12. According to _____ theory, if roles are lost or taken away, the individual should find substitute roles and activities. (1, p. 548)

activity

13. The third social _____ of aging is social breakdown theory. (1, p. 548)

theory

14. According to this _____ , aging is promoted by negative psychological functioning, a poor self-concept, negative feedback from others, and a lack of skills. (1, p. 548)

theory

15. Thus, _____ _____ begins with susceptibility and ends with identification of the self as incompetent. (1, p. 548)

social breakdown

16. In order to prevent _____ _____ , we should arrange the social system so older people are treated with more respect, and feel more competent. (1, p. 548)

social breakdown

17. Ageism is a form of prejudice against _____ people, which is particularly prevalent in the United States. (2, p. 548)

older

18. Although in our culture we do not treat elderly people very well, the same is not true in other _____ . (2, p. 549)

cultures

19. In China and Japan, the _____ are rewarded for their skills and knowledge, often being considered as the most important figures. (2, p. 549)

elderly

20. A major concern of older people is the decrease in _____ which often follows retirement. (3, p. 549)

income

21. Poverty among the elderly is more common for _____ than for men, and for nonwhites than for whites. (3, p. 550)

women

22. In addition to support from the family, there are a wide range of services available to _____ Americans, as a result of numerous government programs. (3, p. 550)

elderly (or old)

23. Patterns of life within marriage change when a person _____ from work. (4, p. 550)

retires

24. The changes produced by _____ are greatest in traditional families. (4, p. 550)

retirement

25. In such _____ families, both spouses may need to learn more expressive roles in order to maintain the relationship. (4, p. 550)

traditional

26. Individuals, particularly _____ , who are married, appear to be happier than those who are single. (4, p. 551)

women

27. But old persons who have never been _____ have less trouble with loneliness. (4, p. 551)

married

28. When your children have children, you will be a _____ . (5, p. 552)

grandparent

29. There are three meanings to the _____ role. (5, p. 552)

grandparent

30. One meaning is biological renewal or continuity, in which the _____ is extended into the future through the grandchild. (5, p. 552)

grandparent

31. Another _____ is emotional self-fulfillment, in which feelings of companionship emerge which were missing in earlier relationships. (5, p. 552)

meaning

32. For some, the role of _____ is remote, meaning little to them. (5, p. 552)

grandparent

33. Three styles of interaction used by _____ have also been identified: formal, fun-seeking, and distant. (5, p. 552)

grandparents

34. Grandparents who are careful not to give parenting advice, but enjoy their grandchildren, are called _____ . (5, p. 552)

formal

35. Grandparents who are informal and playful, emphasizing mutual satisfaction, are called _____ . (5, p. 552)

fun-seeking

36. And grandparents who are benevolent but visit infrequently are called _____ . (5, p. 552)

distant

37. Grandparents older than sixty-five are often _____ , while those younger than sixty-five are more likely to be fun-seeking. (5, p. 552)

formal

38. Aside from family contacts, people of all ages, including the elderly, enjoy spending time with their _____ . (6, p. 552)

friends

39. After the death of a spouse, _____ provide an important source of support. (5, p. 552)

friends

40. As family size continues to shrink, _____ may become even more important to the elderly person. (5, p. 553)

friends (or friendships)

41. Several theorists have written about the development of personality in old age. For example, Freud believed that _____ people returned to narcissism. (7, p. 554)

old

228

42. Consuming love for oneself is what Freud meant by _____ . (7, p. 554)

narcissism

43. Jung thought that in old age thought is submerged in the _____ , gradually sinking until no contact with reality remains. (7, p. 554)

unconscious

44. Erikson has also written (eloquently) about personality development in _____
_____ . (7, p. 554)

old age

45. According to _____ , the last crisis of life is that of ego integrity versus despair. (7, p. 554)

Erikson

46. If we look back and find that we have lived a satisfying life, we will achieve _____ .
(7, p. 554)

integrity

47. If we look back with dismay and gloom over our lives, seeing a series of mistakes and blunders, we will be likely to develop a sense of _____ . (7, p. 554)

despair

48. As _____ says it so well, each of us will ultimately come to appreciate that we are "what survives of us." (7, p. 554)

Erikson

49. Robert Peck has reworked _____ notion of integrity versus despair. (7, p. 554)

Erikson's

50. Peck claims we must confront three issues in _____ age. (7, p. 554)

old

51. One _____ is ego differentiation versus work-role preoccupation. (7, p. 554)

issue

52. People should not dwell on their _____ _____ in defining themselves, but should explore and grow beyond it, according to Peck. (7, p. 554)

work role

53. The second _____ we confront, according to Peck's model, is body transcendence versus body preoccupation. (7, p. 554)

issue

54. If we constantly complain about our ills, we are suffering from _____ _____ .
    (7, p. 554)

body preoccupation

55. But if we find our sense of well-being from relationships and activities, we are accomplishing _____
    _____ . (7, p. 554)

body transcendence

56. The third and last _____ is ego transcendence versus ego preoccupation. (7, p. 554)

issue

57. Peck points out that we must come to grips on a very personal level with the fact that _____
    is inevitable. (7, p. 554)

death

58. Then, directing our lives toward what we can do, and realizing what we have contributed to the future, we
    accomplish what Peck calls _____ _____ . (7, p. 554)

ego transcendence

59. Robert Butler agrees with Erikson that in late _____ the person should look back and
    review life. (7, p. 554)

adulthood

60. This process, which _____ calls the life review, is initiated by the knowledge that death is
    inevitable. (7, p. 554)

Butler

61. As the person gets older, more and more time is spend thinking about the past, accomplishing the _____
    _____ . (7, p. 555)

life review

62. As the life review proceeds, the individual may share with family and close friends, previously unknown
    characteristics of the _____ , and may uncover hidden themes of great meaning.
    (7, p. 555)

personality

63. Of course, we want to see our lives as satisfying. In a study by Markides and Martin, health and income were
    the most important predictors of life _____ . (8, p. 555)

satisfaction

64. Another important determinant of _____ _____ is activity. (8, p. 555)

life satisfaction

65. According to the data from the Terman follow-up studies, _____ _____ focused on two areas: occupation and family life. (8, p. 556)

life satisfaction

66. Work persistence into the sixties was the primary coping style for the variable they called _____ . (8, p. 556)

occupation

67. Unbroken marriage was the family life pattern most often found among those high in _____ _____ . (8, p. 556)

life satisfaction

68. Among the gifted women, those who worked, primarily in professional careers, had higher _____ _____ . (8, p. 556)

life satisfaction

69. Indeed, many of the Terman women who had not worked outside the home would now opt for a career if they had the opportunity to relive their _____ . (8, p. 556)

lives

70. There is a continuing debate over whether there are changes in the sex roles in late _____ . (8, p. 556)

adulthood

71. While the evidence is still somewhat soft, coming from projective tests and self-reports of self-concept, it does appear that there is an increase in sex-typed feminine traits in older _____ . (8, p. 556)

men

72. At the same time, however, there does not seem to be as strong a tendency for an increase in sex-typed masculine traits among older _____ . (8, p. 556)

women

73. Throughout our lives, we struggle to make sense out of what is happening to us. This _____ , which is both mental and emotional, has significant implications for our health, mental stability, competence, and success. (8, p. 556)

struggle

231

74. Sometimes, we are not able to _____ _____ _____ _____
successfully, and become unable to deal with what is happening to us. (9, p. 556)

make sense of things

75. We are becoming more aware of mental health problems among the _____. (9, p. 557)

elderly

76. The absence of mental illness, and the ability to deal with life issues in a satisfying and effective manner, defines _____ _____ . (9, p. 557)

mental health

77. Many _____ adults are depressed. There are often real reasons, due to real losses, for feeling depressed. (9, p. 557)

older

78. Also, _____ people are often avoided by family and friends, adding to feelings of loneliness. (9, p. 557)

depressed

79. Many older people who are _____ have been successfully treated with antidepressant drugs. (9, p. 558)

depressed

80. The tricyclic _____ are currently the most popular drugs used to treat depression, and are available in compounds like imipramine, and under trade names such as Tofranil. (9, p. 558)

antidepressants

81. These _____ antidepressants also produce a sedative effect, helping the depressed person to regulate sleep patterns. (9, p. 558)

tricyclic

82. Group psychotherapy has also proved helpful in the treatment of _____ among both young and elderly adults. (9, p. 558)

depression

83. Aside from depression, the dementias are the most confusing and troubling disturbances which afflict _____ adults. (9, p. 560)

older (or elderly)

84. A _____ is often considered a chronic, irreversible condition, but in reality many of them can be successfully treated. (9, p. 560)

dementia

85. The problem is that a _____ is simply a clinical syndrome, a cluster of symptoms, not in itself the cause of any disorder. (9, p. 560)

dementia

86. About half of all dementias are in fact Alzheimer's disease, for which there is as yet no known _____ . (9, p. 561)

cure (or treatment)

87. Sometimes depression in the elderly also mimics the symptoms of _____ . This same clinical picture may be caused by drugs or physical illness. (9, p. 562)

dementia

88. In fact, a thyroid disorder, hyperthyroidism, can cause the _____ syndrome, but is readily reversed. (9, p. 562)

dementia

89. It is very difficult to estimate the number of older people who have emotional or mental problems. Many of them do not seek _____ . (9, p. 562)

treatment

90. In addition, many have more than one problem, so categorizing the problems is difficult. Yet, community surveys regularly find a large number of _____ people suffering from depression and other disorders. (9, p. 562)

older

91. We have not done well in meeting the mental health needs of the elderly. First, we must encourage psychologists to do more work with the _____ . We must also make such care affordable. (9, p. 562)

elderly

92. To stimulate interest in geropsychology, it might be helpful to build in the study of aging into undergraduate programs in _____ and related fields. (9, p. 562)

psychology

Congratulations on completing another unit review! After you take a break for appropriate reward ceremonies, please look over the learning objectives. Next comes the self test.

Self Test

1. According to Neugarten, Havighurst, and Tobin, which of the following is likely to have the highest life satisfaction in old age? (1, p. 548)
   a. unintegrated
   b. disengaged
   c. passive-dependent
   d. armored-defended

2. Marital happiness in late adulthood is influenced heavily by (4, p. 550)
   a. the availability of friends
   b. how close children live
   c. the choice of grandparent roles
   d. each person's ability to develop expressive abilities

3. The happiest person in later life is likely to be the (4, p. 551)
   a. married female
   b. single female
   c. widowed male
   d. married male

4. Compared to the United States, Japan (2, p. 549)
   a. places more value on the knowledge of old people
   b. is changing more rapidly in its attitudes toward the aged
   c. avoids the trap of reciprocal family patterns
   d. avoids ageism by having no retirement system

5. Grandparents who are careful not to interfere in the parenting of the grandchildren are described as (5, p. 552)
   a. fun-seeking
   b. distant
   c. formal
   d. remote

6. According to social breakdown theory, the social breakdown can be avoided altogether by providing the elderly with (1, p. 548)
   a. jobs
   b. respect
   c. more money
   d. preventative treatment for depression

7. According to Freud, old people become increasingly (7, p. 554)
   a. unconscious
   b. detached from reality
   c. reminiscent
   d. narcissistic

8. According to Peck, we should find a sense of well being from our (7, p. 554)
   a. work roles
   b. health
   c. activities
   d. physical stamina

9. According to Markides and Martin, the two most important factors in predicting life satisfaction are (8, p. 555)
   a. health and income
   b. activity and housing
   c. intimacy with children and income
   d. health and housing

10. A major problem in dealing with depression among the elderly is that (9, p. 557)
    a. depression is caused by organic factors
    b. the causes of depression cannot be treated
    c. people who are depressed are not in contact with reality
    d. family and friends avoid depressed people

Individual Learning Activity

You and I are going to achieve fame and wealth! We are going to be invited to every major talk show, and our work will be featured on the evening news. Our names will be household words, and we will be revered by generations to come. Do I have your interest?

This activity will help you learn and remember all you need to know about older people. We are going to design the world's best living arrangement for elderly people, based on the research reported in this chapter. I know you will actually be able to do this, and I regret to tell you that it is not usually done this way.

In order to guide your work, here are some questions to answer. Don't write down the answers directly, but see if you can use them to organize your planning.

1. What type of arrangement do we want, nursing or home care, or apartment complex?
2. How many stories, and how many units per floor do we want?
3. Please draw a rough floor plan, showing each unit or apartment, hallways, stairs and elevators, bathrooms, etc.
4. What about lighting, windows, and furnishings? To what extent can each person design and alter the arrangements?
5. Where will this complex be in terms of other community resources, housing, stores, etc.?
6. What type of activities will you schedule for the residents of the complex?
7. What common or public spaces will be provided, such as lounges or community rooms for parties?
8. What staff will be provided as resources for the residents?
9. What arrangements will be made for easy transportation for residents who do not have cars?
10. What arrangements will be made regarding the age of the residents? Will you recruit people of all ages? Will children be welcome?

As you can see, the design of an environment for an older person is a difficult task. Most of the places in which elderly people live were not designed for elderly people. Your design will undoubtedly be better!

Answers to the Self Test

1. d	6. b
2. d	7. d
3. a	8. c
4. a	9. a
5. c.	10. d

Section IX Death and the Dying Process

---

19 Death and the Dying Process

Preview

The ultimate truth of life is that each of us will die. Historically, death was defined by cessation of respiration and circulation, followed by rigor mortis, pupillary dilation, and sphincter relaxation. In recent years, we have seen confusion over the definition of death, including the neurological definition of brain death based on a flat EEG. The ability to resuscitate a dying person complicates the definition of death, and raises ethical and legal questions.

Euthanasia traditionally refers to the act of painlessly putting to death people suffering from incurable disease or severe disability. Active euthanasia involves inducing death by some positive action, such as a lethal drug. While passive euthanasia reflects the withdrawal of heroic or extraordinary measures, seen by some as simply letting nature take its course. The current debate over euthanasia has deviated from the traditional focus on irreversible pain, and focused instead on the quality of life or the costs, both financial and psychological, of care.

In some cultures old people are killed or allowed to die when they are no longer productive. In many cultures, the elderly are treated with great respect. While Americans learn early to live as though they will never die, most of the rest of the world knows better. While death is a common event for most people, Americans may reach maturity without witnessing a death.

Most societies have some religious or spiritual concepts of death. Elderly Greenland Eskimos may walk off alone, or be given a departure ceremony at which they are ritually killed. Most societies have some belief in an afterlife. The Gond culture in India believes death is the result of magic or demons, while the Tanala of Madagascar attribute death to natural causes. Hinduism and Buddhism involve the belief in reincarnation. People in the United States react to death with denial and avoidance.

We come to understand the nature of death developmentally. At age two or three, children confuse death with sleep. Children less than six years of age often believe that only people who want to die, or are careless or bad, actually die, and that they can be returned to life. Between the ages of five and seven, a realistic perception of death emerges, but applies only to other people. Only after about age nine do we appreciate that death is universal, inevitable, and final. During adolescence, few individuals confront death on a personal level. In middle adulthood, however, it is common to reflect on remaining time, and to fear death more than in early adulthood. In late adulthood fear of death is reduced and discussions of death are more common.

While most of us live in denial of death, people who are dying often want an opportunity to make decisions, complete unfinished business, and put their affairs in order. Kübler-Ross has documented the patterns of many dying persons, and suggests five stages, which are not necessarily sequential: denial and isolation, anger, bargaining, depression, and acceptance. In a similar vein, Pattison describes three phases of the living-dying interval within the trajectory of life: acute, chronic, and terminal. Schneidman has pointed out that when facing death emotions wax and wane. The concept of learned helplessness applies to the dying situation, in which learning that a negative or traumatic outcome is beyond control may lead an individual to stop responding, give up, and become apathetic, despondent, and depressed. On the other hand, perceived control may prolong a person's life.

Denial, coupled with perceived control, may be a very adaptive coping strategy. Weisman suggests that there may be three forms of denial: denial of facts, denial of implications, or denial of extinction. Denial may also be brittle, involving anxiety and agitation, or adaptive, in which the person elects to emphasize strengths and opportunities. Kalish has pointed out that denial can be adaptive, maladaptive, or both simultaneously.

It is generally agreed that the situation is optimal when the dying person knows he is dying, significant others in his world know it too, and they can interact on the basis of this common knowledge. This open-awareness context of communication permits the person to close his life in accord with his own ideas, complete plans and projects, reminisce, and understand what is happening. Some experts believe that communication with a dying person should focus on the person's strengths and preparation for the balance of life, rather than on direct preparation for death.

Most deaths in the United States occur in hospitals, which offer technical advantages but psychological disadvantages. Most people would rather die at home, but are concerned about being a burden. Hospices provide the best of both worlds, in the form of a humane setting free of pain, anxiety, and depression, with the family always welcome. The effort is focused on pain prevention and psychological readiness for death within the family context. Begun in England, the hospice movement is spreading rapidly across the United States.

The death of a loved one produces a deep sense of loss and grief, like the loss of part of ourselves. The extent of grief is determined by the nature of the relationship, and the nature of the changes brought about by the death. Bereavement is the state of loss, while grief includes the sorrow, anger, guilt and confusion which must be worked through in order to recover from the loss. Mourning is the overt, behavioral expression of grief and bereavement.

Several stage models of grief have been suggested. Averill suggests stages of shock, despair, and recovery, while Parkes suggests four stages: numbness, pining, depression, and recovery. The shock stage involves disbelief, numbness, weeping, and easy agitation, beginning at the time of death and lasting several days. The second stage involves painful longing, memories and visual images, insomnia, irritability, and restlessness, peaking two to four weeks after the death. Grief can be felt in many ways. Grief pangs include somatic distress, tension, sobbing, and crying. Denial and searching are also normal aspects of the grief process. Grief helps motivate people to try to make sense of their world. When a death is unexpected or accidental, the effort to understand it is intensified. Recovery appears within a year after the death, and involves pleasant memories and the establishment of new relationships.

Widowed persons experience more physical and psychological symptoms than married persons, and have an elevated death rate in the first year following the death of a spouse.

There are many cultural differences in mourning practices, such as suttee, a black armband, and funerals. One way to avoid exploitation in funeral purchases is to make the purchases in advance, which very few people do.

Learning Objectives

1. Comment on the difficulty in defining death, and trace the arguments regarding euthanasia. (p. 571)
2. Contrast the American approach to death with that of other cultures. (p. 572)
3. Trace the development of the understanding of death from early childhood to late adulthood. (p. 574)
4. Describe typical changes which occur as death approaches, and trace the stages of dying proposed by Kübler-Ross and Pattison. (p. 579)
5. Describe the roles of learned helpless, perceived control, and denial in preparing for death. (p. 580)
6. List principles for communicating with dying persons, and contrast dying at home, in the hospice, and in the hospital. (p. 581)
7. Define the nature and stages of bereavement, grief, and mourning, and compare mourning and funeral practices in different cultures. (p. 584)

Key Terms

For each key term, please write the definition in the space provided.

brain death (1, p. 571) _____

euthanasia (1, p. 572) _____

denial and isolation (4, p. 579) _____

anger (4, p. 579) _____

bargaining (4, p. 579) _____

depression (4, p. 579) _____

acceptance (4, p. 579) _____

trajectory of life (4, p. 580) _____

living-dying interval (4, p. 580) _____

acute phase (4, p. 580) _____

chronic phase (4, p. 580) _____

terminal phase (4, p. 580) _____

perceived control (5, p. 581) _____

hospice (6, p. 583) _____

bereavement (7, p. 584) _____

grief (7, p. 584) _____

mourning (7, p. 584) _____

suttee (7, p. 588) _____

Guided Review

1. No matter how long we live, we will certainly _____ . (1, p. 571)

   die

2. Historically, the cessation of respiration and circulation, rigor mortis, dilation of the pupils, and relaxation of the sphincter muscles defined _____ . (1, p. 571)

   death

3. In recent years, some controversy has arisen over the definition of _____ . (1, p. 571)

   death

4. When all electrical activity of the brain has ceased, we say that _____ _____ has occurred. (1, p. 571)

brain death

5. With a variety of machines, it is possible to maintain the circulatory and respiratory functions of someone who has suffered _____ _____ . (1, p. 571)

brain death

6. The ability to keep brain dead people "alive" with respirators and intravenous feeding raises many legal and _____ concerns and questions. (1, p. 571)

ethical

7. Such practices also raise the issue of euthanasia. Painlessly putting to death someone who is suffering from an incurable disease or severe disability is called _____ . (1, p. 572)

euthanasia

8. Actually, there are two types of _____ , active and passive. (1, p. 572)

euthanasia

9. The injection of a lethal drug into a suffering person to hasten death would be considered _____ euthanasia, and is usually illegal. (1, p. 572)

active

10. On the other hand, simply withdrawing the respirator or other extraordinary treatment measures would be considered _____ euthanasia, and is rarely illegal. (1, p. 572)

passive

11. Historically, arguments about _____ have stressed the irreversible pain involved in fatal illness or other abnormalities. (1, p. 572)

euthanasia

12. More recently, however, _____ has ceased to be an issue, and the quality of life has become the focus. (1, p. 572)

pain

13. There are many cultural variations in how humans relate to death. In some cultures old people are killed or allowed to _____ when they are no longer productive. (2, p. 572)

die

14. In the United States, we grow up believing we will live forever and rarely witness _____ , which is a fact of daily life for people elsewhere in the world. (2, p. 572)

death

15. In most societies, death is not viewed as the end of existence; only the physical body is said to have _____ . (2, p. 573)

died

16. Most societies have philosophical or religious beliefs or rituals surrounding _____ . (2, p. 572)

death

17. In India, the Gond believe that _____ is caused by magic or demons. (2, p. 573)

death

18. In Madagascar, the Tanala believe that _____ occurs due to natural causes. (2, p. 573)

death

19. Hinduism and Buddhism involve the belief that death is transcended in the form of _____ . (2, p. 573)

reincarnation

20. In the United States, our attitude toward death is one of _____ . (2, p. 573)

denial

21. We see this attitude of _____ in our funeral customs, our language, our rejection of the aged, and our strong faith in medical science. (2, p. 573)

denial

22. Our understanding of _____ grows developmentally. (3, p. 574)

death

23. Often children who are only two or three years old confuse _____ with _____ . (3, p. 574)

death, sleep (either order)

24. Children less than six years old usually think that only people who want to, or who are bad or careless, actually _____ . (3, p. 574)

die

25. Also, children at this age believe that people who have _____ can be brought back to life. (3, p. 574)

died

26. Children between the ages of six and nine begin to appreciate that death is _____ , but believe that it only happens to others. (3, p. 574)

final

27. Children older than nine years, recognize that death is both _____ and _____ . (3, p. 574)

final, universal

28. During adolescence, most people avoid thinking about death, although a few adolescents do confront the prospect of their own _____ . (3, p. 575)

death

29. In middle age, we think much more about _____ and how much time is left. (3, p. 575)

death

30. Most individuals in _____ _____ believe that death comes too soon. (3, p. 575)

middle age

31. In late adulthood, there is less _____ of death, and it is discussed more. (3, p. 575)

fear

32. Kübler-Ross has suggested that people who are _____ go through five stages. (4, p. 579)

dying

33. It should be clear that these _____ are not necessarily sequential. (4, p. 579)

stages

34. The first _____ is denial and isolation. However, denial is a temporary defense. (4, p. 579)

stage

35. Anger is next. The question "Why me???" characterizes the stage of _____ . (4, p. 579)

anger

36. People become _____ at everyone, even God, and may explode and shout at anyone who happens to be there. (4, p. 579)

angry

37. The third _____ is bargaining. The dying person may try to make a private bargain, usually with God, in which they promise to do something in exchange for a cure or just for a little more time. (4, p. 579)

stage

38. The fourth stage is depression. Many psychologists see the stage of _____ as healthy grief work and letting go. You should not try to cheer up the person who is depressed. (4, p. 579)

depression

39. The fifth stage is acceptance, and is characterized by a deep sense of calm and _____ . There is almost never physical pain or discomfort during acceptance. (4, p. 579)

peace

40. To die with peace and dignity, it is very helpful if not necessary to reach the stage of _____ . (4, p. 579)

acceptance

41. Another way of looking at the development of people who are _____ is Pattison's concept of the trajectory of life. (4, p. 580)

dying

42. Pattison says that, when our life plan becomes modified by the sudden knowledge that we are _____ , we enter the living-dying interval. (4, p. 580)

dying

43. According to Pattison, in the _____ interval, we go through three phases. (4, p. 580)

living-dying

44. First is the acute phase. The most severe life crisis, realizing that you will _____ sooner than planned, occurs during the acute phase. (4, p. 580)

die

45. People feel immobilized and have very high levels of anxiety during the _____ phase. (4, p. 580)

acute

46. In the chronic phase, we begin to confront our fear of _____ . Fear of loneliness, suffering, and the unknown must be dealt with during the chronic phase. (4, p. 580)

dying

47. In the terminal phase, the individual begins to withdraw. Recognizing and accepting one's own impending _____ is the key element to the terminal phase. (4, p. 580)

death

48. A dying person experiences a wide range of emotions, as he tries to make sense out of what is happening. One concept that may contribute to our understanding of the _____ person's experience is learned helplessness. (5, p. 580)

dying

49. When a person learns that a negative or traumatic outcome is beyond their control, _____ _____ may develop. (5, p. 580)

learned helplessness

50. The results of learned helplessness include not responding, giving up, and becoming apathetic or _____ . (5, p. 581)

depressed

51. When people are led to believe that they can influence and control some events, they become more alert and cheerful, and develop a sense of perceived _____ . (5, p. 581)

control

52. This sense of _____ _____ can even prolong a person's life. (5, p. 581)

perceived control

53. Coupled with _____ _____ , denial may represent an adaptive coping strategy. (5, p. 581)

perceived control

54. At the same time, _____ can be a very protective mechanism, enabling people to grapple with the feeling that they are going to die. (5, p. 581)

denial

55. Weisman suggests that there may be three forms of _____ . (5, p. 581)

denial

56. The first form is a simple _____ of the facts; the person denies having an illness. (5, p. 581)

denial

57. The second type is _____ of the implications; the person now admits the disease, but denies that it will end in death. (5, p. 581)

denial

58. The third type is _____ of extinction, which involves accepting the fact of having a fatal illness, but acting as though they would survive anyway. (5, p. 581)

denial

59. Another way of looking at denial distinguishes between brittle and adaptive denial. If observable anxiety and agitation are present, the denial is said to be _____ . (5, p. 581)

brittle

60. However, if the individual simply decides not to dwell on dying, but emphasizes strengths and opportunities, the denial is termed _____ . (5, p. 581)

adaptive

61. Most people who know they are _____ want to talk about their feelings and their fears. (6, p. 581)

dying

62. There are many advantages of an open-awareness context for the _____ person. (6, p. 582)

dying

63. The freedom to talk about your impending _____ with others who share the knowledge, permits you to complete plans, reminisce, and understand what is happening. (6, p. 582)

death

64. Some experts believe that communication with _____ people should not focus on impending death, but on strengths and preparation for the remainder of life. (6, p. 583)

dying

65. Most deaths in the United States occur in _____ , where medical technology eclipses family relationships and autonomy. (6, p. 583)

hospitals

66. Given the option, most people would rather die at _____ , surrounded by people they love rather than by professional strangers. (6, p. 583)

home

67. The combination of institutional care and home care, with a unique and strong family orientation, is found in the _____ . (6, p. 583)

hospice

68. One of the major aspects of _____ care is the avoidance of pain, anxiety, and depression. (6, p. 583)

hospice

69. The movement began in the late 1960s, when Saint Christopher's _____ opened in London, and is very rapidly spreading across the United States. (6, p. 583)

Hospice

70. Loss comes in many forms in our lives, but the greatest loss is the _____ of someone we love. (7, p. 584)

death

71. Loss leads to bereavement, grief, and mourning. The state involving loss is known technically as _____ . (7, p. 584)

bereavement

72. The emotional response to bereavement, including sorrow, anger, guilt, and confusion, is called _____ . (7, p. 584)

grief

73. The overt, behavioral expression of grief and bereavement is called _____ . (7, p. 584)

mourning

74. Several stage models of grief have been proposed. Averill proposed a three-stage model of _____ . (7, p. 585)

grief

75. In the first stage, shock, the person feels disbelief and numbness, and weeps or becomes easily agitated. This stage begins soon after the _____ and lasts for several days. (7, p. 585)

death

76. The second _____ is characterized by wrenching pain, and pining for the person who died. (7, p. 585)

stage

77. It is not uncommon to believe that you see or hear the person who _____ during the second stage. (7, p. 585)

died

78. Stage _____ involves resolution of the grief. (7, p. 585)

three

79. Pleasant memories of the person who died, and the making of new relationships, mark the successful _____ of grief. (7, p. 585)

resolution

80. Even when the _____ is resolved, there will always be a sense of loss when that person is remembered. (7, p. 585)

grief

81. Grief can be felt in many ways. A _____ pang involves somatic distress such as tightness in the throat, shortness of breath, and deep sighing. (7, p. 585)

grief

82. An important aspect of _____ is searching for the person who died, which is a normal aspect of pining. (7, p. 585)

grief

83. One positive aspect of _____ is that it motivates people to try to make sense of their world. (7, p. 586)

grief

84. When the _____ was the result of accident or disaster, the effort to make sense of it all is intensified. (7, p. 586)

death

85. Researchers have documented that bereaved individuals experience more problems, both psychological and _____ . (7, p. 586)

physical

86. Moreover, widowed persons experience more physical and psychological symptoms than do _____ persons. (7, p. 586)

married

87. Widowed persons also have a much higher mortality rate in the first year following the _____ of the spouse. (7, p. 587)

death

88. There are many cultural differences in mourning. For example, the Hindu have the optional practice of suttee, which involves burning the dead man's _____ to firmly establish her in his memory. (7, p. 588)

widow

89. In the United States, the most common mourning practice is the _____ , typically with viewing of the body. (7, p. 589)

funeral

90. There is some concern about the advisability and expense of _____ arrangements, and it is possible to avoid exploitation by making arrangements before they are needed. (7, p. 589)

funeral

91. As you can easily suspect, very few people make advance arrangements for their own _____ . (7, p. 589)

funeral

Well, that ends this last review unit. I hope you have enjoyed it, and learned from it too. Please remember to look over the learning objectives before you attempt the self test.

Self Test

1. Debate over the exact definition of death has ensued due to (1, p. 571)
   a. the notion of brain death
   b. the availability of euthanasia
   c. modern technology, such as respirators
   d. the discovery of new diseases

2. According to the Greeks, the behavior of Greenland Eskimos would be viewed as (2, p. 572)
   a. totally unacceptable
   b. passive euthanasia
   c. immoral and unethical, but not illegal
   d. perfectly appropriate

3. The belief that death is both final and universal does not appear common until about age (3, p. 574)
   a. six
   b. nine
   c. fifteen
   d. forty-five

4. According to most psychologists, when discussing death with children the best rule to follow is (3, p. 574)
   a. don't tell the child more than he or she can understand and accept
   b. use religious explanations with children under six
   c. be completely honest
   d. adopt the parents' religious and philosophical beliefs to avoid confusion

5. When asked to estimate how much life they have left, most people base their projections on (3, p. 576)
   a. the ages at which their parents died
   b. having time to achieve their long-term goals
   c. a fantasy derived from anticipatory bargaining with God
   d. the assumption that they could die at any time

6. According to Kübler-Ross, the question "Why me?" pervades the thinking of the person in the stage she calls (4, p. 579)
   a. denial and isolation
   b. anger
   c. bargaining
   d. depression

7. Perhaps the most effective way of dealing with the fear of impending death is (5, p. 581)
   a. learned helplessness
   b. acceptance as the first stage of adjustment
   c. perceived control combined with denial
   d. brittle denial

8. A most humane way to care for people who are dying, which involves their family, is (6, p. 583)
   a. grief work
   b. hospice
   c. euthanasia
   d. in the hospital

9. The fear of death peaks during (3, p. 575)
   a. the living-dying interval
   b. learned helplessness
   c. middle age
   d. the terminal phase of the dying trajectory

10. Believing that you see the person who recently died walking down the street, you run up to talk and then discover that it is not the person you thought it was. This experience is (7, p. 585)
   a. a normal part of stage-two grieving
   b. an initial form of denial
   c. part of the shock of the first stage of grief
   d. a sign of faith in life after death

Individual Learning Activity

For the past several years, I have worked closely with people who are dying, in a hospice setting. We primarily care for people in their own homes, and help the members of the family in whatever way we can, by teaching them nursing skills, giving them some respite (a few hours away from home, for example, or a movie or dinner out), and most of all by just listening as the dying person and the members of the family work out their feelings and make decisions about the meaning of life and love. I have had the privilege and pleasure, and sometimes the fear, of sharing some of the most critical moments of life with others.

As a result of these experiences, I want to suggest to you a most beneficial activity. As you have read, reminiscence and a life review are an important part of aging, and particularly of dying. One of the things which happens if you work with someone who is dying, is that you discover that a life review can be helpful at any age, and can redirect your focus and priorities. That is what I am suggesting to you now.

It is not necessary to imagine that you are dying, but simply to realize that each of us will in fact die, and we do not know when. Confronting our own mortality, the truth that we will die, is not the same as confronting our own imminent death, but it will have to do. I cannot very well convince you that you have a terminal illness, but we all share a terminal condition—life itself.

A life review is not scary, but it is difficult. It requires us to characterize our life in an organized way. What have we done that we are proud of? (I know it is easier to think of negative things, but it is much more productive to think of positive commissions.) What are we most invested in? If we were to die today, what would we most miss? What would we want others to remember us for? What would we want others to continue in our name or memory? To what charity would we want donations to be made in our name?

Another tactic is this. Simply write your own obituary, as though it would appear (you would hope) if you died today, at your present age. My students assure me that this is one of the most powerful and beneficial assignments I give them. Give it a try. It will show you what you have accomplished.

Still another technique, which dying people often use early in their life review, is this. Try writing endings to this sentence beginning:

If I had my life to live over again, I would . . .

1. _____
2. _____
3. _____
4. _____
5. _____

Now, of course, you are confronted with an even more difficult decision. How will you change your life to reflect what you have learned from the review? This is an advantage which dying people seldom have—the time to make changes. Those of us who work with dying people are often grateful for the lessons we learn about the importance of doing today what we believe is important. Each of us will surely die; all that remains to be discovered is when. Thank you for caring enough about yourself to complete this challenging activity.

Answers to the Self Test

1. a	6. b
2. d	7. c
3. b	8. b
4. c	9. c
5. a	10. a